Mallorca
Sport Climbs

Text, crag photography and topos
by Mark Glaister and Alan James
Action photography as credited
Edited by Alan James and Rebecca Ting
Printed in Europe by LF Book Services
Distributed by Cordee (cordee.co.uk)

Maps by Alan James
Some maps based on original source data
from openstreetmap.org

Fax71 - ISBN 978 1 873341 24 7

Published by Rockfax in April 2025
© Rockfax 2025

Rockfax is part of UKClimbing Limited
which is an Employee Ownership Trust

All rights reserved. No part of this publication may be reproduced, stored in a retrieval system, or transmitted in any form or by any means, electronic, mechanical, photocopying or otherwise without prior written permission of the copyright owner. A CIP catalogue record is available from the British Library.

We only use paper made from wood fibre from sustainable forests and produced according to ISO 14001 environmental standard.

FSC
www.fsc.org
MIX
Paper | Supporting responsible forestry
FSC® C014138

Cover: Bridget Glaister on *Hematoma* (5c) - *p.52* - at Mont Port. Photo: Mark Glaister

This page: John McKenna on *Sostre Den Burotet* (6c+) - *p.140* - at Valdemossa.
Photo: Mark Glaister

This book belongs to:

Alan James
Mark Glaister

Contents — Mallorca Sport Climbs

Introduction	4
Rockfax Digital	6
Symbol, Map and Topo Key	7
Acknowledgments	8
Rockfax Publications	10
Mallorca Logistics	**12**
When to Go and Getting There	14
Where to Stay	16
Getting Around	17
Shops and Tourist Information	18
Mallorca Climbing	**20**
Access and Guidebooks	22
Bolts and Bolting	24
Gear and Grades	26
Route Lengths and Lowering Off	27
Graded List	28
Destination Planner	32
The Southwest	**34**
Can Ortigues	36
Capdella	40
Mont Port	48
Cala Llamp	56
C'an Formiga	62
Puig de Garrafa	64
Santa Ponça	80
Ca's Català	84
Sa Cantera	92
Valldemossa Area	**96**
Penyal d'es Grau	98
Es Verger	106
S'estret	114
Valldemossa	132
Bunyola Area	**142**
Sa Gubia	144
Fraguel	168
North of the Mountains	**178**
Port de Sóller	180
C'an Nyic	190
Gorg Blau	192
South of the Mountains	**198**
Alaró	200
Caimari	210
Grau des Ruc	228
The Northeast	**234**
La Creveta	236
El Fumat	240
Puig St. Marti	246
El Caló de Betlem	252
The East Coast	**260**
Son Servera	262
Sa Mola de Felanitx	264
Cala Magraner	272
Cala Bota	282
Torre d'en Beu	290
Tijuana	300
Route Index	310
Buttress and Crag Index	319
Map and General Index	320

Natalie Berry on the outstanding *Octopussy* (7a) - *p.130* - at S'estret. This is another photographic angle on the image that graced the previous guidebook. Photo: Mark Glaister

Mallorca Sport Climbs Introduction

Mallorca, the stunningly beautiful Mediterranean island, is one of Europe's top-flight sport climbing destinations. Its magnificent mountains and sublime coastline are home to a wealth of astonishing crags, presenting climbers with some of the most majestic climbing locations to be found anywhere. With its perfect climate, well-established tourist infrastructure, and friendly locals, it's an ideal spot for any sport climbing enthusiast. On a first visit to Mallorca, climbers are often amazed by the vast amount of rock on display, both in the mountains and along the coastline. However, the actual number of developed crags is relatively small. Even so, there's no shortage of routes to explore, though many of the best spots are not immediately obvious. While the mountains feature their share of prime crags, a large portion of the island's climbing can be found along the rugged east coast or on the dramatic Formentor Peninsula.

Mallorca serves up plenty of climbing that will appeal to those operating at most levels, ranging from grade 3s and 4s to the current hardest at 9a+. Come and test yourself on some of Europe's steepest and best tufa systems in a shady north-facing cave; have a week's holiday ticking pleasant walls and slabs on perfect sheets of compact grey rock; or tackle the island's world famous multi-pitch climb of *Albahida* at Sa Gubia, a line that can be seen from the air on the approach to Palma airport - all while soaking up some summer or winter sun.

Over the years, sport climbing in Mallorca has developed at a fairly relaxed pace, much like the island's easygoing lifestyle. The sheer abundance of climbing opportunities seems to have left local climbers spoilt for choice. However, in recent years, the pace has accelerated, with an increasing number of climbers uncovering and developing new crags. Notable new venues, such as Cala Bota, Mont Port and Capdella have been opened up, while established areas like S'estret, Caimari and Sa Mola de Felanitx have seen a host of excellent new routes added.

One of the biggest draws of a climbing trip to Mallorca is the island's compact size and well-connected road network, making it easy to access all the crags from a wide range of accommodation. The island's "off-season" offers the perfect conditions for a climbing getaway. With its mild climate, affordable accommodation, and budget-friendly flights, it's an ideal destination for winter sun and sport climbing. What could be better than starting the day by unwinding on a serene beach or wandering through a charming village, then spending the afternoon tackling some world-class climbing - finish it all off with a relaxing evening at a quiet port or mountain village, enjoying a cold beer on a terrace as the sun sets.

The Book
The possibilities for winter sport climbing on Mallorca initially came to prominence in the late 1980s. The first Rockfax publication was in February 1995 and covered 12 sport crags across the island. This book is the ninth Rockfax publication to the island and covers just over 1500 sport climbs on 31 crags. The routes in this guide are presented in the familiar full-colour Rockfax style which offers the clearest method available for locating and choosing your routes for the day. Mallorca's Deep Water Soloing is now covered in its own book - *see inside back cover flap*. The information is as up-to-date as we can make it at the time of publication but new roads will be built, new routes will be climbed and new crags will be developed. If you find anything that is incorrect, out of date or confusing then please get in touch via the Rockfax website - **rockfax.com**

Eneko Pou on *Playboy* (8a) - *p.227* - at Sector Cueva, Caimari. This crag is a long established venue for climbers operating in the upper grades with most of the lines being exceptional challenges at 8a or harder. Photo: Pou Brothers Collection

Rockfax Digital brings together 50 guides from 4 publishers covering over 80,000 routes on 1600+ crags and presents it in a user-friendly package for use on mobile devices.

The heart of Rockfax Digital is the crag and route information covering 'areas' which roughly correspond to the printed guidebooks. The main data is sold by subscription so that you purchase access to everything for a period of time, from a month to a year. Once you are subscribed, you will have everything on Rockfax Digital for the duration. You can download the main data and store it on your device so you don't need any signal to be able to read the descriptions and see the topos and maps. There is plenty of free content available without a subscription, enabling you to get a really good impression of what Rockfax Digital is like without shelling out any money.

Rockfax Digital is available as an app which is free to download and incredibly useful in its own right. It contains a detailed crag map linked to the UKClimbing crags database with basic information and route lists for crags

worldwide. The map also displays all the 3,800+ listings from the UKClimbing Directory of climbing walls, outdoor shops, climbing clubs, outdoor-specific accommodation and instructors and guides, amongst others.

How to Subscribe to Rockfax Digital
Go to **rockfax.digital** to find links to download the app and create an account. New users can subscribe and get 7 days free.

Scan to find out more

UKC Logbooks
A popular method of logging your climbing is to use the **UKClimbing.com** logbooks system. This database has 653,000+ routes on over 24,700+ crags. So far, over 68,100 users have recorded more than 11 million ascents! To set up your own logbook, just register at **UKClimbing.com** and click on the logbook tab. You will be able to record every ascent you make, when you did it, what style you climbed it in and who you did it with. Each entry has a place for your own notes. You can also add your vote to the grade/star system which is used by guidebook writers to get opinions on grades and quality of routes. The logbook can be private, public or restricted to your own climbing partners only.

Rockfax Digital can be linked to your **UKClimbing.com** user account and logbook so that you can record your activity while at the crag. To do this you will need a 3G/4G/5G data connection. You can also look at the UKC logbooks to see if anyone has climbed your chosen route recently to check on conditions.

Route Symbols

- A good route which is well worth the effort.
- A very good route, one of the best on the crag.
- A brilliant route, one of the best on the island.
- Technical climbing requiring good balance and technique, or complex and tricky moves.
- Powerful climbing; roofs, steep rock, low lock-offs or long moves off small holds.
- Sustained climbing; either lots of hard moves or steep rock giving pumpy climbing.
- Fingery climbing with significant small holds on the hard sections.
- Fluttery climbing with big fall potential and scary run-outs.
- A long reach is helpful, or even essential, for one or more of the moves.
- Some loose rock may be encountered.
- Old bolts - do not climb. Routes without this symbol may have old bolts as well.
- A route which isn't fully bolted. A rack of gear consisting of wires and cams is needed.

Crag Symbols

- Angle of the approach walk to the crag with approximate time.
- Approximate time that the crag is in the direct sun (when it is shining).
- The buttress has some multi-pitch routes.
- The crag is exposed to bad weather and will catch the wind if it is blowing.
- The crag can offer shelter from cold winds and it may be a good suntrap in colder weather.
- The crag suffers from seepage. It may well be wet and unclimbable in winter and early spring.
- The crag is steep and may well offer some dry rock to climb when it is raining.
- **Deserted** - Currently under-used and usually quiet. Fewer good routes or remote and smaller areas.
- **Quiet** - Less popular sections on major crags, or good buttresses with awkward approaches.
- **Busy** - Places you will seldom be alone, especially at weekends. Good routes and easy access.
- **Crowded** - The most popular sections of the most popular crags which are always busy.

Topo Key

Map Key

The Southwest
Valldemossa Area
Bunyola Area
North of the Mountains
South of the Mountains
The Northeast
The East Coast

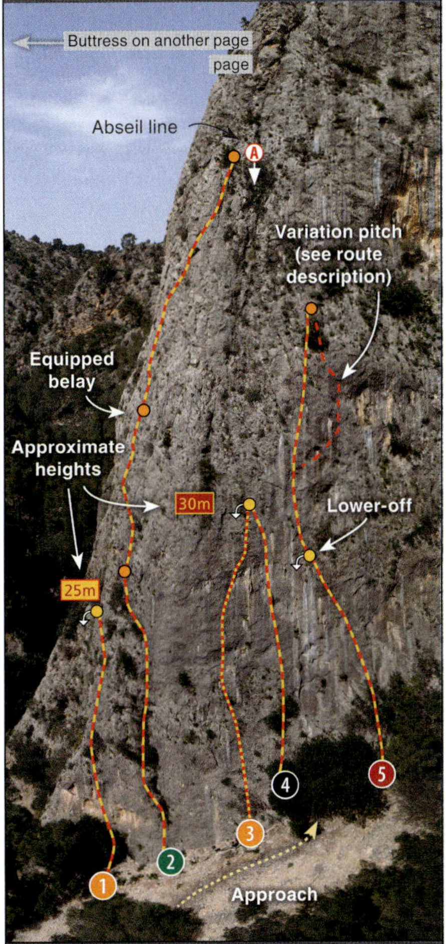

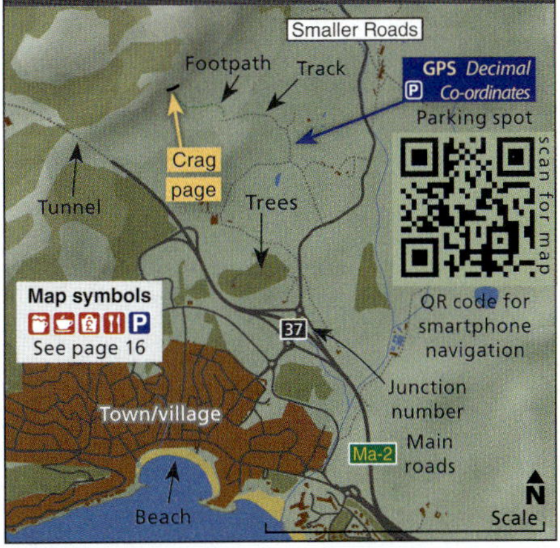

Mallorca Sport Climbs — Acknowledgments

Mallorca is now firmly established as a fantastic holiday sport climbing destination and this is reflected in the number of Rockfax guides that have been published over the last 30+ years. For this edition I spent a month or so a year staying in the village of Binissalem and experienced both magnificent warm spring days out on the coast and in the mountains, as well as a very frigid number of weeks where the mountains were inaccessible due to a hundred year snow storm and its aftermath. Thank you to all who visited to climb with me and share the delights of Binissalem - the prime area of wine production on the island! I must above all thank the hard work that the developers have put in to open up the routes and to those who have taken and been the subjects of the superb portfolio of shots that make such a huge contribution to the appeal of this guidebook. It has as ever been a pleasure to work with Alan and the Rockfax/UKC team on the production.

Mark Glaister, February 2025

The core of a guidebook is its climbing information and we must acknowledge the great work done by climbers on Mallorca in equipping and maintaining the routes. Over many years we have been able to work with local climbers and provide some support to the bolting efforts by giving funds and bolts. Thanks to those we have worked with.

The action photos in this book, other than those by Mark and myself, were mostly taken by Mike Hutton. Thanks to Mike, the McKenna brothers and Paul Dearden for their support on recent trips. Thanks also to Eneko and Iker Pou for their action photos and Rebecca Ting for her proof reading.

Much of the information in this new edition has come from the amazing feedback received via the **UKClimbing.com** web site. Thanks to everyone who has contributed to this.

Mark has once again been great to work with and has put an incredible effort into re-photographing all the crags using our new techniques. Thanks also to Rebecca Ting for her last minute proofing.

Alan James, February 2025

The sublime Formentor peninsular and the massive wall of El Fumat. Photo: Mark Glaister

Advertisers

We are grateful to the following for supporting this guidebook.

BMC Insurance - Inside back cover
thebmc.co.uk/insurance

Petzl - Outside back cover flap
petzl.com/GB/en/Sport

Rock and Water - Page 15
rockandwatermallorca.com

Rock On - Page 2
rockonclimbing.co.uk

Rocòdrom es cau - Back cover
rocodromescau.com

Rockfax Publications

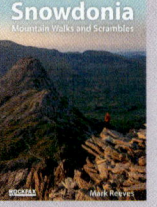

- 📖 Print version date
- Ⓡ Digital version date
- Ⓡ⁺ Digital has extra content

North Wales Climbs
📖 March 2023
Ⓡ⁺ October 2023

Clwyd Limestone
📖 December 2015
Ⓡ⁺ December 2015

North Wales Slate
📖 September 2018
Ⓡ⁺ March 2023

Snowdonia Scrambles
📖 December 2020
Ⓡ December 2020

ROCKFAX digital

Scan to find out more

Order online from **rockfax.com**
30% discount for Rockfax Digital subscribers

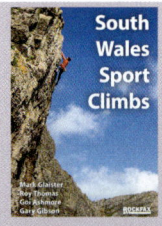

South Wales Sport Climbs
📖 November 2024
Ⓡ November 2024

Pembroke
📖 August 2009
Ⓡ⁺ April 2024

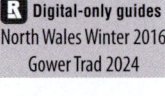
Ⓡ **Digital-only guides**
North Wales Winter 2016
Gower Trad 2024

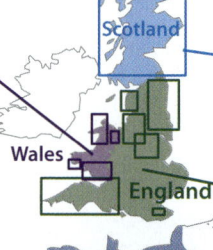

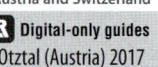
Ⓡ **Digital-only guides**
Otztal (Austria) 2017
Eiger (Switzerland) 2016

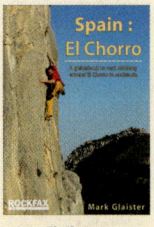

El Chorro
📖 December 2018
Ⓡ December 2018

Ⓡ **Digital-only guides**
Catalunya 2016
Madrid Area 2017
Sierra de Gredos 2024
Zaragoza 2016
Tenerife 2020
Northern Spain 2023

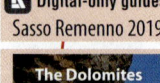
Ⓡ **Digital-only guides**
Sasso Remenno 2019

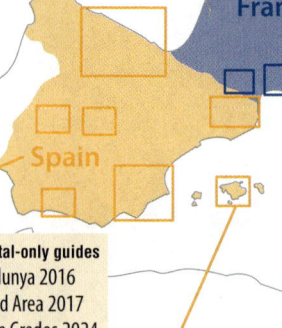

Ⓡ **Digital-only guides**
Santorini 2019
Cyprus 2022

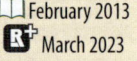

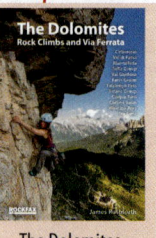
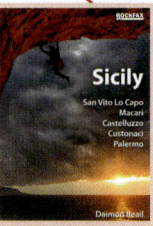

Spain : Costa Blanca
📖 February 2013
Ⓡ⁺ March 2023

Mallorca Sport Climbs
📖 April 2025
Ⓡ April 2025

Mallorca DWS
📖 April 2025
Ⓡ April 2025

The Dolomites
📖 November 2019
Ⓡ November 2019

Sicily
📖 March 2021
Ⓡ⁺ October 2023

Rockfax Publications

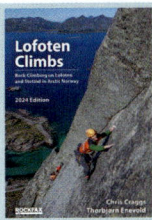

Lofoten Climbs
📖 May 2024
Ⓡ May 2024

Ⓡ Digital-only guides
Rjukan 2016
Nissedal 2016

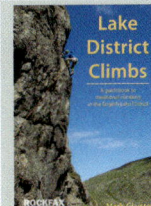

Lake District Climbs
📖 November 2019
R+ October 2023

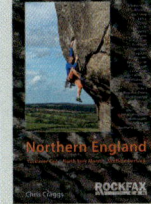

Northern England
📖 February 2008
Ⓡ February 2008

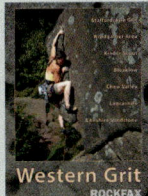

Western Grit
📖 April 2009
Ⓡ June 2023

Northern Limestone
📖 January 2015
R+ June 2023

SMC Digital-only guides
Scottish Rock Climbs 2024
Scottish Winter Climbs 2019
Highland Scrambles 2020
Available on the Rockfax App

Eastern Grit
📖 May 2022
R+ August 2022

Peak Limestone
📖 June 2020
R+ October 2024

Peak Bouldering
📖 August 2023
R+ October 2023

West Country Climbs
📖 December 2022
R+ April 2023

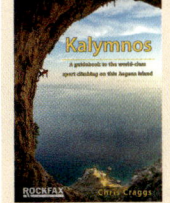

Kalymnos
📖 May 2018
R+ April 2023

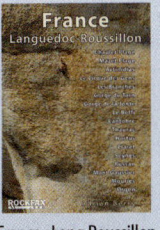

Southern Sandstone
📖 September 2017
R+ May 2023

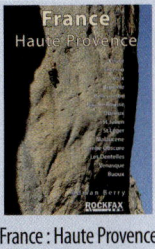

Dorset
📖 July 2021
R+ October 2024

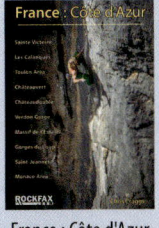

Dorset Bouldering
📖 May 2014
R+ January 2020

Devon Bouldering
📖 January 2024
Ⓡ January 2024

For all trade printed book orders please direct enquiries to Cordee
Telephone: +44 145 561 1585   Email: info@cordee.co.uk
Trade Sales: sales@cordee.co.uk   Web: cordee.co.uk

Ⓡ Digital-only guides
Ailefroide 2021
Maurienne 2021

France : Ariege
📖 December 2012
R+ April 2021

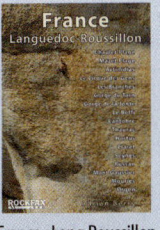

France : Lang.Roussillon
📖 November 2011
Ⓡ November 2011

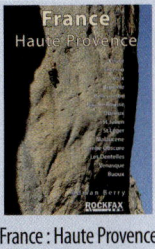

France : Haute Provence
📖 December 2009
R+ November 2022

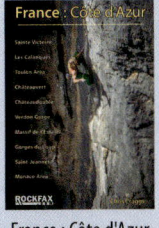

France : Côte d'Azur
📖 February 2017
Ⓡ February 2017

Chamonix
📖 July 2022
Ⓡ July 2022

Mallorca Logistics

John McKenna making his way up the glorious orange wall of tufa and pockets to be found on *Nanga Parbat* (7a+) - *p.53* - at Mont Port. This shot encapsulates what many of the coastal Mallorcan crags are renowned for - sun, sea and tremendous routes. Photo: Mike Hutton

When to Go

The best time to visit Mallorca for sport climbing is in the spring, when the temperatures are usually pleasant and it is likely to be dry. Winter can be cold but with some luck the weather may be good and many people have had great holidays over Christmas and the New Year. If it does rain, then there are steep crags that stay dry but these tend to only offer harder routes. When it is raining in the mountains it is often still possible to find dry rock on the east coast crags - Cala Magraner, Cala Bota, Torre d'en Beu and Tijuana - which have routes across the grade range. Autumn is the stormy season and, though the temperature will be fine, problems can arise with dripping tufas on certain crags, although there is still likely to be plenty to do and week-long washouts are very rare. It is worth bearing in mind that Mallorca has a number of north-facing crags which can be good options during hot spells and a few which only get late afternoon sun like El Fumat and Port de Sóller. In the summer it is simply too hot and expensive for most climbers to justify a visit, although for those out on holiday some climbing might be feasible on the high and shady crags such as Gorg Blau, Grau des Ruc and C'an Nyic.

Mallorca Averages	Jan	Feb	Mar	Apr	May	Jun	Jul	Aug	Sep	Oct	Nov	Dec
Temperature (maximum)	10	15	17	19	22	26	29	29	27	23	18	15
Temperature (minimum)	6	6	8	10	18	17	19	20	18	14	10	8
Hours of sunshine	5	6	7	8	10	11	12	11	8	6	6	4
Sea Temperature	14	13	14	15	17	19	24	25	24	21	18	15
Rainfall in mm / month	40	32	35	30	7	10	5	6	61	73	60	50
Wet days (>0.1mm) / month	8	6	8	5	5	3	1	3	6	9	8	9

Getting There by Air

Mallorca's international airport is on the outskirts of the city of Palma and is on the destination list of many airlines. This means bargain flights at off-peak times, and reasonable value ones at popular times, with the added advantage of being able to book outward and return flights separately.

Getting There Without Flying

It is possible to get to the island without flying although it is time consuming. There are ferries from Valencia, Dénia (on the Costa Blanca) and Barcelona to Palma, and from Barcelona to Port d'Alcúdia. The high speed AVE railway serves Valencia and Barcelona.

Travel Insurance

It is strongly advised that travel, medical and rescue insurance is taken out before undertaking a trip. If you are in any doubt, just ask someone who has had cause to use it!

BMC Travel Insurance *Inside back cover*
Web: services.thebmc.co.uk/insurance

Let us guide you
to the secret spots

DWS *by boat*
SPORT CLIMBING
MULTIPITCH
COASTEERING
CANYONING
CLIMBING CAMPS

Photo by ChrisBurkard.com. Chris Sharma climbing on Soller cliffs.

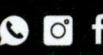

ROCKANDWATERMALLORCA.COM
(+34) 619 751 515

ROCK & WATER
MALLORCA

Mallorca Logistics — Where to Stay

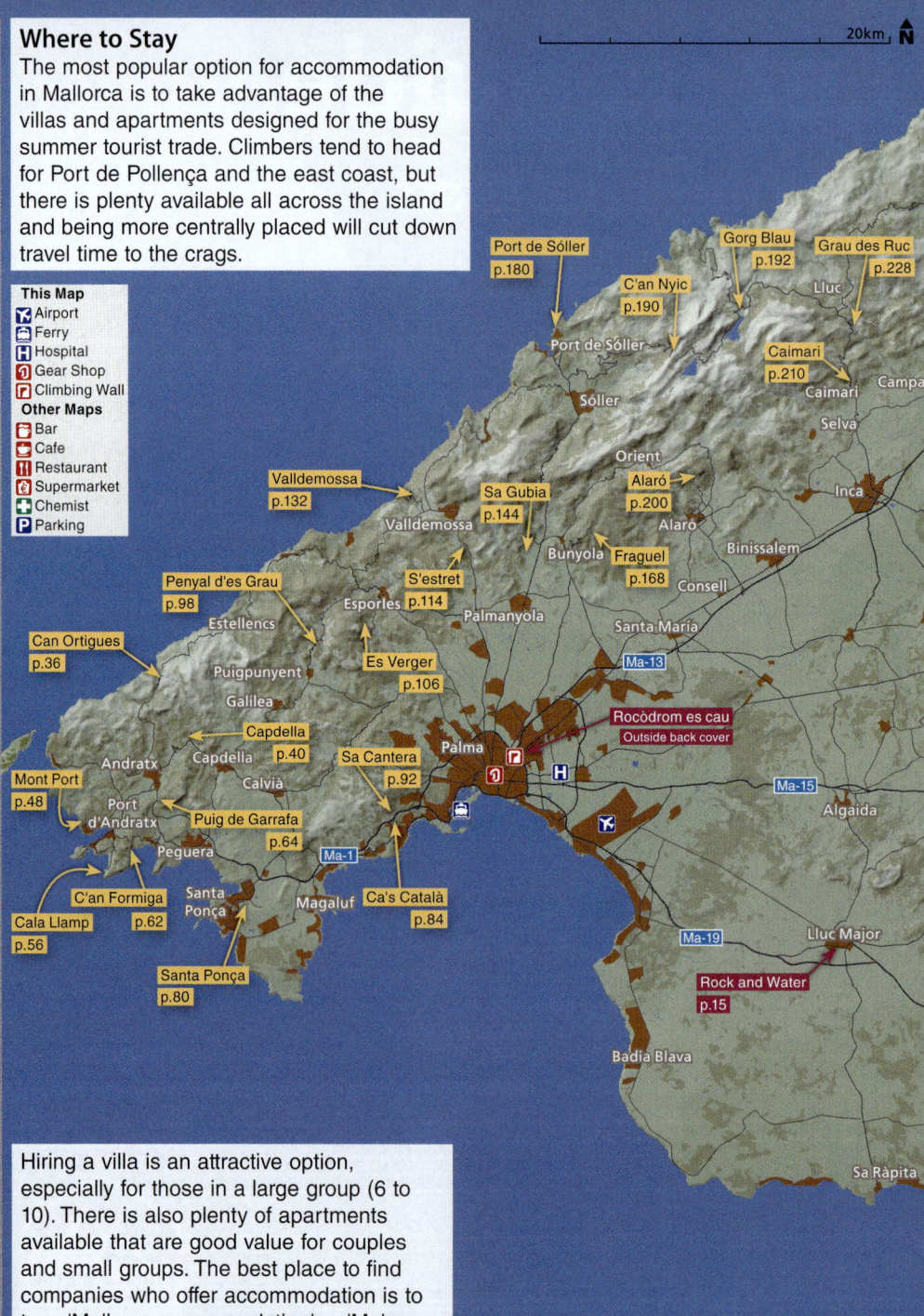

Where to Stay

The most popular option for accommodation in Mallorca is to take advantage of the villas and apartments designed for the busy summer tourist trade. Climbers tend to head for Port de Pollença and the east coast, but there is plenty available all across the island and being more centrally placed will cut down travel time to the crags.

This Map
- Airport
- Ferry
- Hospital
- Gear Shop
- Climbing Wall

Other Maps
- Bar
- Cafe
- Restaurant
- Supermarket
- Chemist
- Parking

Hiring a villa is an attractive option, especially for those in a large group (6 to 10). There is also plenty of apartments available that are good value for couples and small groups. The best place to find companies who offer accommodation is to type 'Mallorca accommodation' or 'Majorca accommodation' into Google.

Locations on map

- Port de Sóller p.180
- C'an Nyic p.190
- Gorg Blau p.192
- Grau des Ruc p.228
- Caimari p.210
- Valldemossa p.132
- Sa Gubia p.144
- Alaró p.200
- Penyal d'es Grau p.98
- S'estret p.114
- Fraguel p.168
- Can Ortigues p.36
- Es Verger p.106
- Rocòdrom es cau (Outside back cover)
- Capdella p.40
- Sa Cantera p.92
- Mont Port p.48
- Puig de Garrafa p.64
- C'an Formiga p.62
- Ca's Català p.84
- Cala Llamp p.56
- Santa Ponça p.80
- Rock and Water p.15

Getting Around **Mallorca Logistics** 17

Getting Around

With a Car - A hire car is advisable for climbing on Mallorca since many of the crags are in remote locations and you will not be able to get the most out of a trip without access to a car. While driving around, it is best to avoid the slow, hairpin-ridden roads in the mountains. The longer, straighter roads to the south of the mountains are much faster. The toll tunnel (free) between Bunyola and Sóller is a bonus for those wishing to reach the crags north of the mountains.

Mallorca DWS
April 2025
April 2025

Without a Car - There is public transport from Palma. Using the public transport system will require a long walk, or a difficult hitch, to get to the crag. The tourist information offices have good information about bus services which nearly all depart from the area around the train stations. The most accessible crags are Port de Sóller, Sa Gubia, Valldemossa, S'estret and Tijuana.

Lunchtime at the famous Es Verger restaurant, high up on the narrow approach road to the Alaró crags.
Photo: Mark Glaister

Tourist Information Offices
Mallorca has almost 50 tourist information offices across the island with two main offices located at the airport and in Palma. For a full list visit:

mallorca.es/en/tourist-information-offices

Shops
There are large supermarkets in most of the major towns and hypermarkets in Palma. Opening times for the majority of shops in Mallorca are from 10am to 1:30pm and 4pm to 8pm. Most supermarkets stay open during the whole day and open a lot earlier. Most shops will be shut on national holidays and many, but not all, will be shut on Sundays.

Climbing Shops
There are several climbing shops that sell climbing gear on the island plus a couple of Decathlons on the outskirts of Palma. You can also get your climbing shoes resoled.

Foracorda - Climbing shop in Palma.
foracorda.com

Guiding Services
If you are after a guide for all types of climbing then here are some options:

Rock and Water *Page 15*
Web: rockandwatermallorca.com
Tel: +34 619 751 515
Email: info@rockandwatermallorca.com

Ròcodrom es cau - Offer outdoor and indoor climbing courses - see below.

Climbing Walls
Of course the weather on Mallorca is always perfect, right? Well not always, in which case you may want to make use one of the local climbing walls.

Ròcodrom es cau *Outside back cover*
C/ Jaume Ferran No. 72, Palma
Web: rocodromescau.com
Tel: +34 648 704 117
Email: rocodromescau@gmail.com

Shops and Tourist Information **Mallorca Logistics**

Sa Mola de Felanitx is located inland from the east coast and is a brilliant destination for teams wanting some excellent pitches in the 5th and 6th grades. The rock is high quality, as is the bolting and the routes often follow strong natural lines as illustrated in this photo of Paul Dearden climbing *Papallona* (5c) - *p.270*. Photo: Mike Hutton

Mallorca Climbing

Paul Dearden picking his way up the numerous pockets of all shapes and sizes encountered on the pumpy *S'ancora* (6a+) - *p.110* - at Es Verger. Es Verger is typical of many of the crags located on the southern lower slopes of the Tramuntana mountains, being easy to approach but often quiet and endowed with exquisite views out across the lower lying land of the island to the Mediterranean. Photo: Alan James

Access

Access is a big issue on Mallorca! There is no formal right of access to most of the crags on the island and there are extra restrictions in the Serra de Tramuntana. In recent times some popular crags have had formal access restricted or been de-bolted. Climbing at La Vall Verde, Galilea, Calvià in the southwest, and Xon Xanquete, Sa Jonquera and Castell de Santueri on the east of the island has been restricted because of a variety of problems. Sometimes it is because of uncooperative land owners, but frequently it is caused by a lack of respect by climbers for their impact on the environment, noise and inconsiderate parking. There are other crags contained within this guidebook that could so easily go the same way if climbers are not careful with parking, litter, noise, fires, natural water supplies and following approach paths to the crags. Please use all the described approaches and avoid antagonising local residents and landowners.

Secret Crags

There are a number of crags not covered in this book or any book. These are known by locals and are climbed on. We haven't documented any here since access is sensitive and inclusion in a book is likely to jeopardise access by increasing visitors.

Guidebooks and Websites

This Rockfax covers sport climbing on Mallorca. Previous editions included the deep water soloing which is mostly along the east coast. This now has its own separate Rockfax publication - Mallorca Deep Water Soloing - right.

A route database can be accessed at **foracorda.com/es/guias**. This site has some information on new developments on the island for traditional and sport venues.

Those looking for adventurous, mainly multi-pitch, trad lines ('Escalada clasica') will also discover a small number of documented routes.

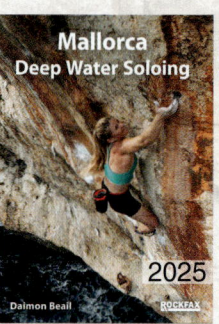

Route Names

In order to create unique identities for the routes in our databases, on Rockfax Digital and printed books, it is essential that they have a route name. It hasn't always been possible to find local names for some routes and others are left without names by their developers. We have taken the liberty of giving names to all of the routes to aid in identification. In most cases, the 'invented' names are descriptive and inoffensive. If you know alternative names for these routes then please let us know via the Rockfax website - **rockfax.com**.

Guidebook Footnote

The inclusion of a climbing area in this guidebook does not mean that you have a right of access or the right to climb upon it. The descriptions of routes within this guide are recorded for historical reasons only and no reliance should be placed on the accuracy of the description. The grades set in this guide are a fair assessment of the difficulty of the climbs. Climbers who attempt a route of a particular standard should use their own judgment as to whether they are proficient enough to tackle that route. This book is not a substitute for experience and proper judgment. The authors, publisher and distributors of this book do not recognise any liability for injury or damage caused to, or by, climbers, third parties, or property arising from such persons seeking reliance on this guidebook as an assurance for their own safety.

Jeremy Wilson on the final steep wall at the top of the well-named *Cut Loose* (6a+) - *p.296* - at Torre d'en Beu. The lower moves on this pitch require a wild swing on a good hold to get established above the initial overhang. Thankfully more conventional climbing follows. Photo: Mark Glaister

Bolts

Many thousands of bolts protect the sport climbs of Mallorca. A good proportion have been in place for a considerable time and are starting to show their age, particularly those on the coastal crags. Many bolts and hangers exhibit surface rust but the vast majority are still serviceable. Some are now in a poor state and a personal decision should be taken as to the safety of the bolts and hangers before embarking on a route. In this guidebook we have only given a little guidance on the state of the bolts as rebolting is ongoing, hence the information can get out of date, and each climber's perception of what is acceptable will vary with experience and their own assessment of the integrity of bolts and hangers.

A rusty bolt - probably sound but difficult to trust

Bolt Funding

The work of bolting and re-bolting is done by local climbers mostly self-funding their activities. There is no central bolt fund run by the locals but climbers can make a donation via **UKBoltFund.org** which will be channelled through Rockfax and passed on directly to the local climbers in the shape of bolts and resin. Over the last few years Rockfax has contributed by purchasing many titanium bolts which have been used on some of the sea-cliff routes. This relationship is ongoing and proceeds from the sale of this book, and the use of the Mallorca area on Rockfax Digital, will generate funds to make more donations in the shape of bolts or equipment.

Replaced lower-off at Creveta

Martin McKenna on the lower section of *La Marmita* (6c+) - *p.296* - at The Cathedral, Capdella. This crag is quick to approach and set amongst some beautiful wooded slopes. The hillside below the cliff leads down to the village of the same name which is a fine spot to relax and grab a drink and snack. Photo: Mike Hutton

Gear

For climbing the sport routes in this book you will need around 12 to 18 quickdraws and a single rope. Of the few routes in this book that require gear, only one is likely to be on the tick list of most climbers - *Albahida* at Sa Gubia (see page 154). If you wish to do this route then consider taking a small rack including several slings. There is a good deal of traditional climbing on the island but it is not described in this book.

Ropes - A 60m or 70m single rope is advised for tackling most routes in this book. You will be able to get up, and more importantly down, many routes on a 50m rope, but it is much safer to use a longer rope. If you intend to climb any multi-pitch routes - sport or trad - then you will need to take an extra rope for the abseil descents.

Other Gear - Beyond these essentials you may find tape useful for bandaging your fingers if the prickly rock starts to take its toll. For multi-pitch routes a small sack with a water bladder, a long-sleeve shirt and some sun cream are good ideas.

Sport Grade	British Trad Grade (for well-protected routes)	UIAA	USA
1	Mod (Moderate)	I	5.1
2		II	5.2
2+	Diff (Difficult)		5.3
3a	VDiff (Very Difficult)	III-	5.4
3b		III	
3c	Sev (Severe)	III+	5.5
4a	HVD (Hard Very Difficult)	IV-	5.6
4b	HS (Hard Severe) 4a	IV	5.7
4c	VS (Very Severe) 4c	IV+	
5a		V-	5.8
5b	HVS (Hard Very Severe) 5b	V	5.9
5c	E1 5a	V+	
6a		VI-	5.10a
6a+	E2 5b	VI	5.10b
6b		VI+	
6b+	E3 6a	VII-	5.10c
6c		VII	5.10d
6c+	E4 6a	VII+	5.11a
7a		VIII-	5.11b
7a+	E5 6b		5.11c
7b	E6 6b	VIII	5.11d
7b+		VIII+	5.12a
7c	E7 6c	IX-	5.12b
7c+			5.12c
8a	E8 6c	IX	5.12d
8a+		IX+	5.13a
8b	E9 7a	X-	5.13b
8b+			5.13c
8c	E10 7b	X	5.13d
8c+		X+	5.14a
9a	E11 7b	XI-	5.14b
9a+		XI	5.14c
		XI+	5.14d
			5.15a

Grades

The routes on Mallorca are graded using the usual sport grade. Mallorcan grades have had a reputation over the years for being extremely hard, especially in the range from 5a to around 7a. Through successive Rockfax guidebooks we have tried to rationalise these middle grades, bringing them into line with other areas, but there may still be the odd surprise out there. Additionally, routes on the newly developed crags may not have been properly assessed yet.

Colour Coding

The routes are colour-coded corresponding to a grade band:

Green Spots *Beginners* - everything at grade 4c and under.

Orange Spots *Experienced* - 5a to 6a+ inclusive. General ticking routes.

Red Spots *Advanced* - 6b to 7a inclusive. The next level routes to push yourself on.

Black Spots *Expert* - 7a+ to 7c+. Hard routes for dedicated and full-time climbers.

White Spots *Elite* - 8a and above. The hardest routes for the World's best climbers.

Mallorca Climbing

Route Lengths and Lowering Off

The photo-topos have approximate heights indicated next to some lower-offs. These are guideline heights only and it is important to remember that crag bases are not always level and people stand in different places when belaying. Also, many climbers don't know exactly how long their rope is, having chopped worn sections off the ends in the past, or because ropes can be longer than the length they are advertised at. The golden rule is always be on your guard on longer pitches and ALWAYS tie a knot in the end of the rope to prevent dropping a climber when lowering them.

Charlotte Macdonald on the long sustained wall and rib climbing of *Espabilaos* (6a) - *p.91* - at Ca's Catala. This is one of the best crags close to Palma that has a host of very good well-bolted routes in the mid-grades. Photo: Mark Glaister

Iker Pou on one of the hardest routes on the island *Big Men* (9a+) - *p.173* - at Fraguel. Fraguel was one of the island's first hard cliffs to be developed and is still a crag worth visiting from afar - if you are up to the entry grade where the quality lines begin. Like many of the crags in the mountains, the approach is now slightly altered following the snow storm of 2023 which bought down huge numbers of trees. Photo: Pou Brothers Collection

Graded List — Mallorca Climbing

This graded list has been assembled from the votes on UKClimbing Logbooks. If you disagree strongly with the list then register your vote online at ukclimbing.com/logbooks/

9a+
- *** Big Men .... *28* ... 173

8c+
- *** Odissy 226
- *** Bobo dodo 173

8c
- *** Sa fosca 196
- *** Perestroika 309
- *** American Express 226
- *** Aresta gore 126

8b+
- ** Tatoo 126
- *** Amnesia 172
- *** La misión 196
- ** S'Entreforc 197
- *** Master Hit .... *223* ... 226
- *** Domus Dei 45

8b
- *** Commando Madrid 226
- *** M & M's 226
- *** French Kiss 173
- ** Moscovita 309
- *** Empire State 226
- *** No Badis 196

8a+
- ** Mr. Magu 197
- ** Head hunter 126
- *** Macchiato 60
- ** Natiu 197
- *** A vista de pájaro 227
- ** Planet G 78

8a
- *** Motorhead 227
- *** Bota Petit 227
- *** Goo Goo Mack 171
- *** Salpicón de menisco 171
- ** Football Fan 172
- ** La Cripta 70

7c+
- *** Flashback Samurai 209
- *** Pinky Winki 194
- ** Cotorrot 176
- *** Big Sebastian 289
- ** Penthouse 227
- *** Pantano boas .... *175* ... 174

7c
- *** Sarcofago 70
- *** Die Toten Hosen 227
- ** Aloha from Hell 174
- *** Cuencamelo 174
- *** Le gorille a une bonne mine . 172
- *** Terre d'adventure 173

7b+
- ** Glasnost 174
- *** Bobo dodo (L2) 173
- *** Canibalismo vaginal 220
- *** On es l'avi 174
- *** Hoodoo Gurus 227
- *** Club super tres 188

7b
- *** Sweetie the Pooh 219
- *** King Conguito 131
- *** Colgao 226
- *** Fes lo que puguis 173
- *** Pasteles de Isabel 148
- *** Phantomas 188

7a+
- *** To pa ti (Alaró) .... *207* ... 207
- *** Jungle hop 171
- *** Chorrera 78
- *** Ganxito Perfecto 131
- *** Si lo sé no vengo ..... *147* ... 146
- *** Via d'en Pepino 71

7a
- *** Las bolas del chino .. *217* ... 219
- *** Buf! 207
- *** Vall-de-mega 136
- *** Octopussy .... *3* ... 130
- *** To pa ti (Puig de G) 71
- *** Ja som five 188

6c+
- ** Nano 89
- *** Yonquis de la Broca 216
- *** Busibus 120
- *** Sostre den burotet ...... *1* ... 140
- ** Hippipunklperriklautico ... 219
- ** Mexicans Forever 120

6c
- *** Cous-cous 177
- *** Via morito 219
- *** Bombay Bicycle Club 129
- *** Blobland .... *180* ... 186
- *** Nosferatu 224
- ** Sun .... *183* ... 188

6b+
- *** Asulla 281
- *** Al tanto que va de canto . *75* ... 76
- *** Algo salvaje .... *142* ... 146
- *** Es pasto (Dog Walker) 256
- *** Xorics 280
- *** Las bolas del chino L1 219

6b
- *** Récords de Bunyola ... *237* ... 239
- *** 3D 270
- *** Vol de nuit 148
- *** Patito feo .... *178* ... 188
- ** ORC 72
- ** Pepa 139

Mallorca Climbing — Graded List

6a+
- *** Colesterol Party . . . . *300* . . . 305
- ** Bon vi. 187
- *** Wave Scalpel 270
- ** King of Quint 122
- ** Repusai 280
- *** Ses tres Maries 281
- *** Tierra al reves . . . . *161* . . . 159
- ** Beachcomber 280

6a
- ** Nautilus . . . . *273* . . . 280
- *** Suphi . . . . *134* . . . 139
- ** El mar del amor . . . . *187* . . . 188
- *** L'amo de Baltix m'envia 281
- ** El bandido de un brazo 122
- ** Duck 72
- ** Virgin (S'estret) 120
- ** Pineapple 72
- *** Hooters 72
- *** La ley del deseo 157

5c
- ** Crack 279
- ** Dali 140
- ** The Juggy One 280
- ** Camisasque . . . . *Opposite* . . . 238
- *** Papallona . . . . *19* . . . 270
- ** Part forana 120
- ** Movimiento sexy 120
- ** Paramuero 279

5b
- ** Tantum ergo 160
- ** Clásica 281
- ** Covas Bros 88
- ** Yum 45
- ** Cagadero de Gineta. 130
- *** Mario moreno 121

5a
- ** Baba 238
- ** Coordina coordinator 238
- ** End Slab 1 120
- ** Curset 238
- *** Pasión interminable 123
- ** Las cagao 120
- ** Potaje Español 160
- ** Fup 72
- *** Mario moreno II 121

4c
- ** Bon profit 91
- ** La mosca . . . . *249* . . . 250
- ** Zarzamora 121
- ** Lord of the Rings 238
- ** 100 duros 250
- *** Albahida (Gubia Normal) 154

4b
- ** Hembras 89
- ** Primer plato 271
- ** Rama Lama Dindon 91
- ** Stone Lion 251
- *** El vigilant de la platja 281

3c
- ** Schnurzelpurzel 286

John McKenna on *Camisasque* (5c) - *p.238* - at Creveta. The slabs and walls of Creveta are located in a gorgeous setting and for many years have been a prime destination for visiting teams. Sadly however, the bolts have degraded and only a small number of lines have been re-equipped, nevertheless those that have been re-bolted are well worth tracking down. Photo: Mike Hutton

Destination Planner

Area	Routes		up to 4c	5a to 6a+	6b to 7a	7a+ to 7c+	8a and up
The Southwest	Can Ortigues	19	2	8	8	1	–
The Southwest	Capdella	38	1	14	8	7	8
The Southwest	Mont Port	25	–	12	8	5	–
The Southwest	Cala Llamp	22	2	5	5	8	2
The Southwest	C'an Formiga	7	2	4	1	–	–
The Southwest	Puig de Garrafa	114	7	28	37	32	10
The Southwest	Santa Ponça	16	–	1	3	7	5
The Southwest	Ca's Català	38	10	16	11	1	–
The Southwest	Sa Cantera	13	2	7	4	–	–
Valldemossa	Penyal d'es Grau	26	–	4	15	7	–
Valldemossa	Es Verger	35	–	1	14	19	1
Valldemossa	S'estret	137	9	32	52	35	9
Valldemossa	Valldemossa	58	3	15	26	11	3
Bunyola	Sa Gubia	147	6	43	61	30	7
Bunyola	Fraguel	62	1	6	13	24	18
North Mountains	Port de Sóller	35	–	3	17	12	3
North Mountains	C'an Nyic	13	–	1	6	4	2
North Mountains	Gorg Blau	67	1	4	17	27	18
South Mountains	Alaró	76	3	16	20	31	6
South Mountains	Caimari	151	1	34	56	39	21
South Mountains	Grau des Ruc	53	–	1	9	35	11
The Northeast	La Creveta	28	2	13	13	–	–
The Northeast	El Fumat	18	–	5	11	3	–
The Northeast	Puig St. Marti	19	6	12	1	–	–
The Northeast	El Caló de Betlem	27	–	5	14	7	1
The Northeast	Son Servera	9	–	1	1	4	3
The East Coast	Sa Mola de Felanitx	47	5	31	11	–	–
The East Coast	Cala Magraner	66	4	25	22	12	3
The East Coast	Cala Bota	36	5	18	11	2	–
The East Coast	Torre d'en Beu	44	2	14	17	7	4
The East Coast	Tijuana	71	1	10	28	22	10
	Route Totals	1517	75	389	519	389	145

Approach	Sun	Sheltered	Dry in Rain	Multi-pitch	Seepage	Summary	Page	
1 - 2 min	Evening					A small, virtually roadside crag that offers a limited number of mid-grade lines. Slope stabilisation work has affected the approach but it is still quick.	38	The Southwest
20 min	To mid afternoon		Dry in the rain			The perfect venue for groups of mixed abilities. Long pitches across the grades on rock that varies from slabs to overhanging walls. A lovely spot.	45	
15 - 18 min	Afternoon					An imposing large cliff perched high above the sea with a stunning backdrop. Tricky approach on a narrow path and a short scramble.	52	
8 min	Not much sun	Sheltered			Seepage	This spectacular headland has a superb atmospheric cave with some good grade 6s, 7s and 8s. Can be greasy but superb when dry.	59	
1 min	Afternoon	Sheltered				A very small crag with easy access and a set of decent routes, though nothing of any great quality.	63	
8 - 15 min	Afternoon		Dry in the rain			Plenty of excellent routes across several buttresses with sunny and shady options. A good grade spread with easy access.	68	Valldemossa Area
2 min	Not much sun	Sheltered				A small lump of rock with mostly hard routes. It has easy access and is well sheltered, with a face that may stay dry in light rain.	82	
10 min	From mid morning	Sheltered				An excellent crag near Palma with good routes in the mid- and lower-grades. Easy access and popular.	88	
20 min	Afternoon	Sheltered				A minor venue in a quiet location with a handful of decent climbs. There may be break-ins at the parking. Fine views out over Palma.	94	
1 - 2 min		Windy				A great crag high in the hills. Some super routes on very good rock with room for new developments.	102	
10 min	Morning					A finely positioned and extensive cliff with quality routes in the mid to higher grades. Sunny but exposed.	110	Bunyola Area
1 - 10 min	Not much sun	Sheltered	Dry in the rain			An extensive and varied area with some popular sunny crags, a lot of newish development on north-facing walls and one very hard old buttress.	120	
2 - 5 min Roadside	Afternoon	Sheltered				A popular roadside crag with pleasant sunny features across four buttresses. Very easy access and a pleasant place to be.	136	
25 - 60 min	Afternoon		Windy	Multi-pitch	Seepage	The biggest and best crag on the island. Superb single pitches and fully-bolted multi-pitch routes in a magnificent setting.	146	
20 min	Morning	Windy	Dry in the rain		Seepage	High up and shady, with some climbing on tufas that is both brilliant and hard. A must visit crag for hard climbers.	170	
5 - 8 min	Afternoon	Sheltered	Dry in the rain			Only a small set of routes, but they are mostly classics. Beautifully situated for sunsets, and easy to get to.	184	North of the Mountains
10 min	Evening	Windy				A shady mountain crag with a trio of great routes, plus a few others of interest. Good for hot weather, but a long drive from most places.	191	
4 - 6 min	Afternoon	Windy		Multi-pitch	Seepage	A large area with only limited development so far. Superb routes on a big wall, offering cool climbing in hot weather. A long approach drive.	194	
20 - 25 min	Afternoon	Windy		Multi-pitch	Seepage	A magnificent bastion of rock in the centre of the island. Three great sectors with loads of classic routes.	202	
1 - 10 min	Afternoon	Sheltered	Dry in the rain		Seepage	Four varied sectors: a mega-steep cave for shady hard stuff, and three excellent sections with good easier routes and afternoon sun.	214	South of the Mountains
5 - 15 min	Sun and shade		Dry in the rain		Seepage	A shady north-facing wall with some brilliant harder routes. Great for escaping the heat and dry in the rain, but an awkward approach walk.	229	
20 min	Afternoon	Windy				A popular slab and some vertical walls. The situation is stunning but unfortunately only a small number of the lines have been rebolted.	238	
20 min	Evening	Windy				A huge face with some small developments at its base. An excellent set of routes for hot days or cool evenings.	244	
2 min	Afternoon	Sheltered				A small and secluded crag, with a short walk-in. The views are fantastic. The first bolts are occasionally missing. Plenty on offer in the lower grades	248	The Northeast
10 - 15 min	Afternoon	Sheltered				A delightful buttress which has a classic slab climb and some other good routes. There is also a steep sector that features some harder stuff.	255	
10 min	Afternoon	Sheltered	Dry in the rain			A tough section of crag with a selection of higher grade pitches. The crag is a nice place to hang out although the parking is on an industrial estate.	263	
5 min	Afternoon	Sheltered				A superb crag that now has a host of low and mid-grade routes on excellent rock. Interesting setting and approach.	268	
25 min	Lots of sun	Sheltered	Dry in the rain			Seaside sport climbing in an isolated river inlet. A relaxed atmosphere and plenty of routes across the grades. Good for swimming off the beach.	276	The East Coast
30 min	To mid afternoon					A pleasant seaside venue with lots of pitches in the middle grades. The approach involves a short scramble down to spacious ledges.	286	
5 - 10 min	Afternoon	Sheltered				A set of appealing walls set above a seaside platform. Good routes across the grades and mostly with solid new bolts.	295	
5 - 6 min	Lots of sun					Seaside action above a rock platform. Great routes up steep red walls, often with hard starts. A few easier routes as well. Lovely beach nearby.	302	

Faded symbol means only some of the routes are affected by the symbol characteristic

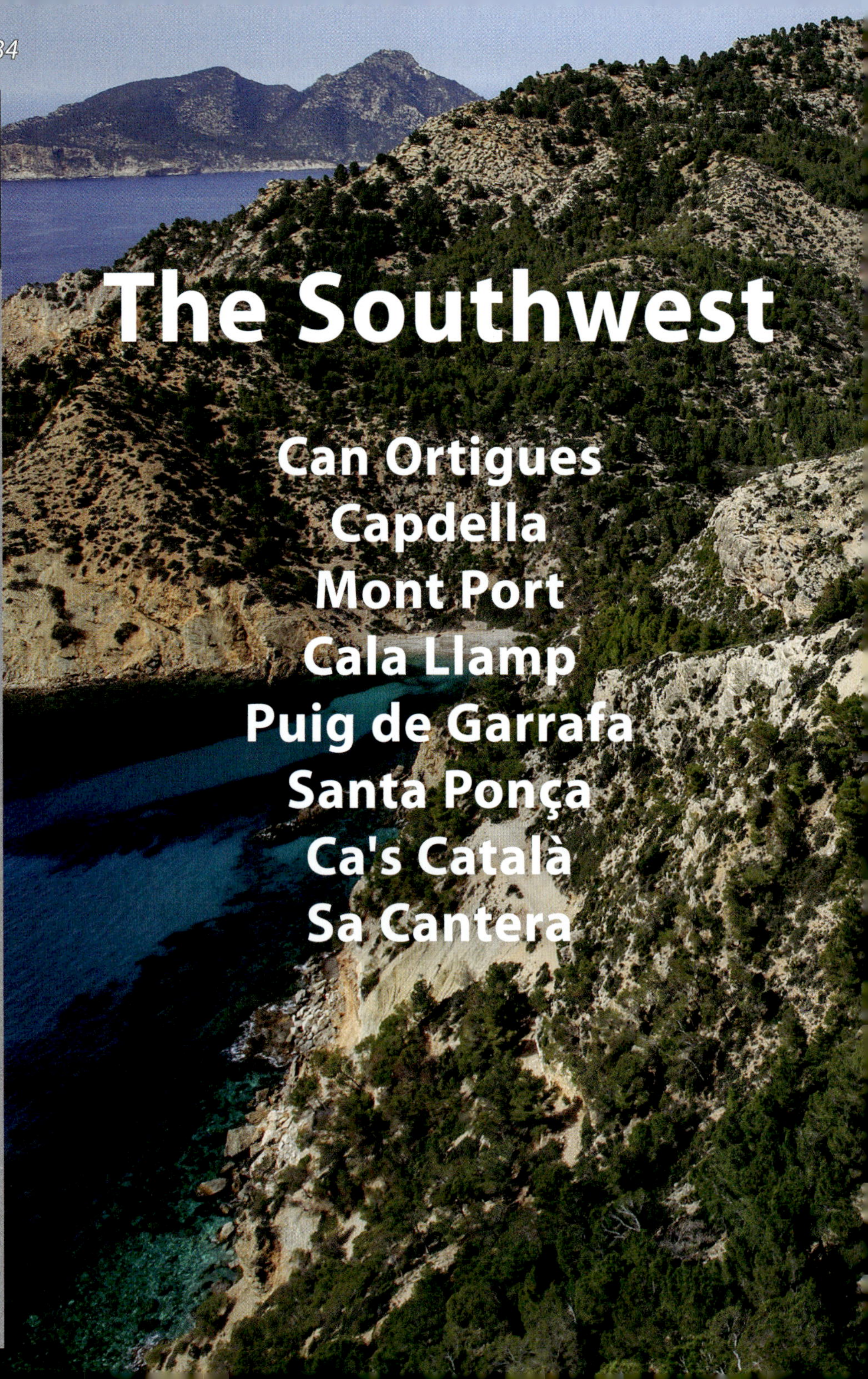

The Southwest

Can Ortigues
Capdella
Mont Port
Cala Llamp
Puig de Garrafa
Santa Ponça
Ca's Català
Sa Cantera

The southwest of the island presents a diverse landscape, ranging from towering sea cliffs to rugged, barren mountains, all within reach of Palma and its coastal resorts. The climbing spots reflect this variety, with locations like Cala Llamp and Mont Port perched high above the sea, Ca's Català and Sa Cantera just a stone's throw from Palma, and Capdella and Puig de Garrafa offering a more rural atmosphere, nestled amongst the inland hills. In this image John McKenna is on the steep upper section of *Namec* (6c) - *p.53* - at Mont Port. Photo: Mike Hutton

Can Ortigues

Grade Spread 2 8 8 1 -

Can Ortigues is a small crag that offers the chance of some brief entertainment for climbers passing this way along the spectacular coastal road. The routes are well bolted and on clean rock although the rock is sharp and some of the routes have hard and slippery starts.

Approach
From Andratx, drive north on the Ma-10 towards Estellencs, Banyalbufar and Sóller. Park in a rough lay-by on the right just after the sharp right-hand bend, following the 103km marker post. If approaching from Sóllervthe lay-by is just after two short arched tunnel sections. From the parking spot, pass a fence and scramble up the short steep slope to the crag.

Conditions
The crag faces northwest and only gets the late afternoon sun. It doesn't offer any shelter from the rain but is a good option in hot weather.

Sal Swannick on *La tuya y la mia* (6a) - *p.39* - at Can Ortigues. Although only a small crag, the outlook is fantastic and the rock excellent. It also benefits from being a shady spot that is virtually roadside. Photo: Mark Glaister

Can Ortigues

A small crag in a lovely setting that has a limited selection of mid-grade lines on compact rock. Its roadside location makes it an ideal airport day crag.

Approach (map and overview p.36) - From the parking spot, pass a fence and scramble up the short steep slope to the crag.

1 Los abajo firmantes .... 6a+
The left-hand line on the wall.

2 Balrog .... 6b+
The right-hand line on the wall.

3 No siento las piernas .... 6a+
The bulging left-hand side of the block.

4 Hobbiton 4a
The right-hand side of the block.

5 Quin clau 6c
Steep and fingery with a hard section after the second bolt. Moving right at this point to the crack gives a nice 6b.

6 Ultimos días de la vítima 6b
The wall is tricky. Above this is a nice rib.

7 Regina 7a
Very technical and fingery. If there is no lower-off then continue up one of the routes on either side.

8 Barbol 6a
A nice groove after a hard and slippery start.

9 La ley de la frontera 6a
After a tricky start to the groove, climb the awkward rib on the right.

Can Ortigues 39

10 La tuya y la mía 6a
Start up a blunt rib then trend left across the slabs. You can climb direct into the next route at the same grade. *Photo p.37.*

11 Armageddon 6a
From a blob, move up left to gain a steep rib where the holds improve.

12 Cultural urbana 5a
Climb the left wall of the corner.

13 Puercoespin 6a
The crozzly wall right of the corner using a hundred holds.

14 Steep Rib 7a
The right-hand side of the rib.

15 Tierra media 6c
Climb the steep wall right of the cave.

16 Club privado 7b
Climb the wall using modified holds.

17 Guancho 6c
Good technical climbing past the blobs. Very sharp holds on the upper wall.

18 The Wanderer .... 6c+
A wandering line with a difficult blank section.

19 Area de servicio 4c
Climb the broken rib on the right end of the crag by either start. The left-hand start is slightly harder at **5a**.

Capdella

Grade Spread | 1 | 14 | 8 | 7 | 8

A crag for all that offers excellent climbing across the grades, featuring everything from gentle slabs to impressive overhanging walls. The crag environment is tranquil and the village of Es Capdella a lovely place to grab a pre or post climb coffee or beer.

Approach
From Junction 22 on the Ma-1 Palma to Andratx road, take the Ma-1012 to Es Capdella. At the crossroads in the middle of Es Capdella turn left on to the Ma-1031 to Andratx. After 1km park at a pull-off on a bend with an information board. Walk up the path and just after it turns left, take a path off right. Follow this along and then up steeply ignoring a branch off right. Where the path fades go right on the better path and take this to the base of the crag.

Conditions
The sun leaves the crag by mid-afternoon. There is a chance of finding dry rock here if it is raining.

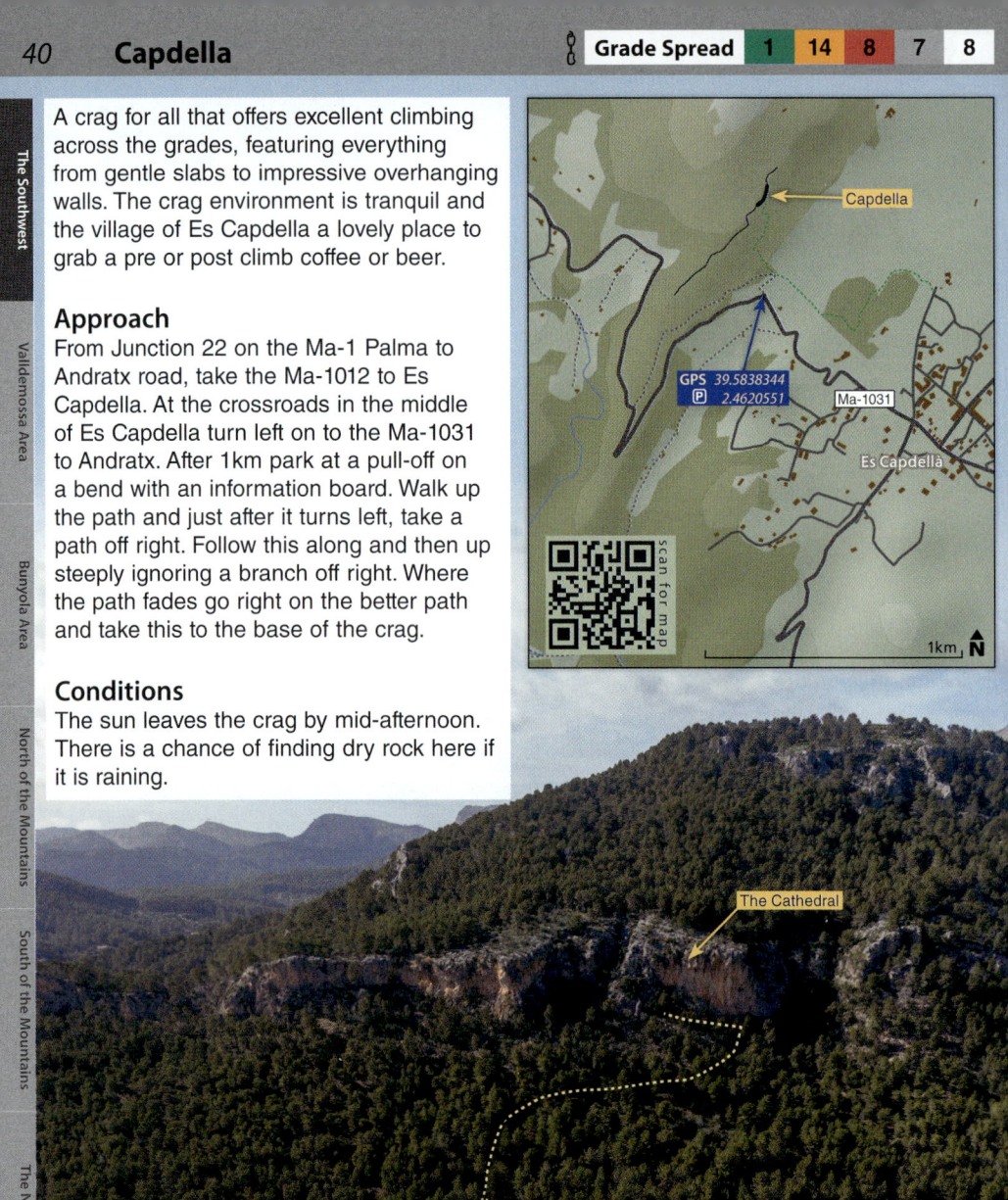

Mark Glaister on the impressive central pillar of *Memento Lower* (6a+) - *p.45* - at Capdella. Photo: Jeremy Wilson

42 Capdella

Capdella

Capdella is a crag for all, having a broad selection of routes in the 5th to 8th grades. Much of the harder climbing is concentrated on the severely overhanging upper walls, whilst the lower, less steep reaches are home to easier mid-grade lines such as that captured in this picture of Paul Cox on *El Monje* (6a+) *p.45* at Capdella. Photo: Mark Glaister

The Cathedral — Capdella

A climber on the well-travelled overhanging tufa of *Total Pro* (7a+) - *this page* - at Capdella.
Photo: Mark Glaister

The Cathedral

The main crag presents a huge prow with magnificent overhanging rock on its upper section and a pleasant slabby apron underneath. The upper pitches are all in the highest of grades whereas the contrasting lower section makes the crag very worthwhile for mid-grade climbers. The grey wall on its right-hand side also has some very good routes on quality rock.

Approach (map and overview p.40) - Walk up the path and just after it turns left, take a path off right. Follow this along and then up steeply ignoring a branch off right. Where the path fades, go right on the better path and take this to the base of the crag.

❶ **Petita Raixa** 5b
A line of bolts on the far left. Currently missing its hangers.

❷ **Yum** 5b
The slab and long slim groove/corner is a fine pitch and one of the best at the grade on the crag.

❸ **El Monje** 6a
The slab and left-leading line of overlaps is capped off by a steep pull to reach the lower-off where *Domus Dei* begins.

❹ **Domus Dei** ...... 8b+
The impressive steep ground above *El Monje*.

❺ **Pranayama** 6a
Gradually steepening climbing leads to a juggy finish.

❻ **Baltasar** .... 6a+
The toughest of the lower wall challenges follows the slab and wall of tufa to a stiff final pull to reach the lower-off.

❼ **El Hombre del Saco** ... 8a+
Move out left from low on *Memento*.

❽ **Memento Lower** .... 6a+
The initial half of *Memento* to the first lower-off is a tremendous bit of climbing on gigantic tufa holds. *Photo p.42*.

❾ **Memento** .... 7c+
Head out left from the initial lower-off. A stunning line up the central prow.

❿ **Memenet** .... 8c+/9a

⓫ **Telnet** .... 8c+/9a

⓬ **Naranja** .... 8a+/b

⓭ **The Best** .... 7c+
Start up *Naranja*. The short extension to the lower-off at the top of the crag is 8a.

⓮ **Total Pro** .... 7a+
Start up *The Best* and go right. *Photo this page*. Continuing to the lower-off of *The Best* gives *The Total Best* 7b+.

⓯ **Afrodita** .... 8a+

Capdella — The Cathedral

16 La Puta del Pueblo — 6a+
A great pitch with holds in just the right place. The tough-looking initial wall with a pocket is much easier than it appears.

17 Sam Sara — 8b+/c
The severely overhanging tufa system directly above the lower-off of *La Puta del Pueblo*.

18 Siddhartha — 7c
Head out right from above the lower-off of *La Puta del Pueblo* to the second lower-off on *Hijo de Cain*.

19 Hijo de Cain (L1) — 6c+
Connect small pockets and crimps to the first lower-off.

20 Hijo de Cain (L2) — 7b
Continue to the second lower-off.

21 Hijo de Cain — 8a
Continue up the blank grey wall to the top.

22 Cain — 6b+
To the first lower-off. A slightly unbalanced pitch that exits the depression on the left.

23 Cain Extension — 7a+
Continue above the *Cain* lower-off.

24 Abel — 6b
Good climbing exiting the depression on its right.

25 Judas — 7a
A long pitch beginning up the grey tufa.

26 El Obelisco — 7b+
Head out right from high on *Judas*.

27 La Marmita — 6c+
A brilliant varied climb culminating with some exhilarating moves up a steep pillar. Photo p.24.

28 El Caldero — 6c+
Thin in its first half.

29 Cadena Perpetua — 6c
Move out right from *El Caldero*.

30 Al Capone — 6a+
Fine climbing on excellent rock that is steeper than it appears.

31 Tierra Doy Una/Sutra — 6a
A full-height pitch with a mid-height lower-off.

32 Lucas — 6a
A long pitch that thins out towards the top.

33 Escoleta — 4c
A shorter offering of similar style to its neighbours.

The Cathedral Capdella

34 Rosa Blanca 5c
Nice climbing between a bush and tree in its upper reaches.

35 Sapporo 5c
The left-hand of two close lines.

36 Ladri di Arange 5c
The right-hand of two close lines.

37 La Porrusalda 6b
A very long route which features a precise crux on the headwall. Take great care when lowering off.

38 Moretti 5b
The final line on the right.

Mont Port

Grade Spread - | 12 | 8 | 5 | -

Set in a stunning location, Mont Port is well worth a visit for all climbers searching out some fine climbing in the 5c to 7a+ grade range. The outlook takes some beating, the view being uninterrupted by the hand of man save for the lighthouse on the distant Island of Dragonera. Bolts on some of the harder lines are old but the most popular routes have good bolts including some with staples. A little beyond the routes described here is a steep cave with a myriad of very hard routes crossing its roof. These are not described here.

Mont Port

Approach
Follow the Ma-1 towards Andratx and then Port Andratx. At a roundabout take the Ma-1022 to Saint Elm and at the next roundabout head towards Son Llarg, still on the Ma-1022. Follow the road for 2km to a crossroads and go straight across onto Carrer Cala d'Egos. Follow this road which starts to climb on some hairpin bends, to parking prior to the crest of the hill (at this point the road deteriorates to a very rough track). Walk up the track to the crest of the hill. The track continues but leave it and take the path that runs parallel to it on its left. After 60m follow a smaller path to the right, marked by cairns. The path leads across the hillside and eventually reaches a short section where rope handrails aid the final ascent to the crag.

Conditions
The sun comes around onto the crag from early afternoon. It is an exposed spot and would not be a good place to head for if a wind is blowing.

John McKenna on the perfectly positioned and much photographed *Pequeño Coatí* (6a+) - p.52 - at Mont Port. Photo: Mike Hutton

Mont Port

The crag of Mont Port sits high above the sea at the western tip of Mallorca, with the small island of Dragonera as a backdrop and little hint of the bustling Port d'Andratx just over the ridge above the cliff. The climbing is exposed and on tall, steep pocketed walls and slabs. In this image, Jeremy Wilson is starting the initial pocket-covered wall and thin crack on *Namec* (6c) - *p.53* Photo: Mark Glaister

Mont Port 51

Mont Port — Sector Dragonera

Sector Dragonera
A beautifully positioned buttress with some impressive steep routes through honeycomb caves on the left, a magnificent organ-pipe wall and then a great grey slab on the right. Some of the bolts are old and in need of replacement.

Approach (map and overview p.48) - The approach path leads to a good flat area under the main cave. The routes on the right are reached by a narrow path along the base.

1. **Approach Slab** 5b
Just before rounding the final corner on the approach to the main crag.

2. **Pequeño Coatí** .... 6a+
A highly photogenic wall climb midway up the final approach scramble. *Photo p.49.*

3. **Alegría** 5c
The corner line starting in the recess.

4. **Hematoma** 5c
The leaning rib is a short but memorable pitch that has a fantastic backdrop. *Photo on cover.*

Sector Dragonera Mont Port

5 Planeta Roja 6a
The well chalked line of pockets and ledges is trickier than it appears. The top pitch is **6a** but rarely climbed.

6 Asteroide .... 6b+
The steep corner has old bolts.

7 Mako 11 .... 7a
The same start as *Sherpa*, following the mouth of the cave to finish above the right-hand side.

8 Sherpa .... 7a+
The same start as *Mako 11*. It has a bouldery section between the third bolt and the lower-off. A very nice route.

9 Shisha Pangma .... 7a+
The well featured wide rib and wall above.

10 Namec 6c
Superb positions and holds once the lower section has been overcome. Staple bolts. *Photo p.35 and p.50.*

11 Nuvol Kinton 7a
The extension to *Namec*. Spectacular views from the rest in the cave before the crux.

12 Kaito .... 6c+
The same start as *Namec*, splitting off to the right about halfway up.

13 Wild Planet .... 7a+
The blank-looking line left of the staples of *Nanga Parbet* on older bolts.

14 Wild Spirit .... 7b+
The extension to *Wild Planet* to the lower-off of *Nanga Parbat*.

15 Nanga Parbat .... 7a+
A magnificent climb taking on the centre of the wall via the mid-height tufa drape. Staple bolts. *Photo p.12.*

16 Ní-Mu 6c
Pleasant steady climbing to a distinct crux at the top.

17 Parque de diversión . 6a+
Pull out of the recess and proceed up the slab to a steeper finish on the upper wall.

18 Diagonal Combination . 6a
A long and interesting pitch. Break out right from *Parque de diversión* and then head up rightwards to the top.

19 Los Deshauciados 6a
The left-hand of three long slab lines begins up the right rib of the recess. Delightful climbing and very sustained.

20 Je suis Charlie ..... 6a+
Some immaculate rock that leads to and from a small red corner at two thirds height.

21 Between the Trees ... 6a
Head up past some trees to get started. *Photo p.55.*

Mont Port — Sector Dragonera - Right

Sector Dragonera - Right
The far right-hand side has two great long routes which make good two-pitch challenges plus two other routes. Take care when pulling your rope down since it can get caught in spiky bushes.

Approach (map and overview p.48) - Do not try and get to these routes from the higher slabby routes. Instead, pick up a vague path which is lower than you expect and contour across to the base - see p.53.

1 Mig día 6a
A steep start on sharp holds soon accesses the slab and some brilliant sustained climbing. Can be split at a stance at 20m.
1) **5c**, 20m, 2) **6a**, 20m.

2 Nice One 6a
A single pitch that ends at a lower-off at 20m.

3 Hielo Negro Left .... 6c+
An alternative start to *Hielo Negro* with a very hard boulder problem start.

4 Hielo Negro 6b
An unbalanced line with a tough start but great climbing on the second pitch. Can be split at a stance at 20m.
1) **6b**, 22m, 2) **5c**, 18m.

Between the Trees - p.53

No access from here

Approach along low path

Paul Dearden on *Between the Trees* (6a) - *p.53* - one of a set of great long slab climbs on the right-hand side of Mont Port. Photo: Alan James

Cala Llamp

Grade Spread 2 | 5 | 5 | 8 | 2

Cala Llamp is a collection of crags which are dotted across the southern headland of the bay that holds the resort of the same name. Access to the various crags is fairly complex and only two of the sectors are covered here. Sector Oasis has a very good selection of harder climbs ranging from some worthwhile grade 6s and 7s to a handful of super-steep grade 8s. Sector Iniciación is a small sector but has some reasonable easier lines and a fine outlook.

Approach
Drive to Port d'Andratx and pick up signs towards Cala Llamp. Follow this road steeply uphill through an area which has a lot of building work and continue driving straight on as it turns into a dirt track, and the crag appears on your left. Keep going on here to the parking spot just before some concrete blocks that stop cars going to the very end of the track.

Conditions
Sector Oasis sees little sun and is very steep and unlikely to get wet in the rain. However it can retain humidity at times and good conditions are not easy to predict. Sector Iniciación gets the sun late in the day and offers no protection from the rain.

Cala Llamp 57

Natalie Berry on *American* (7b) - *p.60* - one of the typically steep offerings at Sector Oasis, Cala Llamp. Photo: Alan James.

Sector Iniciación **Cala Llamp**

Sector Iniciación

This wall offers some routes of interest for those operating at the lower grades. There is plenty of room for development, so expect new routes.

Approach (map and overview p.57) - From the parking spot, walk back down the track for about 70m. Locate some boulders in a gully on the uphill side of the track (possibly marked by a small cairn) and scramble up these to a vague path that heads leftwards. Follow this path through the trees until you reach a prominent sign. Head left here for Sector Iniciación.

❶ Aprendiendo a Volar 6a
The far left-hand line gives the best route on the sector up steepening orange rock. High in the grade.

❷ Humor Amarillo 5c
Steady climbing to a lower-off left of a bush. Well bolted.

❸ Sa via de n'Andreu 3c
A short route for learning to lead.

❹ El Canto de la Hormiga . . 4c
Nice climbing up the left-hand side of the grey slab.

❺ Ratapinyada 5c
The right-hand route on the grey pillar has tricky moves where it steepens.

❻ Lucia 6a
A long pitch well to the right on a pillar. Very good.

Cala Llamp — Sector Oasis

1 Zona de Moda 7a
The first line on the cliff which loops rightwards to finish at the lower-off shared with *Voltor Negra*.

2 Voltor Negra 7c
The leaning shallow arete with small tufa fins and blobs from midway.

3 El Autoestopista 8a
The very steep wall with diagonal thin cracks..

4 Tornillo Torcido 7c
Big holds lead up the lower corner to below the severely overhanging crack/break under the roof.

5 American 7b
The overhanging arete with a potential shake-out on the hanging tufa at mid-height. *Photo p.58.*

6 Cortado 7c
The huge leaning corner/groove starting from the sloping ledge.

7 Macchiato .... 8a+
Start on the edge of the sloping ledge. Climb double roofs and the still steep headwall.

Sector Oasis
A very impressive sector that has some fine steep routes which gradually reduce in grade as the cliff gets less steep as it nears the sea. The approach is a little unnerving on first acquaintance but turns out to be fairly straightforward. Steep, shady and rainproof although humidity can be a problem at times and getting to the base of the crag would be trickier in the wet.

Approach (map and overview p.57) - Walk to the end of the track and use a rope/handrail to go up past some trees to a path that goes right to another rope/handrail. Follow this (exposed) to another path that gains a short easy slab (down-climb) and the base of the sector.

8 Espresso .... 7c+
Extremely steep moves gain a shakeout at some tufa blobs before more overhanging ground. Fixed sling and chain quickdraws.

9 Capuccino .... 7c+
A super-long overhang-infested line marked by a fixed sling and chain quickdraws.

10 El Naturista 6c
A steep start on jugs leads to more involved climbing above.

Sector Oasis **Cala Llamp**

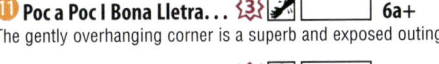

11 Poc a Poc I Bona Lletra . . . . 6a+
The gently overhanging corner is a superb and exposed outing.

12 Cachogenesis Explosiva . . . . 7a+
Climb the steady lower wall to the roof and pass it on reasonable holds to access the fine headwall.

13 Maldito Newton 7a
The tough few initial moves lead to below the long upper wall.

14 Al Mar . . . . 7a+
A huge pitch to the left of the arete.

15 Cafe del Mar 6c
A shorter pitch up the arete.

The next line starts from an exposed ledge around the arete - rope handrail in place.

16 Sin Metros No Hay Paraido . . . . . . 6b+
Steep climbing on pockets gains an easier section of wall. Finish via a couple of big pulls on good holds.

There is another cave below named Sector Rock and Roll. It is reached down a steep gully below the route El Naturista (rope handrail) before traversing right facing in (another rope handrail) to the cave which has routes from 6b to 8a+.

C'an Formiga

Grade Spread 2 | 4 | 1 | - | -

A compact crag that has a small number of intense climbs on good rock, with the added bonus of only being a short stroll from the car. There will not be enough here to fill a day for most, however Cala Llamp and Puig de Garrafa are both close by.

Approach
Turn off the main Palma to Andratx road towards Camp de Mar (the turn off is just before the parking spot for Puig de Garrafa when travelling north). At the next junction bear right, still towards Camp de Mar, but at the next junction turn right towards Port de Andratx. Follow this road for around 2km until a road leads off on a bend by the 2km post. Go down here and round a sharp bend and park where the road forks. The crag is straight ahead and can be reached by a short walk up the slope.

Conditions
C'an Formiga is a sheltered crag that dries quickly and gets plenty of sun in the afternoon. There is very little chance of seepage but it is not possible to climb in the rain.

The idyllic view from the crag of C'an Formiga. Photo: Mark Glaister

C'an Formiga

① **Formigas** 4c
The rib on the left is well bolted.

② **Tiquis Miquis** 5a
Steady climbing with a tricky move past an undercut.

③ **Tata** .... 6a+
Make a stiff pull to leave the ground, then tackle the wall above.

④ **Cap Pelat** 4b
The central diagonal feature. Start up the wide crack and continue up the right-leaning corner finishing on the face as for *Cul Pelut*.

⑤ **Cul Pelut** 6a
The rib to the right of *Cap Pelat* is very thin and it is hard not to drift off to the left. Better but harder (**6b**) is to take the flake-crack on the right of the bolts.

⑥ **Sexo Rapido** .... 6b+
From the hollow, pull up to good holds just above and then make a powerful couple of pulls on hard-to-find holds to easier ground.

⑦ **Inclino** .... 6a+
The final route on the right-hand side of the wall.

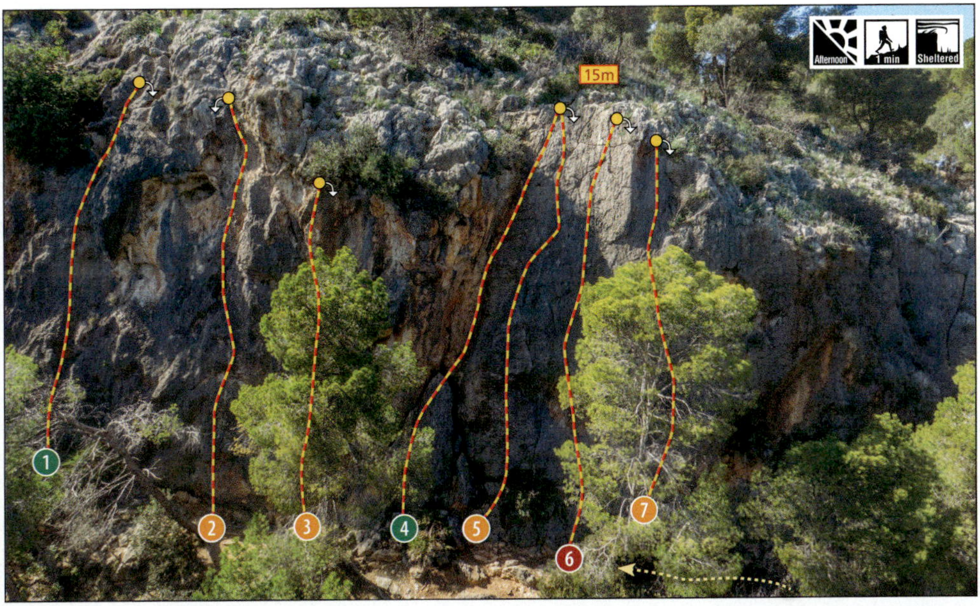

64 Puig de Garrafa

Grade Spread | 7 | 28 | 37 | 32 | 10

Puig de Garrafa is an extensive crag consisting of a number of buttresses spread over a wooded hillside. There are plenty of routes providing high-quality climbs across the grade range making it a good choice for groups of mixed abilities. Most climbing styles are catered for and the best include long pocket walls, a number of steep tufa lines and some fine groove lines. Access is quick, and one of the crag's main benefits is that while shade can be found throughout the day, you can also seek out varying levels of sun from late morning onwards.

Conditions

Sector Sombra is very sheltered and should give some dry climbing in light rain. It faces north and gets no sun. Sectors Corral, To pa ti, Rigor Mortis and Radio 3 may give some sheltered climbing in light rain and all get the sun in the afternoon. All the sectors will seep after heavy rainfall.

Marti Hallett on the steep *Stalactites and Pockets* (6b) - *p.69* - at Sector Radio 3, Puig de Garrafa. This sector has been very recently developed, further enhancing the already fine climbing available at this top-tier Mallorcan climbing destination. Photo: Mark Glaister

Puig de Garrafa 65

Puig de Garrafa

Approach
Leave Palma on the main Ma-1 towards Andratx. After emerging from the second tunnel (a long one) a massive face of rock appears ahead. Continue for 2.4km to the brow of a hill which is halfway between the 27km and 28km posts. Just after the brow, turn right sharply into a small road and park by some waterworks buildings.

For the left-hand sectors - Follow a path from the parking that heads back parallel and just above the approach road to the waterworks. After a short distance various paths break right up the wooded slope to below the crag.

For Sector Sombra and Sector Corral - From the parking next to the waterworks, cross a wall and fence and walk up a wide track to a flat area. Sector Sombra is just to the right and Sector Corral is to the left.

Puig de Garrafa 67

Sector Colmena p.74

Sector Corral p.76

Sector Sombra p.78

Flat area

Track

Path above approach road

Parking next to waterworks

Puig de Garrafa — Radio 3

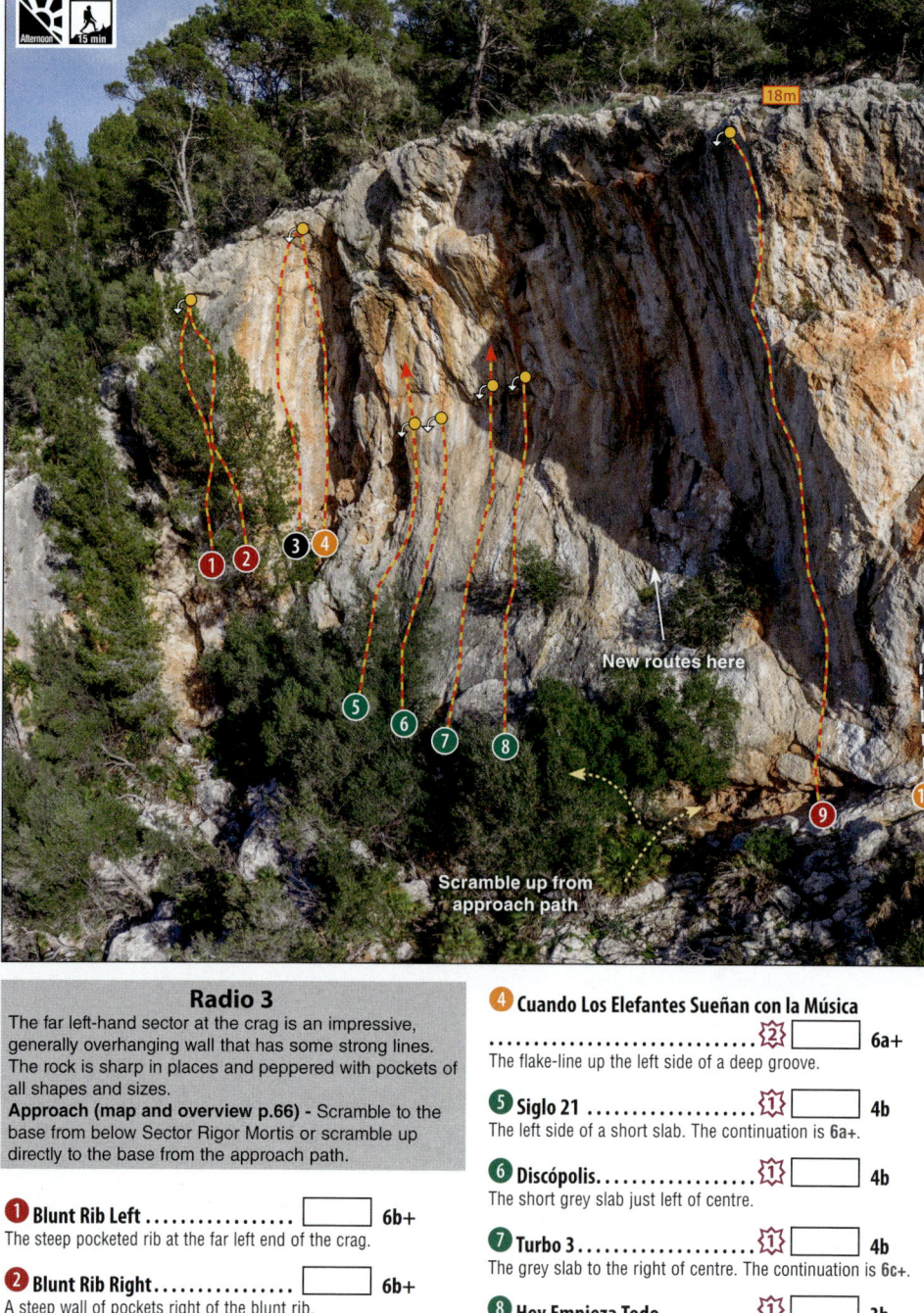

Radio 3
The far left-hand sector at the crag is an impressive, generally overhanging wall that has some strong lines. The rock is sharp in places and peppered with pockets of all shapes and sizes.

Approach (map and overview p.66) - Scramble to the base from below Sector Rigor Mortis or scramble up directly to the base from the approach path.

1 Blunt Rib Left .... 6b+
The steep pocketed rib at the far left end of the crag.

2 Blunt Rib Right .... 6b+
A steep wall of pockets right of the blunt rib.

3 El Vuelo del Fénix 7b
Climb the smooth wall to the left of the deep groove.

4 Cuando Los Elefantes Sueñan con la Música
.... 6a+
The flake-line up the left side of a deep groove.

5 Siglo 21 .... 4b
The left side of a short slab. The continuation is 6a+.

6 Discópolis 4b
The short grey slab just left of centre.

7 Turbo 3 .... 4b
The grey slab to the right of centre. The continuation is 6c+.

8 Hoy Empieza Todo 3b
The right side of the short slab on bigger holds.

The steep wall to the right has new routes from 6a+ to 7c+.

Puig de Garrafa

9 Anusqui .... 6c+
Climb the steep white wall on spaced small pockets and edges to a burly finish pulling up the short sharp arête.

10 Short Pillar Left 5b
The left-hand line up the central half-height pillar that has three lines on it which all share a lower-off.

11 Short Pillar Centre 5b
The central line up the pillar.

12 Short Pillar Right 4b
The right-hand side of the pillar beginning up a flake-crack.

There have been a number of new routes added to the wall to the right.

13 Central Pockets...... 6a
The leaning wall on good pockets to a powerful move over a bulge. Move left and up a slight groove to finish.

14 Rampline.................. 5c
A short wall of pockets gains a rightward-trending ramp. Finish up the steep groove and small slab above.

15 Stalactites and Pockets .. 6b
Steep pulling up big pockets and little stalactites. *Photo p.64.*

16 White pillar .... 6c+
The white pillar on the right side of crag.

17 New Gray Slab 5c
Around to the right, overlooking sector Rigor Mortis, is a lightly featured grey slab. Climb the rightward-trending line to a lower-off.

Puig de Garrafa — Sector Rigor Mortis

Sector Rigor Mortis

This is a tall overhanging wall that is home to a number of excellent hard lines in the 7b to 8b range.

Approach (map and overview p.66) - Gain the wall via an awkward scramble past some large blocks, left of the route *The Lion Slayer*.

❶ Na Marta en el país del Indoorterror
.... 7c
The first route on the wall.

❷ La Noche de los Muertos Vivientes
.... 8a+
The line just right of a tufa up a steep dark wall.

❸ La Cripta.......... 8a
A very good line with a bouldery section.

❹ Zombieland.......... 8a+
Direct up the wall.

❺ La Morgue.......... 7c+
Head up the tufas and then rightwards.

❻ Sarcofago.......... 7c
A great, very sustained pitch. Climb direct to some black streaks then slightly right.

❼ Rigor Mortis .... 7c+
Start left of a block. Climb the long leaning wall left of a bush. There is a left-hand finish. Painful drilled finger slots.

❽ Morir Martir.......... 7b
Superb. Climb the tufa organ pipes from blocks then the steep headwall above, to the right of a bush.

❾ The Undertakers..... 8b
More steep organ pipes and a thin headwall.

❿ Extrema Unción .... 7b+
A recent line between *The Undertakers* and *La boite*.

⓫ La Boite 7b
Start up a detached flake.

⓬ Inteligencia Artificial........ 7a
The right-hand line with some bolts and threads up a crack.

Sector To pa ti Puig de Garrafa

Sector To pa ti

Along with Sectors Rigor Mortis and Sombra, this wall has Puig de Garrafa's best selection of harder routes. Well worth a visit by teams looking for long pumpy pitches in the 7s.

Approach (map and overview p.66) - Follow the approach path up through woods to below the wall.

⑬ **The Lion Slayer** 6b
A tough steep start in the bushes gains the rib above.

⑭ **El Cazador** 6a
Climb direct to a lower-off at the top of a groove. Worthwhile.

⑮ **Skidmark** 6a
Start as for *El Cazador* but break out right.

⑯ **Itchy feet** 6a
The rib to a lower-off is a rather sharp experience on the fingers.

The main event at this end of the crag is the huge featured wall.

⑰ **Es Mirall** 8b
The long-standing project has now been finished. There are some more unknown lines to its left.

⑱ **Equilibrium tremens** .... ?
The thin wall direct to the *To pa ti* finish.

⑲ **To pa ti** 7a
Magnificent climbing up the steep cracks and pockets past two small caves.

⑳ **Hay que joderse pa no caerse**
.... 7b+
A gentle start leads to the first cave. Tough moves gain the tufa and a crimpy finish.

㉑ **Na rua** 7b
The wonderful curving groove all the way. A real line!

㉒ **American Airlines** 7c
Bisects the previous route.

㉓ **Via d'en Pepino** .... 7a+
An easy start leads to a pumpy crack and a hard crimpy section to gain the headwall.

㉔ **Equipo Coliflor** 6c
The line on the far right of this sector. Easier to the right of the bolts at the top.

Puig de Garrafa — Sector Duck

Sector Duck
The right-hand side has a handful of good pitches on water-worn rock. The left side is much steeper.
Approach (map and overview p.66) - Follow the approach path up through woods to below the wall.

❶ Fisura 6c
Step off a tree then wander right across the wall.

❷ Giramita 7c
The hard direct start to *Fisura* is a good-looking line.

❸ Popona .... 7b+
Another very stiff line up the central nose.

❹ El invierno en Alemania es una Kaka
.... 7a+
Begin as for the abandoned project and then follow the right-hand line of bolts.

❺ Dame argo .... 7b+
A steep start left of the cut-away.

❻ Princesa Mara .... 6b+
The wall and capping overhang left of the crack of *Vivan las jarras*.

❼ Vivan las jarras 6c
The steep crack-line. Good if you are into jamming.

❽ Vivan los Shandis 6a
The flared rib is technical and precarious.

❾ ORC 6b
Name plaque at base. Climb the vertical fingery wall on small but positive holds to an easing. The upper rib maintains the interest.

❿ Fup 5a
A fine climb. Follow the crack to a break at mid-height and then the juggy rib above to the top.

⓫ Duck 6a
A good wall pitch on superb rock and holds. Make steep moves up the wall to the left of a broken tufa to a mid-height break. Climb the upper wall on surprisingly good holds.

⓬ Pineapple 6a
Make technical moves up the initial wall and continue more easily up the face above and left of a palm.

⓭ Cheers 6a
The wall and face on good but small finger holds.

⓮ Hooters 6a
Climb the tempting orange wall on some huge sinkers.

⓯ Hooters Right 5a
Begin as for *Hooters* then move right and climb the wall.

Sector Salto **Puig de Garrafa** 73

Sector Salto
A small sector that is severely bulging on its right-hand side.
Approach (map and overview p.66) - Follow the approach path up through woods to below the wall.

16 Chicharra loca 6a
Start up a flake right of a tree. Climb the pillar above.

17 Los Requena 7a
Make a steep pull to gain a hole on the left.

18 Super Lopez .... 6c+
A steep rib to crozzly wall. There is a **7b+** variation.

19 El Salto del Angel .... 8a+

20 Nakles .... 7c+
There may be another line in here - grade unknown.

21 Doog 6c
Make steep moves to a jug rail and finish up right and back left.

Puig de Garrafa Sector Colmena

Sector Colmena
This short section of the crag has a few stiff lines on compact and bulging rock. A number of the lines have recently been upgraded.

Approach (map and overview p.66) - This sector can be approached from either Sector Salto or Sector Corral via the path that runs under the crag.

❶ Lucas 6b
Start on the far left of the wall and pull around two steep bulges, one at the start and one at the finish.

❷ Colmena 6c
Start up the rounded arete then move left out onto the wall. Climb up this to a steep finish.

❸ Ella ya no vive aqui ..... 6b+
The rounded arete shared with *Colmena* leads to a steep finish.

❹ Debil Mente 8a
The severely overhanging wall past monos and crimps.

❺ Juanchi no pudo! .... 6c+
The front of the steep buttress left of a wide crack. Formerly known as *Aresta*.

❻ Cuatre pichos 6b
A fingery and sustained line just right of a wide crack.

❼ Calimocho .... 6c+
Make some perplexing moves to good holds and then finish up the easier (but still tricky) upper arete.

❽ Pitbull 7a
A very steep line following large pockets and a series of bulges.

❾ Ni Araceli se agarra ..... 7b+
Thin rounded cracks and pockets to the right of the large pockets and bulges of *Pitbull*.

❿ Apnea 7a
The rather brutal crack is very steep but short lived. Great if you are into this kind of style

Alan James on one of the crag classic 6s *Al tanto que va de canto* (6b+) - *p.76* - Sector Corral, Puig de Garrafa. Photo: Mark Glaister

Puig de Garrafa — Sector Corral

Sector Corral
A very pleasant section of the crag that features a good selection of routes throughout the grades.
Approach (map and overview p.66) - Head left on a small path from a flat area encountered on the approach path. The crag is a short distance along the path just up the slope, in amongst some trees.

1 Dona Simena 5c
The first line up the less steep left end of the crag. A good little pitch that is 6a for those who cannot reach the good holds off the floor.

2 Polvoron .... 6a+
The right-hand line starting as for *Dona Simena*. After the tricky start, move right and take the groove and orange crack.

3 Ilegales 7b
Pull steeply leftwards out of the cave.

4 El Legado .... 7b+
Hard climbing on small holds after a steep start.

5 Cala Bruix 6a
A varied pitch up the left-hand side of the hole-infested recess. Start up the tree, then pull onto the rib. Climb the rib to a hard bulge near the top.

6 Va de block .... 7a+
An impressive line.

7 Al tanto que va de canto . 6b+
An excellent route up the striking orange corner and left-leaning ramp. *Photo p.75*.

8 El canto del loco 6c
Good climbing up the stepped and bulging buttress to the right of the main groove, at first steep and then technical.

Sector Corral **Puig de Garrafa**

The right-hand section of the sector is shorter and located just up and right amongst trees.

12 Endemicus .... 6c+
Gain the leftward-leaning ramp and make an interesting move to finish out rightwards near the top.

13 Bilitron 6c
A tough little line passing a midway bulge. Use the first couple of bolts on *Bilitron* at the start.

14 Vampiro .... 6b+
Another testing little number. Start up the thin crack-line which is thankfully not too long, and soon eases.

15 Vampiro Right .... 6c+
A thin move up the wall right of the original line.

16 Vampiresa 6b
A tricky little line that has a technical sequence midway..

17 Vampiresa Direct .... 6a+
Heads up from the start of the original line.

18 Macaco 6a
Climb the wall to a perplexing final section.

19 Puta guiri .... 6a+
Take the wall just to the left of the corner-crack.

20 Erectus 6a
The final short line that starts 4m to the right of the corner-crack.

9 Camino al infierno ...... 7b+
Steeper than it looks with a nasty lurch for a finger lock.

10 Bufon .... 6b+
Romp up the jugs and onto the pressing layback.

11 Aprendizaje por tercios 4c
Begin up some huge blocks and finish via the buttress above.

Puig de Garrafa — Sector Sombra

Sector Sombra
Some of the better hard climbing at Puig de Garrafa is on Sector Sombra - 'shade sector'. This is an extremely impressive area with numerous pitches, and one classic tufa climb. There are reports that the grades on some of the harder routes are very stiff!

Approach (map and overview p.66) - The buttress is above a flat area encountered on the approach path.

❶ Alacran 5c
The cracked wall just right of the bushes.

❷ Teresetes .... 6b+
Some sharp holds.

❸ Sindrome .... 7b+
The thin wall and bouldery bulge. Upgraded due to hold loss.

❹ Euribor .... 7b+
Left of the cave.

❺ Mission Possible 7c
The big bulging wall to the left of the classic *Chorrera*.

❻ Chorrera .... 7a+
An impressive and unlikely line at the grade. The tufa has a very steep start but is easier than it looks once you commit.

❼ Columna .... 7a+
Superb and sustained climbing with a very steep start.

❽ Happy End 7c
The bulging wall involves a tough bouldery sequence.

❾ Café del Sol 7b
Steep climbing past a large hole, with a noticeable blank section that is overcome by a bouldery sequence.

❿ Easy White .... 6c+
A fine looking new line up the white rounded scoop/groove to meet a steeper pocketed upper wall.

⓫ Chu, chu, chu... .... 6c+
The left-hand line on the rib gives a thoroughly nasty and desperate bit of climbing to reach the easier-angled rounded rib.

⓬ Chúpamela 6a
A welcome easier pitch up the rib to a lower-off well below the steep top section of the crag. The start is hard.

⓭ Cunilingus 4b
A fun pitch up the easy-angled rib.

(14) Planet G .... 8a+
A very steep section of rock. The line is based on the upper edge of the huge orange recess.

Sector Sombra — **Puig de Garrafa**

⑮ **Sex on the Beach** .... 8a+
Hard bouldery climbing through the low overhang to the slightly easier wall above.

⑯ **Labdance** 7c
A superb and very hard line following the blank open groove.

⑰ **Pussycat** 7b
The striking arete right of the groove is another stunning line.

⑱ **Pussycat/Soledad Combo** 6c+
An excellent link. From midway on *Pussycat* move into *Soledad*.

⑲ **Soledad** .... 7a+
A very long pitch, on good compact rock, up the wall left of a perched block. The initial wall is hard.

⑳ **Dios, no puedo!** 6c
A short intense pitch to a lower-off at mid-height.

㉑ **Dios, si puedo!** 5c
A good long pitch passing the lower-off of *Dios, no Puedo!*.

㉒ **A un metro de la Gloria** .. 6a
The final line on the crag.

Santa Ponça

Santa Ponça is a small crag with a handful of reasonable routes. The crag itself consists of a large 'sugarloaf' lump of rock, perched high on the hillside, overlooking the town and coastline of Santa Ponça. It has a handful of testing routes, the best of which have got reasonable bolts. It doesn't see much attention and is seldom busy.

Approach

The Santa Ponça lump is prominently positioned above the town of Santa Ponça. Leave Palma westwards on the Ma-1 motorway, towards Andratx. Continue to the Santa Ponça exit and head towards 'Santa Ponça'. At the next roundabout, turn left under a gateway and pick up the signs for 'Golf'. Continue along a wide dual carriageway to another roundabout. Go straight on up the hill (signed 'Golf I' - not under the splendid entrance gate to 'Golf II'). At the brow of the hill, turn left at another roundabout (unsigned) to a road with parking on the corner by a school entrance. The signs here suggest that parking is not allowed during school hours. If you cannot park, then continue along the road until it is possible to pull in. Back at the parking spot, follow the track through the gates to the park which leads uphill, past a few junctions, to the Santa Ponça lump.

Cars parked at this crag have been broken into. Leave your car empty with the glove compartment open.

Conditions

The crag faces northeast, so apart from the east-facing wall, it is in the shade for most of the day. Its position on the top of a hill makes it exposed to the wind, although there is some shelter from trees at the base of the crag. If the wind is southerly, the overhanging faces stay dry in the rain. It is also well clear of the mountains, so is worth considering when rained off from there.

Santa Ponça

Santa Ponça

Santa Ponça is a small crag with a handful of reasonable routes. Although not a major destination, is a useful local spot for those staying nearby and wanting a good finger workout. The crag itself consists of a large 'sugarloaf' lump of rock, perched high on the hillside, overlooking the town and coastline of Santa Ponça.

❶ **Flake Route** 6a
Start up a flake, then step onto a steep, pocketed wall. Old bolts.

❷ **Flake Route Right** .... 6b+
Start as for the previous route, but move further right before tackling the wall with the orange streak. Old bolts.

❸ **White Arete** 7b
The prominent, white arete is hard from the outset. Old bolts.

❹ **Wall Left** .... 7a+
The steep wall between the arete and the cave has a hard lower section past a bulge, then a pumpy finish. Old bolts.

❺ **Wall and Cave** .... 7a+
This one tackles the cave with a roof, then finishes up the crack above. Old bolts.

❻ **Cave Right** .... ?
The right edge of the cave and wide rib above. Old bolts.

❼ **Bulge and Wall** .... ?
The lower bulge and wall just left of *White Wall*. Old Bolts.

❽ **White Wall** .... 6c+
The crimpy white wall.

❾ **The Groove** 6c
The deep groove/crack is a strong line but has old bolts.

⑩ The Scoop .... 2★ [ ] 7b
A fine line. To the right of the gully is an awkward scoop that leads to a steep finish. High in the grade. Staple bolts.

⑪ The Wall .... [ ] ?
The central line of old bolts between the stapled lines of *The Scoop* and *The White Groove*.

⑫ The White Groove .... 2★ [ ] 7b+
Follow the technical white groove with a dearth of holds but on an appealing line. Staple bolts.

⑬ The Orange Rib .... [ ] ?
The right-hand rib has a hard start and old bolts.

⑭ Tall Wall Left .... [ ] ?
The left-hand line on old bolts.

⑮ Tall Wall Middle ..... 2★ [ ] 7a+
The fine looking central line. Okay bolts.

⑯ Miseducation .... 1★ [ ] 7a+
The right-hand line has okay bolts.

Not much sun | 2 min | Sheltered | Dry in the rain

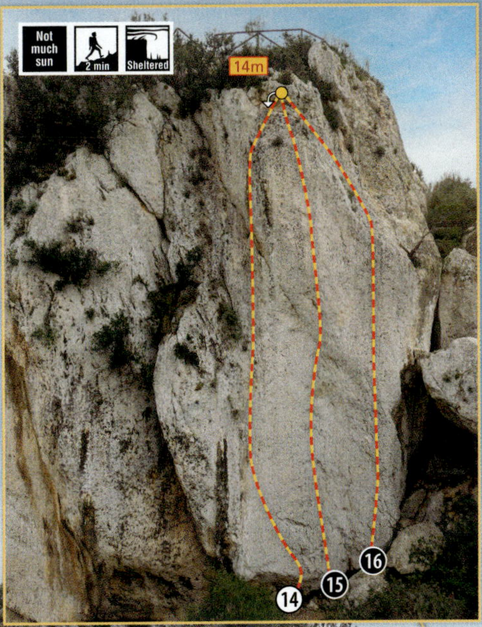

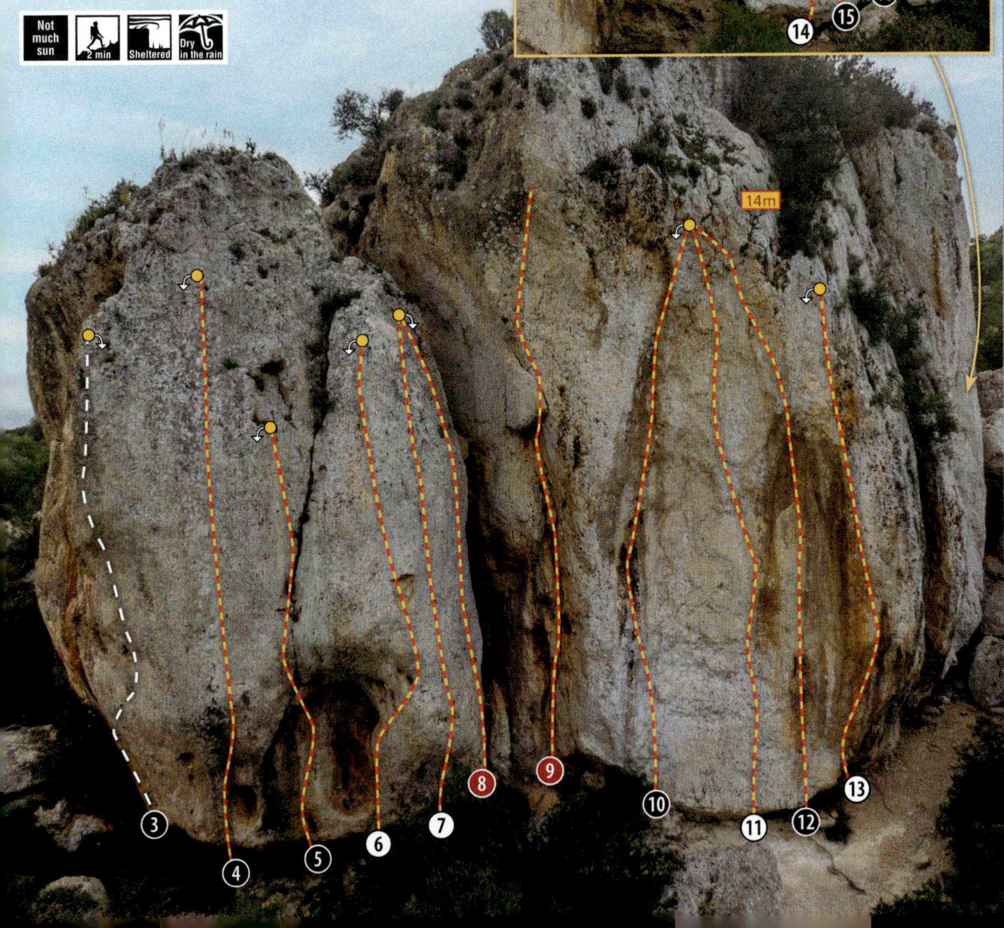

The Southwest
Valldemossa Area
Bunyola Area
North of the Mountains
South of the Mountains
The Northeast
The East Coast

Ca's Català

| Grade Spread | 10 | 16 | 11 | 1 | - |

The Ca's Català crag is set fairly low down amid the coastal development that overlooks Palma Bay and is a fine spot for ticking off some pleasing lower and mid-grade routes. Although surrounded by some impressive villas, the location is scenic and quiet, and the cliff base is a great place to hang out and soak up some sun.

Approach
Turn off the Ma-1 to the west of Palma towards Sant Augusti. Follow the road down into the town and turn right onto the main street. Continue along here for about 1km to an unsigned road on the right of Carrer del Barranc. This can be reached by taking either turning after the large Hotel Zhero on the right. Follow this road as it winds uphill for around 600m, to a flat area in trees with some stone steps on the right. Park here and walk up the curious steps to reach a path. Turn left along this path and the top of the crag starts to appear on the left. A short path marked by cairns leads down to the crag.

Conditions
The crag is low lying, sunny and sheltered, making it hot at certain times but a good spot in the colder months. There is not a lot to go at in the rain. Seepage is unlikely to be a problem.

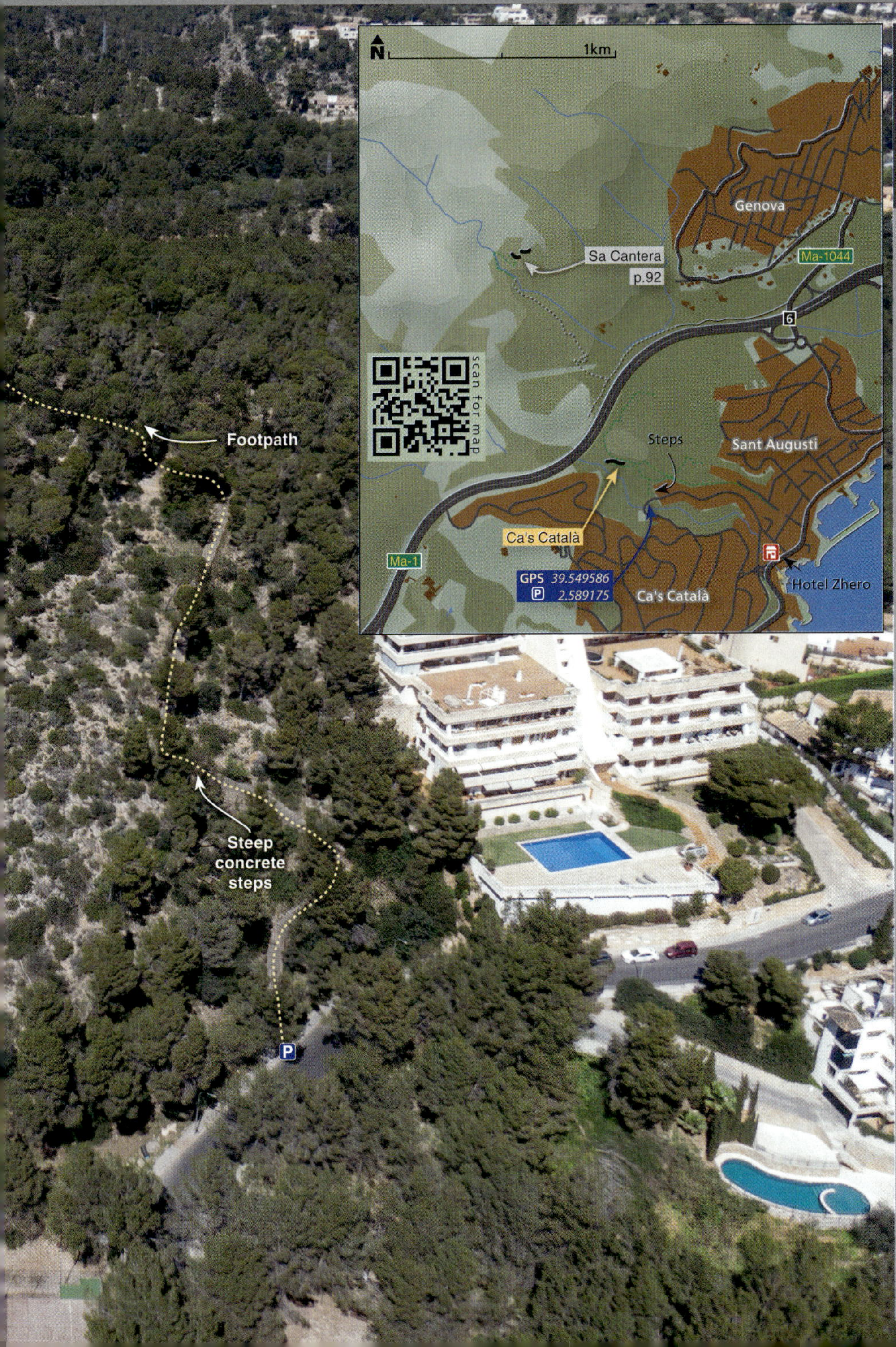
Footpath
Steep concrete steps
P
N
1km
scan for map
Genova
Sa Cantera
p.92
Ma-1044
6
Steps
Sant Agustí
Ca's Català
Ma-1
GPS 39.549586
P 2.589175
Ca's Català
Hotel Zhero

Ca's Català

Charlotte Macdonald about to do battle with the technical crack of *Con el rabo entre las piernas* (6a+) - *p.91* - at Ca's Català. Ca's Català is a very appealing venue that is packed with mid-grade routes. Although it is set between a motorway and the coastal tourist development, it is quiet and has a lovely outlook. Photo: Mark Glaister

Ca's Català 87

Ca's Català

The routes are spread out along a long line of cliff that provides plenty of sport for those seeking out routes in the 4th, 5th and 6th grades. The crag environment is very pleasant even though it is set close to some development.

Approach (map and overview p.85) - From the main approach path, drop down left (easy to miss) to below the cliff. A good small path then leads below all of the climbs.

The first lines are very close together and the bolts and lower-offs can be easily used on neighbouring lines.

❶ Fora nirvis 3b
A short line next to low twin bolts used for demonstrating lowering off.

❷ La roca manda 4a
The parallel line to *Fora nirvis*.

❸ Las fuerzas de la oposición ... 4a
The right-hand line on this section of rock.

❹ Poder fanático .... 6a+
Make some tough pulls past the lower overhangs and then up the (still) difficult and thinner wall above.

❺ La zona mágica .... 6b+
A tough but worthwhile mission. Climb directly to the second bolt and then out left to a rest. Continue up the interesting line of weakness above to a shared lower-off.

❻ Overhang Zig Zag .... 6c+?
Head up steep ground to a flat hold and then concoct a way up onto the headwall and climb it to a shared lower-off.

❼ Morris .... 6a+
A very sustained and varied pitch. Move up the leaning face left of *Ebam 1*, and then continue up the fingery face and rib to a lower-off.

❽ Ebam 1 .... 4c
A long route that follows the rightward-trending open groove and corner.

❾ Ebam 2 .... 4c
Climb the grey wall to an open corner, passing an intermediate chain lower-off.

❿ Covas Bros 5b
Smart climbing up the grey slabby rock to the left of an orange section of wall.

Ca's Catalá

11 Tofal Boxer 6a
A pleasant little orange pocketed wall that leads to an overlap and bulge at the top.

12 Pollo Amarillo ...... 6c+
The orange pocketed lower wall to steeper upper bulges.

13 Nano .... 6c+
A lower rib gains a tough finish on black rock.

14 Roxy Foxy .... 6b+
Move up and left to a finger-rail. Move left again to a good pocket and then on up over a bulge to the lower-off of *Nano*.

15 Cris Tocino 5a
Starting up a short steep crack, climb the rib to the left of the deep chimney/corner.

16 Hembras 4b
The very traditional chimney/corner.

17 La Manada .... 6a+
Interesting climbing from start to finish. Start up a short crack and then take the fingery wall to below a corner. Finish up the corner via some jamming and bridging.

18 Pincho Moruno ...... 6a+
A juggy start precedes a fingery middle section and easier finish.

Ca's Català

19 Toxica .... 6c+
The left-hand of the three very steep bolt-lines.

20 To the memory of Miquel Riera
.... 7a+
The centre of the roof on poor holds.

21 Bateria baixa 6c
Steep, bouldery moves up a right-leaning line gain easier ground.

22 Sensei 6b
Good steep climbing with an awkward move and clip to get started.

23 Trash Out .... 6a+
Climb up past holes, the move to leave the largest of them being the toughest.

24 El rey de bastos 6a
Enjoyable climbing with a long move at the beginning.

25 La virgin del felpudo 6a
The wide rib is an excellent pitch.

26 Macaco radiactivo 6a
Follow the steep flake-line on left side of the hollow.

27 Desconocido .... 6b+
The overhanging line up the left side of the hollow.

28 Orangutan nuclear 6b
The very steep line in the centre of the hollow.

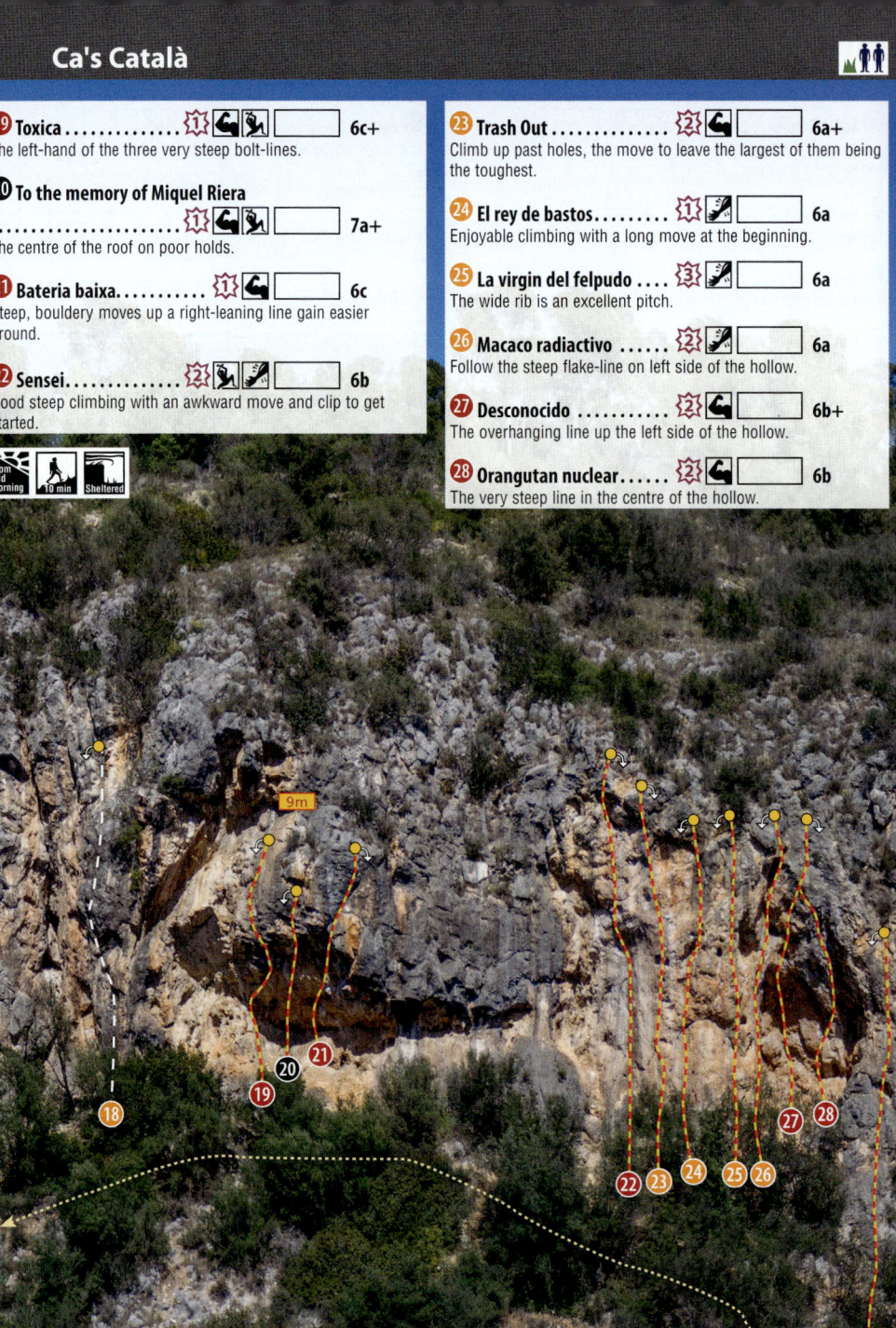

Ca's Catalá

29 Rama Lama Left 4a
An easygoing line up grey rock.

30 Rama Lama Dindon 4b
A lovely long pitch culminating in a small overhang that has good holds.

31 Bon profit 4c
A good route that has a technical section to gain and leave the small corner/groove midway.

The next four routes are reached by a short scramble up to below a steep wall with a depression at its base.

32 Mister 40 .... 6a+
The left-hand line starting in the depression. A very varied and rewarding climb, but not easily accomplished.

33 Twins .... 6b+
Make hard moves to exit the depression and climb the upper grey wall trying to avoid using holds on the routes either side.

34 Con el rabo entre las piernas
.... 6a+
Start up the wall just right of the depression and then take the beefy steeper corner-crack above. *Photo p.86.*

35 Espabilaos 6a
The long grey rib is a lovely intricate pitch. *Photo p.27.*

36 Groove and Wall 5a
Fine techy moves up the left-facing groove and easier ground above.

37 Makarenko 5b
The open, orange groove to grey rock above.

38 Aitornillo 4a
The shallow grey rib.

Sa Cantera

Grade Spread 2 | 7 | 4 | - | -

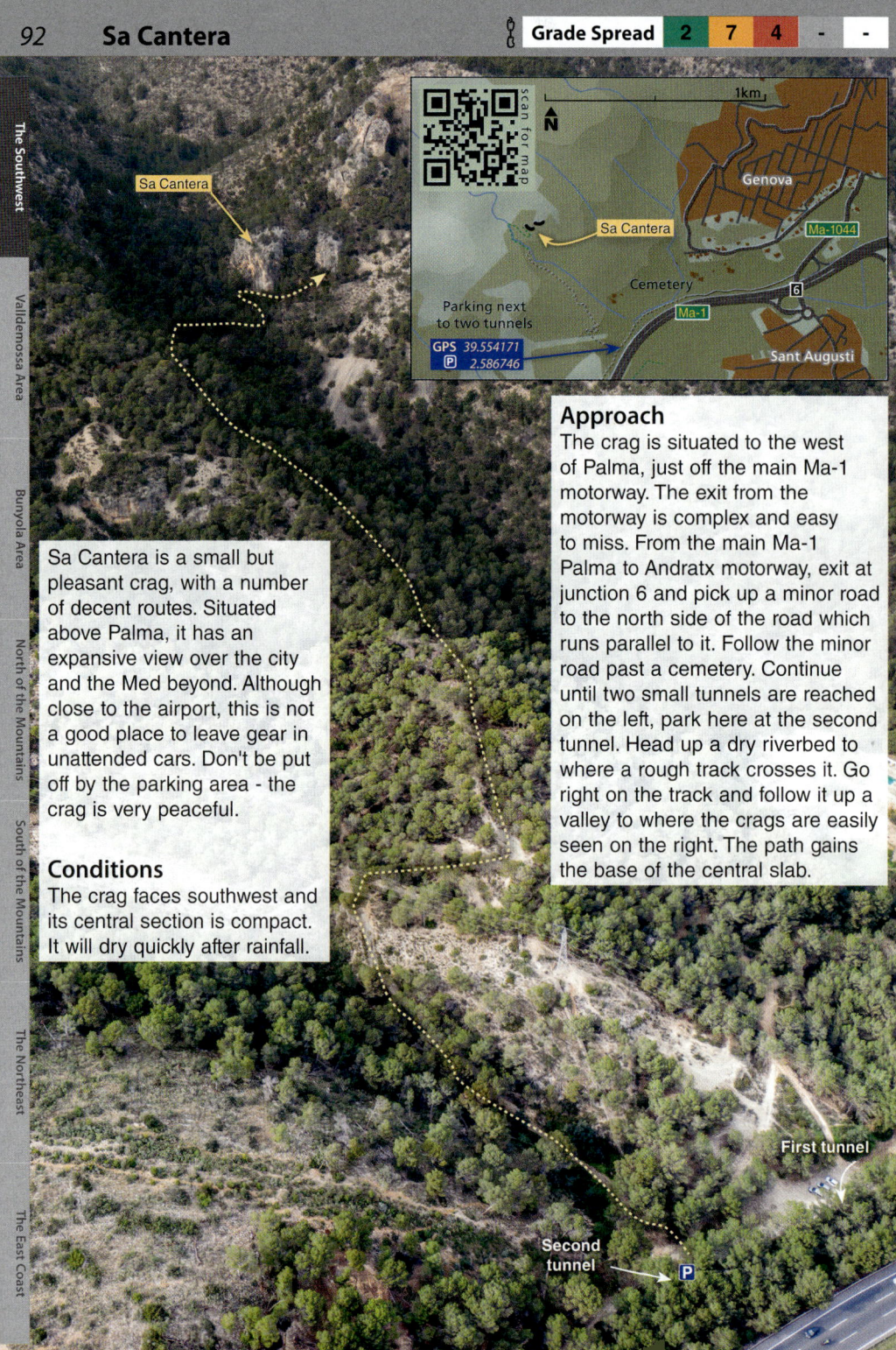

Sa Cantera is a small but pleasant crag, with a number of decent routes. Situated above Palma, it has an expansive view over the city and the Med beyond. Although close to the airport, this is not a good place to leave gear in unattended cars. Don't be put off by the parking area - the crag is very peaceful.

Conditions
The crag faces southwest and its central section is compact. It will dry quickly after rainfall.

Approach
The crag is situated to the west of Palma, just off the main Ma-1 motorway. The exit from the motorway is complex and easy to miss. From the main Ma-1 Palma to Andratx motorway, exit at junction 6 and pick up a minor road to the north side of the road which runs parallel to it. Follow the minor road past a cemetery. Continue until two small tunnels are reached on the left, park here at the second tunnel. Head up a dry riverbed to where a rough track crosses it. Go right on the track and follow it up a valley to where the crags are easily seen on the right. The path gains the base of the central slab.

Parking next to two tunnels
GPS 39.554171 2.586746

Sa Cantera 93

Starting out on the crux wall of *Sa Bruta* (6b+) - p.95 - at Sa Cantera. Photo: Mark Glaister

Sa Cantera

Sa Cantera
The main area has a tall grey slab of reasonable rock. The other routes are up and left on a steeper section.

The first routes are on the left-hand wall, up and left of where the approach path meets the base of the crag. They are accessed via a short scramble to a broad ledge system.

1 Manada salvaje 5a
Gain and climb the rib on the far left of the face.

2 Putero perdut 5a
Move up to gain a hanging slab from a pillar on the right.

3 Lucas 6a
Climb the right-hand edge of the cave.

4 Sa Cantera .... 6c+
Ascend the steep, pocketed wall to a lower-off on the lip.

5 Sa nina va moguda... 6c+
Good climbing up a long open corner. Given 6a+ elsewhere but proves to be much stiffer.

6 Caperucita 4a
Just left of the main slab.

7 Variante Neo 5c
Climb the corner/groove to join up with the upper half of *Neo*.

8 Neo 5c
A sustained line with technical moves at the start...and the finish too, come to think of it.

Sa Cantera

9 Fantasmas al amanecer.. 6b
The central line up the dominating wide open corner, mainly on its left wall. Excellent technical climbing.

10 Sa fisura............. 6a+
Climb up to a hole and pass it on the left to gain a short crack. Finish at the lower-off above this - not the higher one, as the rock is broken.

11 Sa Bruta........... 6b+
Pull out direct from the hole, then move up rightwards, otherwise you will find yourself on *Sa fisura*. Steep moves right of the bolts lead back onto the headwall to finish. *Photo p.93.*

The next section of crag is 70m up and right of the central slab.

12 Fondo sur............ 5a
A very nice pitch on some excellent but very sharp rock.

13 La abuela y sus pelotas .. 4c
The final line at the crag, again on very sharp rock.

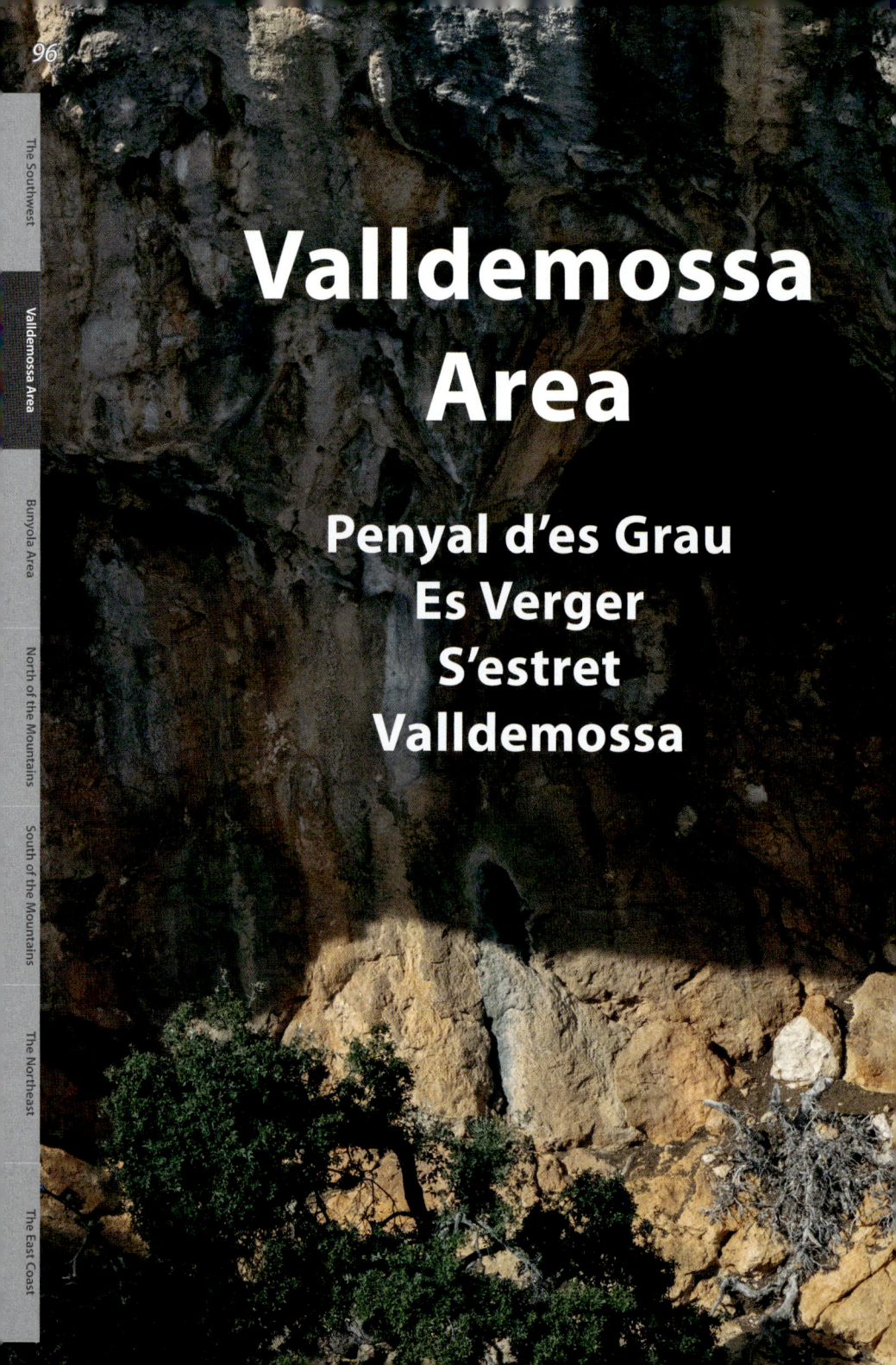

Valldemossa Area

**Penyal d'es Grau
Es Verger
S'estret
Valldemossa**

The Valldemossa Area encompasses a quartet of brilliant crags which have plenty of routes to keep all abilities happy. Each crag is also endowed with a magnificent outlook and nearby lively village for a post climb coffee or beer. Here Paul Dearden is sampling the steep pocket-pulling moves on *S'ancora* (6a+) - *p.110* - at Es Verger. Photo: Mike Hutton

Penyal d'es Grau

One of the best smaller crags in the area, which although not extensive, has something to keep most looking for some quality 6s and lower end 7s happy for a day or so. The cliff is located in a remote wooded section of the mountains but is only a matter of seconds from the parking.

Approach
Take the road from Palma to the town of Esporles. Continue through the town to a turn on the left towards Puigpunyent. Follow this narrow road up for around 6km and over the col 'Es Grau - 468m'. Drop down and park anywhere you can on the first hairpin after the col. There is limited space on the bend with a few more places possible further down. The first buttress is almost directly above the bend with the main area being further along.

Conditions
The main crag faces west and although fully in the sun in the afternoon, has a number of trees at its base that will give some shade. The crag is up in the mountains so will catch any westerly winds and is exposed to poor weather. Seepage could be a problem following prolonged rainfall.

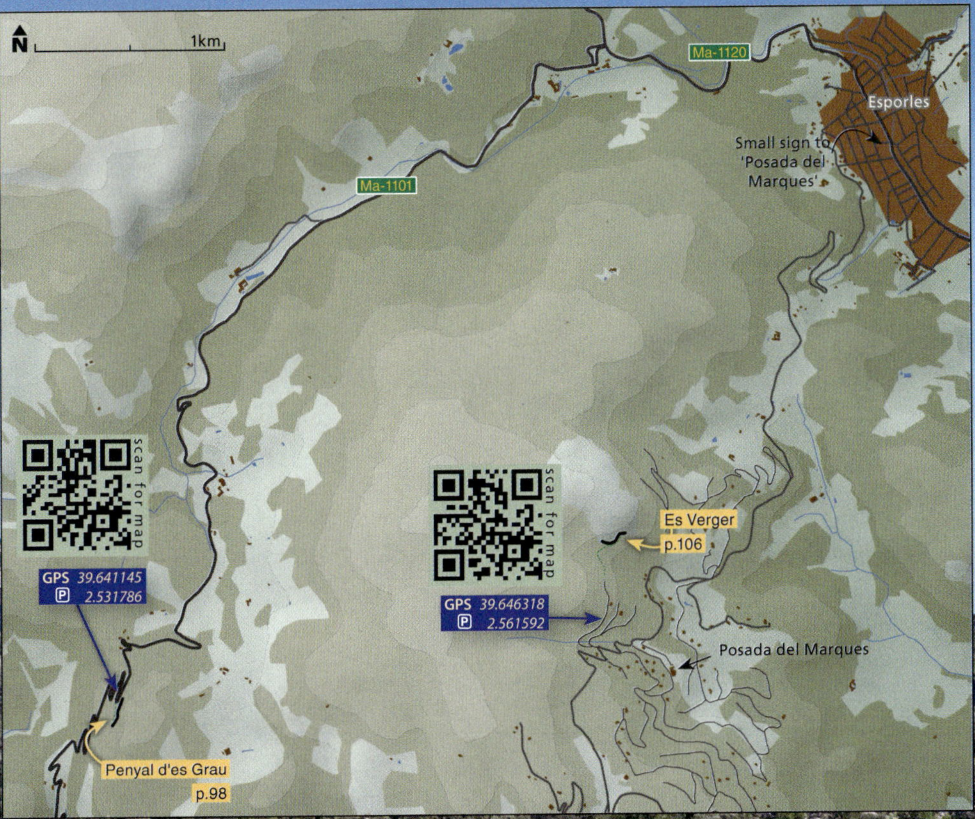
N
1km
Ma-1120
Esporles
Small sign to 'Posada del Marques'
Ma-1101
scan for map
GPS 39.641145
P 2.531786
scan for map
Es Verger
p.106
GPS 39.646318
P 2.561592
Posada del Marques
Penyal d'es Grau
p.98

Main Wall
p.102

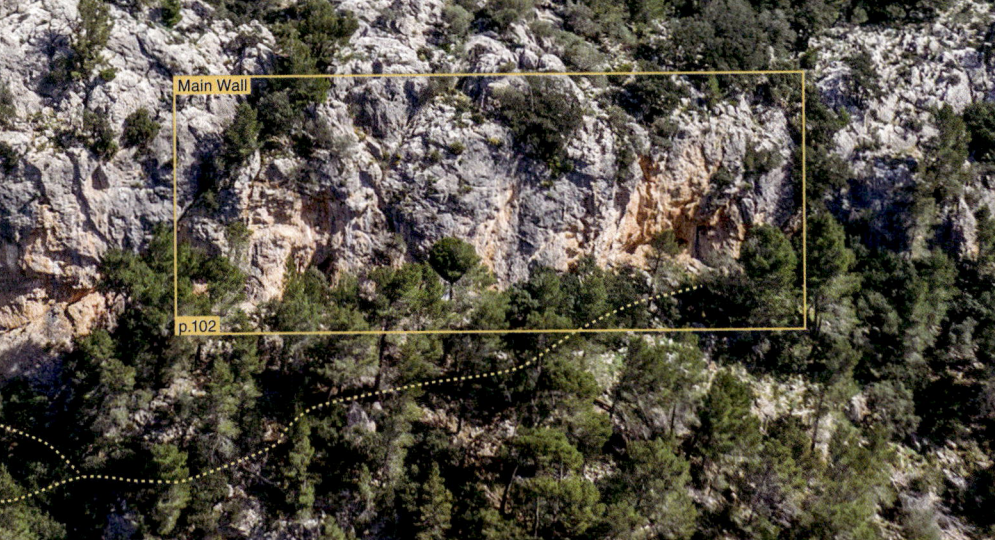

Penyal d'es Grau

Valldemossa Area

Penyal d'es Grau

Martin McKenna approaching the well-named final hanging groove of *Intricate* (6a) - *p.103* - at the remote Penyal d'es Grau. Penyal d'es Grau is a fine roadside escarpment located close to the top of a col reached by a very windy road. All of the routes have plenty of character and those in the 6th grade feel pretty tough. Photo: Mike Hutton

Penyal d'es Grau — Above the Road

Above the Road
The wall almost directly above the bend in the road has three long routes described and some new development.
Approach (map and overview p.99) - Scramble up to a ledge under the face.

❶ Voltor Negra .... 7a+
Good moves and plenty of them.

❷ Aguila Bonelli 7b
A short route with a bouldery section.

❸ Misteri .... 7a+
An excellent pitch starting up a fat slippery tufa. A sustained wall on varied holds leads to a shakeout then final overhang.

Main Wall
The main section consists of a wall of bulging orange and grey rock giving a series of good short routes that pack a lot in for their length.
Approach (map and overview p.99) - Follow the path from the routes above the road bend along to the wall which quickly appears above you on the left.

❹ E.O.S 6c
On the far left of the wall is a hanging acute groove.

❺ Mariol.lo 6a
A nice little wall of flowstone that gradually increases in difficulty as height is gained.

❻ White Bulging Wall 6c
The blank wall right of some tufas to a shared lower-off

Main Wall Penyal d'es Grau

7 Tufa Time .... 6b+
The steep short tufa to the wall.

8 Intricate 6a
More intricate than it looks, especially in the slanting corner near the top. *Photo p.100.*

9 Txorrack 5c
Climb the wall on positive holds. Steeper than it appears.

10 Cafetut .... 6a+
The thin moves and bulge meet the left slanting crack. Move out right and push on up the wall before your strength runs out.

11 Aquiles 6b
The steep hanging corner/groove on the far right of the wall to a shared lower-off with *Cafetut*.

12 Arran 6c
Climb just right of the leaning arete on some sharp holds.

13 Saltimbanquis .. 7b
A hard line up the centre with a thin pull at the top.

14 Fatima 7a
A good varied line that features a slopey start and a thin finish.

15 O.A.T. .... 6b+
Start up a thin vertical wall to a rest, then continue up steeper ground on better holds.

16 Tall en Verduc 6c
An intense sequence off the deck reaches the left end of the slim overhang. Easier (but still interesting) ground above.

17 Flake to Overlap 7a
Take the wall and right side of the slim overhang.

18 Orange Hollows 7a
Make some powerful pulls to some orange hollows then take the steep wall above to an easing and lower-off.

Penyal d'es Grau — Main Wall

19 Es Grau — 6b+
Head up the leaning wall via holes and a fin of rock, until a depressingly hard move allows access to the lower-off. Pumpy.

20 Link In — 6c+
A couple of bolts that allow a link-up from *Es Grau* to *Black Block*.

21 Black Block — 7a
The long wall to the left of tufa.

22 FMI — 7b
A great looking pitch up the left side of the long tufa and overhanging headwall.

23 Talaiot Corcat — 6c
A challenging pitch that takes very steep rock just to the right of the tufa. Only really uses the tufa for feet. *Photo opposite*.

24 Orange Pockets — 7b+
A low overhang and then pockets up the smooth bulging orange wall to join and finish up *Talaiot Corcat*.

25 Overhang, Crack and Corner — 7a+
The low overhang as for *Orange Pockets*, then right to the crack and final overhang.

26 Wassabi — 6c
Climb the corner via a steep entry.

Martin McKenna nearing the finish of *Talaiot Corcat* (6c) - *opposite* - at Penyal d'es Grau.
Photo: Mike Hutton

Es Verger

Es Verger is a lovely crag, set way up in the hills above Esporles. Despite this, it is relatively straightforward to get to. The crag has a mix of mid to high grades, which are well bolted and range from steep tufa to more fingery and technical wall climbs. The views from the cliff are superb, and the valley is a very tranquil place.

Approach   Map p.99

Take the road from Palma to the town of Esporles. Drive up the long main street and keep an eye out for a small sign on the left signposted to 'Posada del Marques'. Follow the road up the hillside for 4.5km to Posada del Marques (a small country hotel) and 100m beyond its entrance, turn right. Continue up the steep hill (ignoring two left turns) to a fork. Take the left fork and drive up the road to a clearing near the end of the road. This last section is very rough so don't push your car too far and park earlier if in doubt. Follow the old track and pick up a footpath across the slope. This can be hard going due to fallen trees but gradually a clear path is being formed.

Conditions

The main crag faces due south and gets all the sun going. However, it is also exposed to the elements. Seepage will be a problem following periods of prolonged rainfall. It's possible to climb on some of the steep sections in light rain, but Es Verger is up in the hills so will generally have poorer weather than lower crags.

John McKenna on *S'àmfora* (6b) - *p.111* - at Es Verger. Photo: Mike Hutton

Alan James on *S'àncora* (6a+) - *p.110* - at Es Verger, one of many long and sustained pitches on steep red rock.
Photo: Mike Hutton

Es Verger — Sa Cova

Sa Cova

A good section of crag on the left with a decent selection of pitches in the mid to higher grades. The base of the crag is flatish and shaded by trees, which is useful in hot weather.

Approach (map p.99, overview p.106) - Take the rough path from the parking heading slightly rightwards initially, avoiding the fallen trees. Once you can see the crag over to the right, make your way up the rough slope towards the crag. This approach has been ravaged by tree fall but it will hopefully clear up as more climbers visit.

❶ Retruc .... 7a+
Climb a short wall to the right side of a ledge at 4m, then climb the bulging grey wall above.

❷ Truc 7a
Start up *Retruc,* then follow the right-hand line up orange pockets to a grey wall above an undercut.

❸ Vull fer més 7b
The bulging wall starting just right of a bush.

❹ Si t'aplec 7b
Steep tufa climbing to a hard and reachy finish.

❺ Es Verger .... 7b+
A steep entry to the crack above the upper cave.

❻ Amoniac amb sal 7c
Move leftwards across the lip of the cave to join and finish up *Es Verger.*

❼ Aferrar i xapar 7b
Direct above the traverse of *Amoniac amb sal.*

❽ S'àncora .... 6a+
Big holds on some steep ground to a bulging finish. A bit steep for a warm-up, but it is the only one you have got.
Photo p.20, p.96 and p.108.

Sa Cova Es Verger

9 S'àmfora 6b
The pocketed wall up the hanging pillar. Finishing left is an easier option but the proper finish has its own lower-off. *Photo p.107.*

10 Sa figuera borda .... 6c+
The wall and shallow corner via a move leftwards at mid-height. It can be a bit dusty.

11 Es cul mos cou 7a
The wall and holes via a runnel on the right at mid-height.

12 Xurrito .... 7b+
The thin wall into the runnel.

13 Campamento para gordos 6c
Climb a vertical crack and then pull into a long corner-groove. Keep going further than you think.

14 Balanceta .... 6b+
The left-trending line of bolts crossing *Campamento para gordos*.

15 Campamento Balanceta . 6b+
The best combination is to start as for *Balanceta* and finish up *Campamento para gordos*.

16 Sobremunt 7c
Right of a project is a bulging pillar.

17 Sangonera 7c
The very thin wall.

18 Esclatabutses .... 6c+
The wall has some hard moves to a slightly steeper finish. Great climbing with rests but save a bit for the finish.

19 Blunt Arete .... 7b+
The steep, blunt arete to the right of a corner.

20 Anamvichi 7b
The thin wall.

Es Verger — Es Sotil

Es Sotil

This section of the crag is less popular and has some very long routes - watch the end of the rope!

Approach (map p.99, overview p.106) - Take the rough path from the parking heading slightly rightwards initially, avoiding the fallen trees. Once you can see the crag over to the right, make your way up the rough slope towards the crag. This approach has been ravaged by tree fall but it will hopefully clear up as more climbers visit. The first sector is Sa Cova - walk up past this to reach Es Sotil.

The next two pitches are very long - take care when lowering off. It is possible to scramble up the ledge at 1/3 height and start from there, which makes the route do-able on a 70m rope.

❶ Slap 7b
The massive wall and overhang on its left-hand side.

❷ Sa rota magnètica ...... 7a+
A hard, fingery start to a ledge - as for *Slap*. Climb to the overhangs where blind moves gain the final difficult slab.

❸ Petit quer .... 7a+
A long line through the right-hand end of the upper overhang.

Es Sotil **Es Verger** 113

| ④ | S'única | 6c |

The left side of the steep wall.

| ⑤ | Flake and wall | 6b |

The right-hand side of the crack to a wall.

| ⑥ | Genma | 7a |

Climb up a white streak.

| ⑦ | Entre dos | 7a+ |

Move right out of *Genma*.

| ⑧ | Entre tres | 7a+ |

Move right from *Entre dos* into *Paparrina*.

| ⑨ | Paparrina | 7a+ |

Start up a steep rib to gain a long wall.

| ⑩ | El enterrador | 6c |

A beautiful grey slab and wall.

| ⑪ | Lumbago permanent | 7a |

Follow a slab to a niche.

Across a gully is a huge corner capped with a roof.

| ⑫ | Es ferreret | 7a |

The left-hand side of the arete is spectacular.

| ⑬ | S'àtic | 7c+ |

The right-hand side of the arete on the same bolts as *Es ferreret*. There is a project up the corner.

| ⑭ | Es sòtil | 8a |

The right-hand side of the corner to a big steep finish.

| ⑮ | Es cantò | 7b+ |

Climb the right-hand side of the arete.

S'estret

Grade Spread | 9 | 32 | 52 | 35 | 9

S'estret is an area of easily accessed crags, located just to the south of the beautiful village of Valldemossa. The various walls offer different attractions for climbers: a series of pleasantly-situated west-facing walls overlooking the road in the valley bottom; an old abandoned quarry that has a number of exceptional hard routes; and some more recently developed walls of eye-catching white limestone. Sector Cuarentón has a large set of routes spread across three separate walls, including some excellent easier-grade slab routes. Above these are some good longer pitches on Sector Pasión. The steep Sector Mejicano gives some ultra-hard pitches that are well worth seeking out when it is hot or wet. The four sectors to the right of the quarry are excellent with lots of high-quality mid-grade lines As a final attraction, there is some bouldering available in the woods below the crag which isn't documented here.

Conditions

Sectors Mejicano, Cabra Zombi, Raska y Gana, All Right, Xurasco and Conguito face due north and their bases are shrouded by trees making for sheltered and cool climbing. The hard routes are also likely to stay dry in heavy rain. Sector Cuarentón gets the afternoon sun but is exposed to the wind down the valley and is not rainproof.

Bridget Glaister on *Fallen Angel* (4c) - *p.121* - at Sector Mario, S'estret. S'estret is a fantastic venue for those operating at either end of the grade spectrum. The numerous sectors are spread out on either side of the valley running up to Valldemossa, and shade and sun can be found throughout the day - a bonus for those seeking out shade in warm weather, or heat on cold days. Photo: Mark Glaister

Approach

Take the Ma-1110 from Palma towards Valldemossa. If approaching from the northeast, you can cut across from the motorway via Palmañola to pick up the Ma-1110 at S'Egleieta. After 4km, just past the 14km post on the roadside, pull into a lay-by on the left, next to a bridge over a dry river bed. This lay-by is 3km before Valldemossa.

Sector Cuarentón - From the parking, cross the road and locate a path at the upstream end of the crash barrier. Follow the path, and after 100m, drop down some old tiled steps and continue along the path to just before the second pylon. The sectors begin near this point - see the detailed description with the sectors.

Sector Cabra Zombi - Walk into the woods and, just before the old gate, head up left to the crag.

Sectors Mejicano, Raska y Gana, All Right, Xurasco and Conguito - From the parking, follow a track through the trees. The boulders are on the left after 250m. For Sector Mejicano, break off left up the hill after passing the boulders.
For Sectors Raska y Gana, All Right, Xurasco and Conguito, continue walking through the trees and break up leftwards to the white walls.

S'estret 117

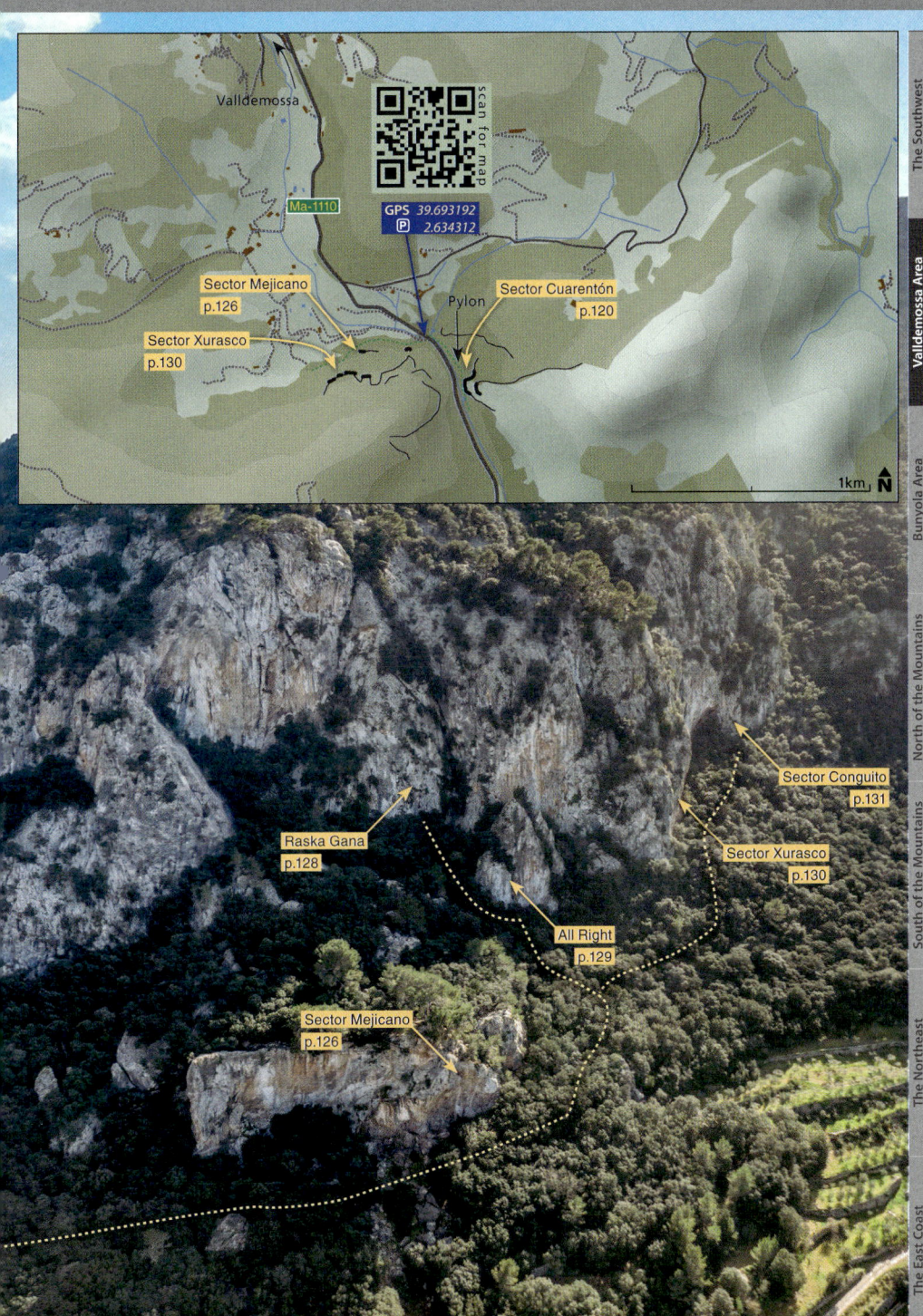

Martin McKenna on *Odio a cobi* (7b) - *p.127* - at Sector Mejicano, S'estret. This sector has a line-up of the harder pitches on offer at S'estret, along with the added benefit of being in the shade all day. Nearby are lots of other shady sectors with a slightly easier selection of grades.
Photo: Mike Hutton

S'estret — Sector Cuarentón

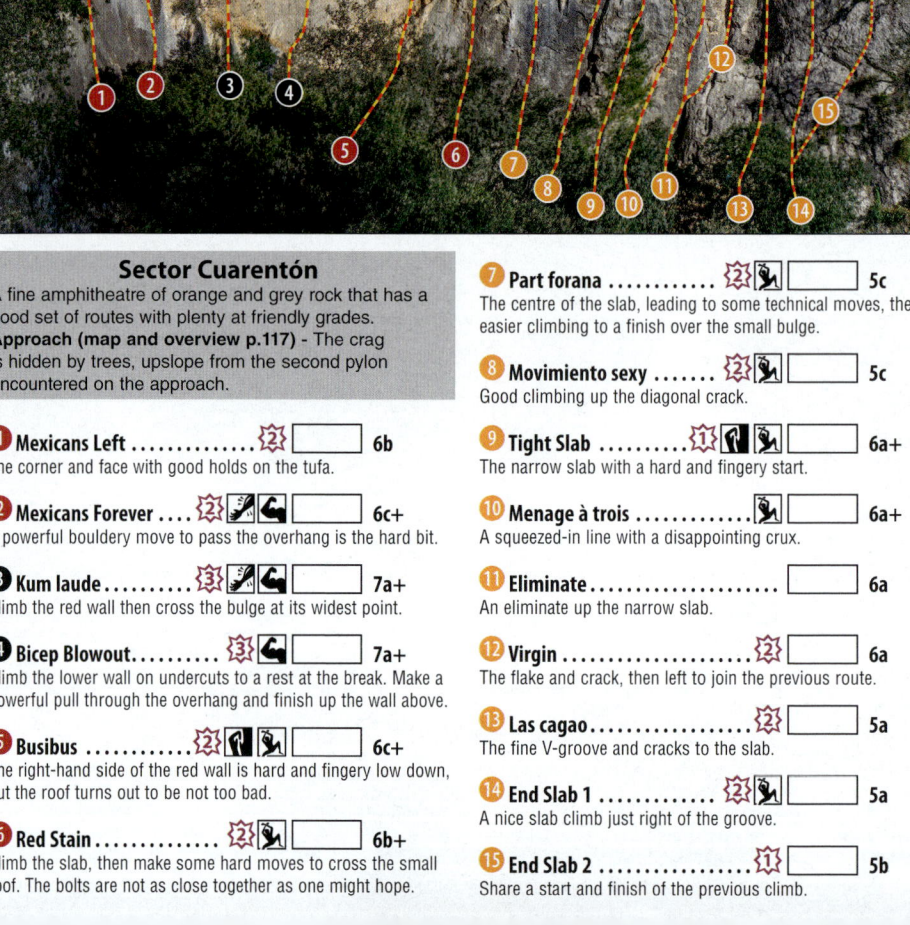

Sector Cuarentón

A fine amphitheatre of orange and grey rock that has a good set of routes with plenty at friendly grades.
Approach (map and overview p.117) - The crag is hidden by trees, upslope from the second pylon encountered on the approach.

1 Mexicans Left 6b
The corner and face with good holds on the tufa.

2 Mexicans Forever .... 6c+
A powerful bouldery move to pass the overhang is the hard bit.

3 Kum laude .... 7a+
Climb the red wall then cross the bulge at its widest point.

4 Bicep Blowout .... 7a+
Climb the lower wall on undercuts to a rest at the break. Make a powerful pull through the overhang and finish up the wall above.

5 Busibus .... 6c+
The right-hand side of the red wall is hard and fingery low down, but the roof turns out to be not too bad.

6 Red Stain .... 6b+
Climb the slab, then make some hard moves to cross the small roof. The bolts are not as close together as one might hope.

7 Part forana 5c
The centre of the slab, leading to some technical moves, then easier climbing to a finish over the small bulge.

8 Movimiento sexy 5c
Good climbing up the diagonal crack.

9 Tight Slab .... 6a+
The narrow slab with a hard and fingery start.

10 Menage à trois .... 6a+
A squeezed-in line with a disappointing crux.

11 Eliminate 6a
An eliminate up the narrow slab.

12 Virgin 6a
The flake and crack, then left to join the previous route.

13 Las cagao 5a
The fine V-groove and cracks to the slab.

14 End Slab 1 .... 5a
A nice slab climb just right of the groove.

15 End Slab 2 .... 5b
Share a start and finish of the previous climb.

Sector Mario S'estret

16 Fallen Angel 4c
A fine sustained pitch without any crux. *Photo p.115.*

17 Mario moreno II 5a
The central line on this very pleasant slab is a bit polished, but most of the holds are enormous so it doesn't matter too much.

18 Mario moreno 5b
The right-hand line is even better, but it does have one tricky section towards the top.

19 Zarzamora 4c
A steady lower slab is followed by a very steep short corner, luckily furnished with some huge holds.

Sector Mario
An attractive apron of rock with some excellent, long and friendly slab routes.
Approach (map and overview p.117) - The slab is directly above the point at which you arrive at the crag.

20 Zarzamora Center 3c
The central line. Finish at a lower-off below the steep headwall.

21 Zarzamora Right 4c
The line on the right of the *Zarzamora* slab is a lovely long pitch which avoids the steep headwall on its right side.

S'estret Sector Pipe

Sector Pipe

A short wall with some insignificant lines. Worth a quick look if they are at your grade.

Approach (map and overview p.117) - The wall is behind the pylon and above the pipe. The pipe floods after heavy rain.

1) El imperio contrataca 4c
The left-hand line up the slab.

2) El retorno del Jedi 5a
The steeper right-hand line on the slab. Low in the grade.

3) La guerra de las galaxies 4c
Follow the vague rib.

4) Pezón 5c
The poor bulging wall. Left at the first bolt is harder.

5) Quarried Wall 5c
A lone route on the quarried wall above the pond. The finish is steeper than it looks, but has some good holds.

Sector Pasión

Sector Pasión is set above Sector Pipe, and consists of a collection of tall buttresses that are home to a number of good long routes. These routes are very long, so take great care when lowering off.

Approach (map and overview p.117) - Follow a path past the pond below Sector Pipe, then scramble up to below the upper buttresses. *El bandido de un brazo* is up to the left, and *Pasión interminable* is up to the right.

6) El bandido de un brazo 6a
Climb the left-hand side of the groove and the good upper arete to a high lower-off. **Take care when lowering off especially if you belayed down the slope a bit.**

7) El culo 5c
Make a hard pull over the overlap, and follow the pleasant slab above. Upgraded due to hold loss at the start.

8) King of Quint .... 6a+
Make a steep pull up the juggy wall on sharp holds. The slab above is considerably easier.

9) Con el culo al aire 5a
1) **5a**. Pull up the steep crack. Follow the thin crack on the right-hand side of the slab to a lower-off.
2) **4c**. A new second pitch follows the edge of the slab above to a high lower-off. The original **5c** finish on the left has old bolts.
Descent - It is 45m to the ground from here, hence best done in two sections.

Sector Cuarentón p.120

Sector Mario p.121

Sector Pipe

10m

Sector Pasión **S'estret** 123

Sector Pasión

50m to the right, above the approach walk to the upper section, are the final routes in the area.

10 Pasión interminable 5a
Excellent climbing up the slab, crossing a groove (awkward) to gain the upper hanging slab which leads to a high lower-off.

11 Pasión oculta 4c
A poorer, right-hand finish.

12 Pasión Direct 4b
Climb the arete to a shared lower-off.

13 Short Rib Route 4c
10m further up the slope is a blunt slabby rib. Start up the short groove to gain the rib.

Sector Cabra Zombi

This small bulging wall is very close to the parking area. It was developed many years ago and has now been rebolted with some extra lines added.

Approach (map and overview p.117) - Walk into the woods but turn left before the gate to arrive at the wall.

1 S-Groove .... 6a+
Climb the S-shaped scoop.

2 Scoop Groove .... 6c+
Start up a steep rounded bulge, then follow grooves and scoops to the top.

3 Negracula 6c
Rounded scoops and pockets.

4 Chisparitas 7a
The blunt arete. A key hold has broken and the grade is unknown.

5 Arete Right 6c
The right-hand side of the arete on pockets.

6 Paprika .... 6b+
Follow the diagonal crack.

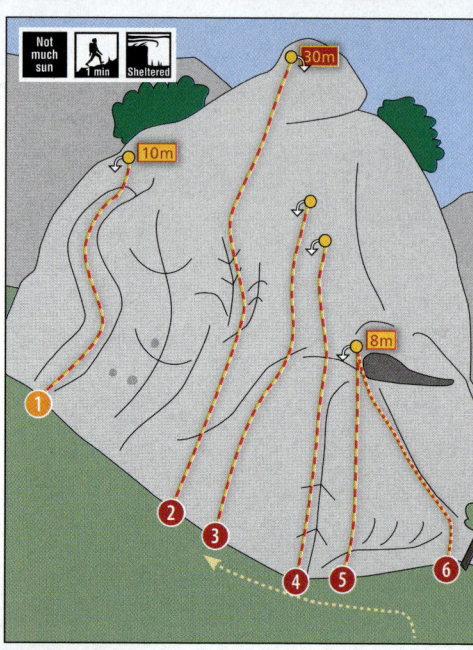

John McKenna on *Cubeza de Patata* (6a) - *p.128* - at Sector Raska y Gana, S'estret. This slabby pitch and its near neighbours are very different to much on offer hereabouts. Photo: Mike Hutton

Martin McKenna on *Flaying Machine* (6c+) - *p.129* - at the tall and shady Sector All Right, S'estret. Photo: Mike Hutton

S'estret — Sector Mejicano

The first three routes are located on the walls on the left - the scene of the rockfall. Seven more routes up and left of these in the grade range 7c to 8a+ have been reported, and there are also two easier lines.

① Perro flauta 8a

② Steep Arete .... ?
The arete of the steep groove may still be a project.

③ Diedre 6c
The steep groove is easier than it looks.

④ Anti-natural .... 7c+
Start up the groove but break right onto the wall.

⑤ Super Natural 8a
A totally artificial route. Bolts removed.

⑥ Aresta gore 8c
An awesome pitch up the mega-arete in the centre of the crag.

⑦ Head hunter .... 8a+
A big pitch that finishes up a prominent left-facing groove high up on the face.

⑧ Tatoo L1 .... 7b+
This version uses all available holds. 8a without holds to the left.

⑨ Tatoo .... 8b+
The full route is much harder.

⑩ Defcon one 8a
The long, blank wall.

⑪ Si yo fuera presidente .... 7b+
To the first lower-off is 7a+.

Sector Mejicano

An imposing crag, even on sunny days, Sector Mejicano provides plenty of very steep and sustained lines on some unusual limestone. This is one of the better spots to hunt down some dry rock in wet weather, as well as shade in hot weather, although the grades are almost all in the upper 7s and 8s.

Rockfall - In January 2005, the left-hand side of the cliff collapsed and ripped a huge channel down the hillside below. The rockfall destroyed ten extremely difficult climbs. The rest of the routes are still standing, and the crag to the right of the rockfall scar appears to be stable, although perhaps it isn't a good idea to hang around the place during very big thunderstorms. The section of cliff that suffered the rockfall has sprouted a few very steep lines.

Approach (map and overview p.117) - Take the path from the parking. Then, once past the boulderfield, head up the slope through the open area, over the huge pile of debris, to the base of the crag. The right-hand section of the crag is just up and right of the main face.

⑫ Odio a cobi 7b
A superb route that finishes up a steep, open groove at the top, via some sharp and positive pockets. *Photo p.118*.

⑬ El sudaca .... 7a+
Originally a right-hand start to *Odio a cobi*. It now has its own set of bolts although the moves are much the same.

⑭ Txino tzapa 8a
The extension to *El sudaca*.

⑮ Tetrix .... 7c+
It is 7b to the lower-off on *La sudaca*.

⑯ Buñocracia .... 6b+
This is the approved warm-up, following the large groove and crack-line. As is often the case with the one relatively easy route on a hard crag, it is no pushover. The rock is not the best.

⑰ Trio infernal 7c
The line of staples has some lovely moves.

⑱ Casi 7c
Technical climbing with a hard crux to onsight.

⑲ Maximo riesgo 7c
The last route on this section of wall direct over the roof.

The next four routes are around the corner to the right on a smaller 'boulder-like' wall.

⑳ La gigante verde 7a
The left-hand side of the overhanging rib.

㉑ Directe verde .... 7a+
The same start as the previous route, but pull right and hack on upwards to the top.

㉒ Bomber torrat .... 7a+
Use a pile of boulders to gain the first holds. There is said to be a right-hand finish at 7a.

㉓ Steep and slabby 6c
A very steep start past a hole.

There is one more line to the right.

㉔ Right Line 5a
The right-hand line up the less steep face.

S'estret — Sector Raska y Gana

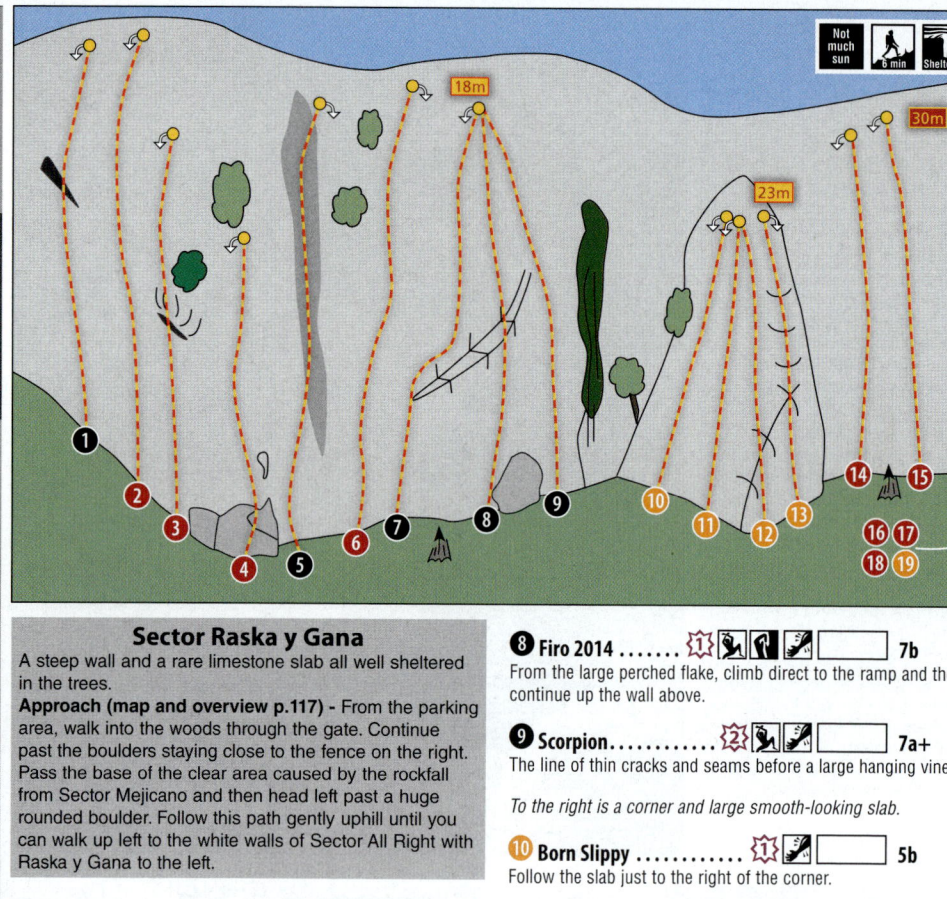

Sector Raska y Gana
A steep wall and a rare limestone slab all well sheltered in the trees.

Approach (map and overview p.117) - From the parking area, walk into the woods through the gate. Continue past the boulders staying close to the fence on the right. Pass the base of the clear area caused by the rockfall from Sector Mejicano and then head left past a huge rounded boulder. Follow this path gently uphill until you can walk up left to the white walls of Sector All Right with Raska y Gana to the left.

❶ Spoon Man .... 7a+
A long route on the left starting from the vegetated gully.

❷ Super Unknown ..... 6c+
From the base of the gully, follow the grey streak and wall above.

❸ Corbata Columbiana 6c
Start at some flakes at the base of the crag. Head up the white wall passing a short crack and bulge.

❹ Recluta Patoso 6c
A shorter pitch from flakes and past a tiny tufa on the left.

❺ Os habeis comido mi cerdo
.... 7b
From right of the flakes, pass the tiny tufa on the right and finish up the grey streak.

❻ Multi Racial ..... 6c+
The multicoloured wall just left of the rightward-rising ramp.

❼ Glasgow Kiss 7b
Climb to the base of the ramp, then take the wall above direct.

❽ Firo 2014 .... 7b
From the large perched flake, climb direct to the ramp and then continue up the wall above.

❾ Scorpion .... 7a+
The line of thin cracks and seams before a large hanging vine.

To the right is a corner and large smooth-looking slab.

❿ Born Slippy 5b
Follow the slab just to the right of the corner.

⓫ Chelsea Smile .... 6a+
The centre of the slab has a technical section low down.

⓬ Cubeza de Patata 6a
Fine sustained climbing starting up the slight arete. *Photo p.124.*

⓭ Dog Sniffer 6a
Start to the right of *Cubeza de Patata* and gain the slab before finishing up a shallow runnel.

5m to the right and just up the slope are two long routes.

⓮ Raska y Gana.............. 6c
Start up the gully.

⓯ The Double Life of Marvel .... 6c+
Start up the face.

Further up a gully on the right are some more routes.

⓰ Molsa blanca 6b
The thin seam left of the corner to jugs. A very good pitch.

Sector All Right S'estret

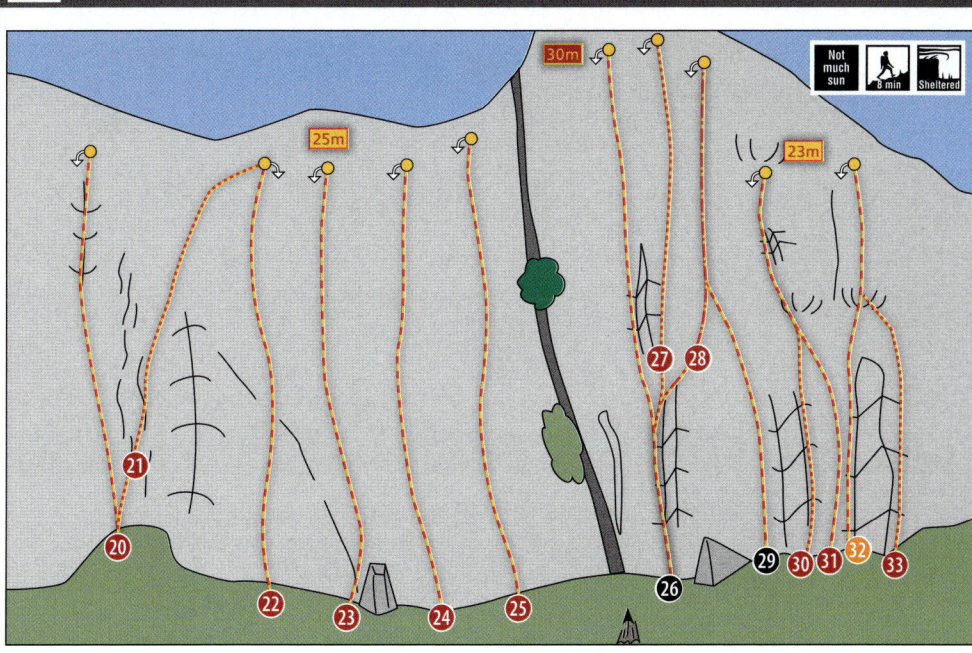

⑰ Tourist Go Home .... ☐ 6b+
The well featured rib and orange rock to the right of the corner.

⑱ Barco de rejilla .... ☐ 6c+
Right of *Tourist Go Home*.

⑲ Carrero de nit .... ☐ 6a
Right of *Barco de rejilla*.

Sector All Right
This vertical wall has some superb varied routes.
Approach (map and overview p.117) - From the parking area, walk into the woods through the gate. Continue past the boulders staying close to the fence on the right. Pass the base of the clear area caused by the rockfall from Sector Mejicano and then head left past a huge rounded boulder. Follow this path gently uphill until you can walk up left to the sector.

⑳ Ignatius .... ☐ 6c
Pocketed cracks lead to a shallow groove.

㉑ The Holland Tigger ...... ☐ 6b+
Start up *Ignatius* and then follow the right-hand line of bolts to the shallow corner and a shared lower-off.

㉒ Botifoll .... ☐ 6c
Follow some orange runnels to a thin wall.

㉓ Gran Prepucio .... ☐ 6c+
From a rock spike, climb direct to a shallow scoop.

㉔ All Right .... ☐ 6c+
Climb the slabby wall to a grey streak in the upper face.

㉕ Fat Climbers .... ☐ 6b+
Take the thin seam left of the chimney and continue up the broad arete.

㉖ Proyecto Salto Base .. ☐ 7b+
Climb the shallow left-facing corner right of a tufa.

㉗ Flaying Machine .... ☐ 6c+
From midway up the shallow corner, climb direct to the upper pillar. Has a good rest on route. *Photo p.125*.

㉘ Bombay Bicycle Club .... ☐ 6c
Brilliant. From midway up the shallow corner, head right and up the pillar to finish.

㉙ Quaranta Putes .... ☐ 7a+
Climb direct up the rounded shallow groove to join and finish as for *Bombay Bicycle Club*.

㉚ Pasta Gansa Left ..... ☐ 7a
The left-hand start to *Pasta Gansa*.

㉛ Pasta Gansa .... ☐ 6b
Start up the bolted line just left of the corner (share holds with *La Xancia de Ghandi*) before heading leftwards up steep ground.

㉜ La Xancia de Ghandi .. ☐ 6a+
Climb the corner and then direct past a grey overlap.

㉝ Super calvo .... ☐ 6b+
The pillar just to the right of the groove of *La Xancia de Ghandi*. Finish up *La Xancia de Ghandi* from the midway ledge.

S'estret — Sector Xurasco

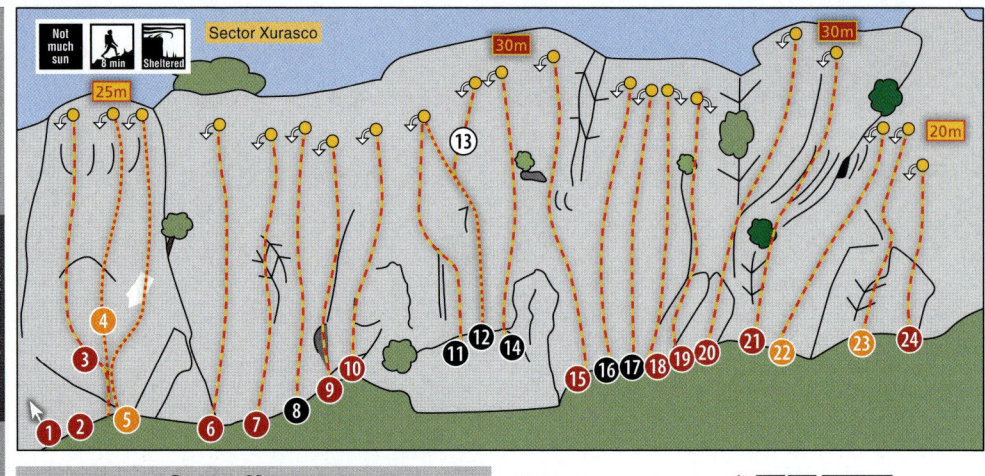

Sector Xurasco

A fine vertical wall of superb rock with many sustained routes. The climbing is technical and the routes follow good lines with excellent gear throughout.

Approach (map and overview p.117) - From the parking, walk into the woods through the gate. Continue past the boulders, staying close to the fence on the right. Pass the base of the clear area then head left past a huge rounded boulder. Follow this path past the white walls of Raska y Gana then go up a steep zigzag path.

❶ **Strigol** .... 6b+

❷ **Pello frito**.................... 6c

❸ **Human Centipede** ...... 6b+
Pull left along the ramp then climb the wall. A long pitch.

❹ **Amon Ra** .... 6a+
Climb direct on good holds to a steep finish.

❺ **Haz tu Zurollo con orgullo**.... 6a+
Climb right past a white patch. Good climbing but close to the gully in places and the grade on the plate is wrong!

❻ **Vidio Nasty** 6c
The clean wall is a classy bit of climbing.

❼ **DVD Nasty** 7a
The wall to a left-facing groove. AKA Por detras me gusta mas.

❽ **Maños moñas** 7b
Start up a rib. A finger trasher.

❾ **Puntas de Pollas**........ 6c+
Start past a small cave and crack, then move up and left.

❿ **Gatos en Llamas** 7a
Pull up steeply past a perma-draw.

⓫ **Mombasa Calling** .... 7b+
The wall right of a tufa. Move left to gain the crozzly headwall.

⓬ **Niño Melôn** 7c
Climb direct to a niche then move up leftwards to the same lower-off as Mombasa Calling.

⓭ **Morcilla** 8a
Break back right from Niño Melôn. The direct line is a project.

⓮ **Cementerio de Sabo**.. 7b+
Start left of the pillar. Climb past the big 'horn'.

⓯ **Octopussy** 7a
Start right of the pillar and climb up to the break then make hard moves onto the steep headwall. Superb. *Photo p.3*.

⓰ **Leche de Milf**........ 7a+
Climb the brown wall finishing left of the bolt-line.

⓱ **El negore albino** ..... 7a+
Tackle the grey streak.

⓲ **Burandanga** 6c
The wall left of the grooves.

⓳ **Mas loco k el loco** .... 6b+
Climb the groove and technical headwall.

⓴ **Viagra de Abuelo** 7a
Climb the slab then some broken rock to gain a rib and an excellent headwall.

㉑ **Viagra Direct**.............. 7a
Break right from Viagra de Abuelo and climb steep orange rock above a fig tree.

㉒ **Cagadero de Gineta** 5b
A superb slab climb with a tricky bulge near the top.

㉓ **Cantimplora rosa** 5a
A steady slab starting up a short groove.

㉔ **Butter Fingers**....... 6b+
Surprisingly sustained climbing up a fingery rib. Escapable.

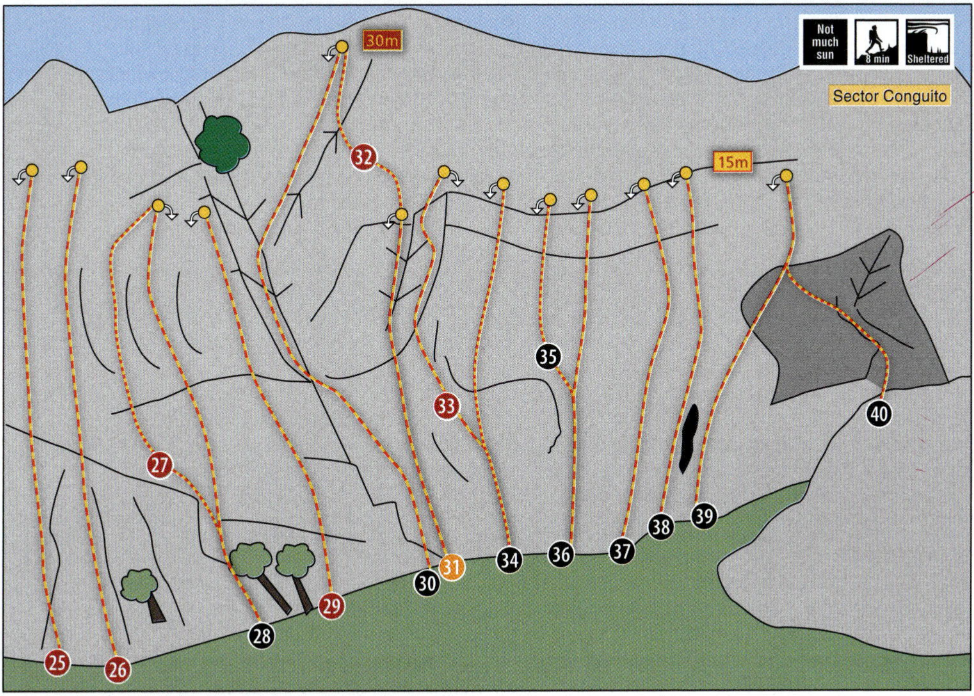

Sector Conguito — S'estret

Sector Conguito

The main feature of this section is a leaning wall with a set of powerful routes on it. Further left are some longer but less continuous lines.

Approach (map and overview p.117) - This is the continuation rightwards from Sector Xurasco.

㉕ Monkey largo 6b

㉖ Suegra 747 .... 6b+
A broken start up clean slabs reaches an excellent headwall.

㉗ Interstellar Overdrive ... 7a
Easy ground leads to a technical wall.

㉘ Doctor Jeremiah ..... 7a+
A slabby start topped off with a desperate technical bulge.

㉙ Zapatiazo 6b
Climb the rib then the right edge of the upper wall.

㉚ Boudica .... 7a+
Climb the white slab past a stump then step across left onto the rib. Climb the rib then step back onto the upper wall.

㉛ Karma Cabra P1 .... 6a
The white slab leads to a groove and lower-off.

㉜ Karma Cabra 7a
Make a big span across left onto the hanging slab. There may well be a second left-hand finish at **7b**.

㉝ Lichen Muncher 6b
The tricky lower wall leads to a crack (come in from the left for a **6a+**). Follow the rib above trying to avoid the groove until it becomes too artificial to keep out of it.

㉞ Sika-phobia 7b
The real line starting as for *Lichen Muncher* and continuing direct.

㉟ Congo Mongo 7b
Break left from the flake of *Ganxito Perfecto*.

㊱ Ganxito Perfecto .... 7a+
Climb to a flake then direct up the wall.

㊲ King Conguito .... 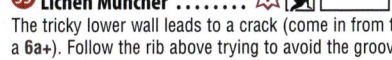 7b
The streak to a ledge then move back left.

㊳ The Lorenzo Pinch ... 7c
Climb the steep pockets and wall above to a final difficult pull onto the slab at the top.

㊴ Gallos Go Home! 7c
Climb past the hole then up steeply.

㊵ Cubo de Sabo .... 7c+
Swing along the lip of the cave to join *Gallos Go Home!*

Valldemossa

Valldemossa is an accessible and popular crag that has a good selection of fine middle-grade routes. The crag is delightfully positioned, high above the village of Port de Valldemossa, with great views over the village and the sea beyond. The only drawback to this idyllic setting is the proximity of the narrow road that passes extremely close to the bottom of the Main Crag. The climbing is spread over four main buttresses, which vary from steep slabs to vertical walls. The Main Crag has its famous roof-over-the-road route; an excellent and popular slab with some honeycomb features in the middle; and some interesting scooped runnels on the left-hand side. Up and left from the Main Crag are two considerably more isolated areas that contain some longer pitches. The other sectors are less interesting but worth a look if you have the time.

Approach

Valldemossa village is easy to get to by following signs from the Palma ring road. If approaching from the north east, you can cut across from the motorway via Palmañola to pick up the Ma-1110 at S'Egleieta. Turn right towards Valldemossa. Once in the town, head towards the coast. Ignore the first right turn (signed 'Sóller') and take the second right turn (signed 'Port de Valldemossa'). The crag is about 1km down this road. The main section of the crag is reached where a conspicuous beak of rock overhangs the road. Please park very carefully and keep in mind that some quite wide lorries come down this road. There is some extra parking further down the hill, or further up before the Roadside Buttress.

Conditions

The crag faces west and gets the sun just after midday. It is reasonably sheltered and could well offer dry climbing if the more mountainous crags are wet. If it is actually raining there is one route to do, but that is about it. In the summer it will get as hot as everywhere else.

Valldemossa 133

Valldemossa

John McKenna tackling the thin midsection of the classic *Suphi* (6a) - *p.139* - at Valldemossa. If roadside is your thing then this is the crag for you, with many of the lines starting from next to the tarmac. Away from the road are a number of other sectors which are home to some excellent and unusual climbs including a massive roof.
Photo: Mark Glaister

Valldemossa — Upper Crag

1. Scoop Left 7b
Climb the rib left of the big scoop then swing right over the top across the thin wall.

2. Rusty 7c
Rusty bolts on the steep pillar.

3. Bulging Wall ..... 7b+
The long bulging wall.

4. Central Flake .... 6b+
The central flake-line is a pumpy but rewarding pitch. It can be extended above the lower-off at **5c**.

5. Vall-de-mega 7a
Fine climbing up the steep wall. One of the best at the crag.

6. Wall Eliminate .... 7a+
Good climbing but escapable where it matters.

7. Chimenea 1 .... 5c
Good 3D climbing up the central gully/chimney. Be careful with blocks at the top.

8. Central Right 6b
A fine route (to the first lower-off) with some tricky moves just right of the central gully. There are two lower-offs - lower off the first as the climbing above is grassy.

9. Spanky 6a
An excellent pitch on great rock.

10. Lanky 6a
Another quality climb starting up an area of scoops and flutings. There is a belay at 25m but you can continue to the top.

11. Average .... 6b+
Climb straight up the wall to a difficult finish up and over a bulge. Good rock.

12. Shorty 6a
A nice wall pitch up the right-hand edge of the wall. Finish at the first lower-off if the continuation out to the right has not been rebolted.

Upper Crag Valldemossa

The next bay has a series of poor routes on some crumbly rock.

13 Arroz con leche 7b
A very poor route with a hard move low down.

14 Circ .... 7a+
Thin wall climbing.

15 Jarcha .... 6c+
A very poor and escapable route to the left of the cave.

16 Why Not 6c
Start up the diagonal crack but branch left.

17 Diedro y placa 6c
Climb the diagonal crack.

18 Arista y diedro .... 7a+
A poor eliminate up the rib right of the crack.

19 Fisura fina 7b
The very steep crack.

Upper Crag

In complete contrast to Roadside Buttress and Main Crag, the Upper Crag is strangely isolated from the hullabaloo below. The routes here vary from slightly pointless filler-ins to good long wall climbs on Verdonesque rock.

Approach (map and overview p.133) - Walk up the slope leftwards, through the trees to beneath the the bays - the left bay is furthest up the slope.

20 Travesia 6c
The right-hand crack.

The next routes are on the opposite wall, and are the most worthwhile routes in this bay.

21 Kirsten 6a
Good climbing up the grey slab.

22 Kirsten II 5c
A worthwhile pitch up the front of the buttress.

Valldemossa Main Crag

Main Crag

The Main Crag consists of a fine buttress with a number of middle-grade wall climbs and one spectacular roof. Most of the climbing can be viewed comfortably from the wall by the side of the road. The routes tend to be technical and fingery except the lines on the right which are pretty butch.
Approach (map and overview p.133) - This is the buttress directly above the parking spot on the road.

① Leftest Edge .... ?
The steepening wall.

② Left Edge 6b
The middle of the not-so-good rock on glue-in bolts. Take care with the rope over the top roof edge.

③ Wall and Overhang .... 6c+
Two distinct cruxes. Climb the technical wall to good holds that lead to a rest. Finish left through the overhang.

④ Kiko 6b
The edge of the good rock. The first bolt hanger may be absent.

⑤ Scooped Runnel 6b
The scooped runnel climbed direct.

⑥ Palmolive 7b
The left-hand finish to *Intrepido* gives superb climbing that features a short technical sequence.

⑦ Intrépido 6c
An excellent route interrupted by a grassy bit in the middle. The finish is exciting, though the start is the crux.

⑧ Something 7a
The line of staples via a short groove and wall.

⑨ Vía des clau .... 6b+
An excellent and sustained climb that has some very tenous moves on fine rock.

⑩ El jubilado 5c
Follow the natural line rightwards across the crag on the bolts of other routes, then climb direct to the lower-off on *Pepa*. Some wires may be useful but are not essential.

Main Crag **Valldemossa** 139

11 Suphi Left-hand 6b
Good and committing moves to gain the wall above the holes and bulges.

12 Suphi 6a
A very good route through the crozzly holes. The upper wall looks unlikely but there are holds. *Photo p.134.*

13 Fito .... 6b+
A technical start proves very frustrating. Above this the bolts are spaced and the final moves are tricky.

14 Jubilado Direct 6b
Climb direct up to the groove on *El jubilado*.

15 Pepa 6b
Technical climbing up the wall right of the groove.

16 Pepino .... 6b+
The right-hand branch to *Pepa*.

Valldemossa Main Crag

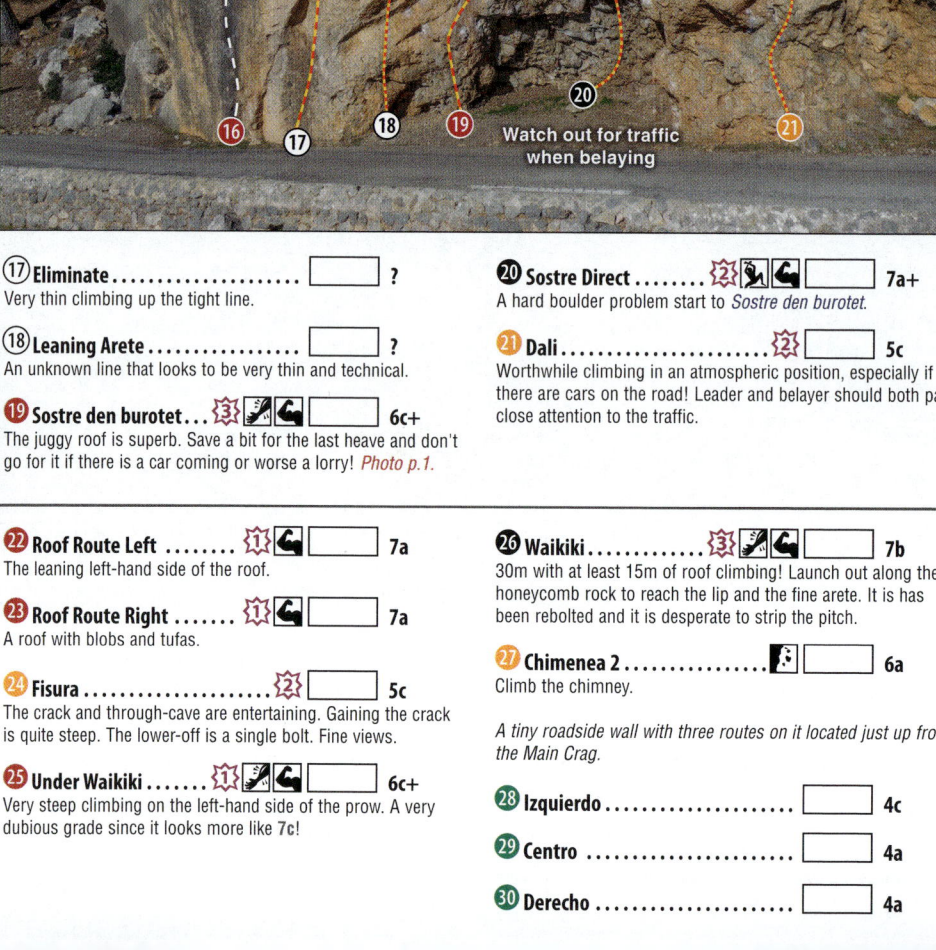

17 Eliminate .... ?
Very thin climbing up the tight line.

18 Leaning Arete .... ?
An unknown line that looks to be very thin and technical.

19 Sostre den burotet .... 6c+
The juggy roof is superb. Save a bit for the last heave and don't go for it if there is a car coming or worse a lorry! *Photo p.1.*

22 Roof Route Left 7a
The leaning left-hand side of the roof.

23 Roof Route Right 7a
A roof with blobs and tufas.

24 Fisura 5c
The crack and through-cave are entertaining. Gaining the crack is quite steep. The lower-off is a single bolt. Fine views.

25 Under Waikiki .... 6c+
Very steep climbing on the left-hand side of the prow. A very dubious grade since it looks more like 7c!

20 Sostre Direct .... 7a+
A hard boulder problem start to *Sostre den burotet*.

21 Dali 5c
Worthwhile climbing in an atmospheric position, especially if there are cars on the road! Leader and belayer should both pay close attention to the traffic.

26 Waikiki 7b
30m with at least 15m of roof climbing! Launch out along the honeycomb rock to reach the lip and the fine arete. It is has been rebolted and it is desperate to strip the pitch.

27 Chimenea 2 .... 6a
Climb the chimney.

A tiny roadside wall with three routes on it located just up from the Main Crag.

28 Izquierdo 4c

29 Centro 4a

30 Derecho 4a

Sector Waikiki and Roadside Buttress **Valldemossa**

Sector Waikiki
A fine buttress in a magnificent position above the Main Crag. It is worth the walk up just to look at the route *Waikiki*.
Approach (map and overview p.133) - Just to the right of the main Valldemossa crag is a rib and a path going steeply up by a big pine tree. Scramble up this path.

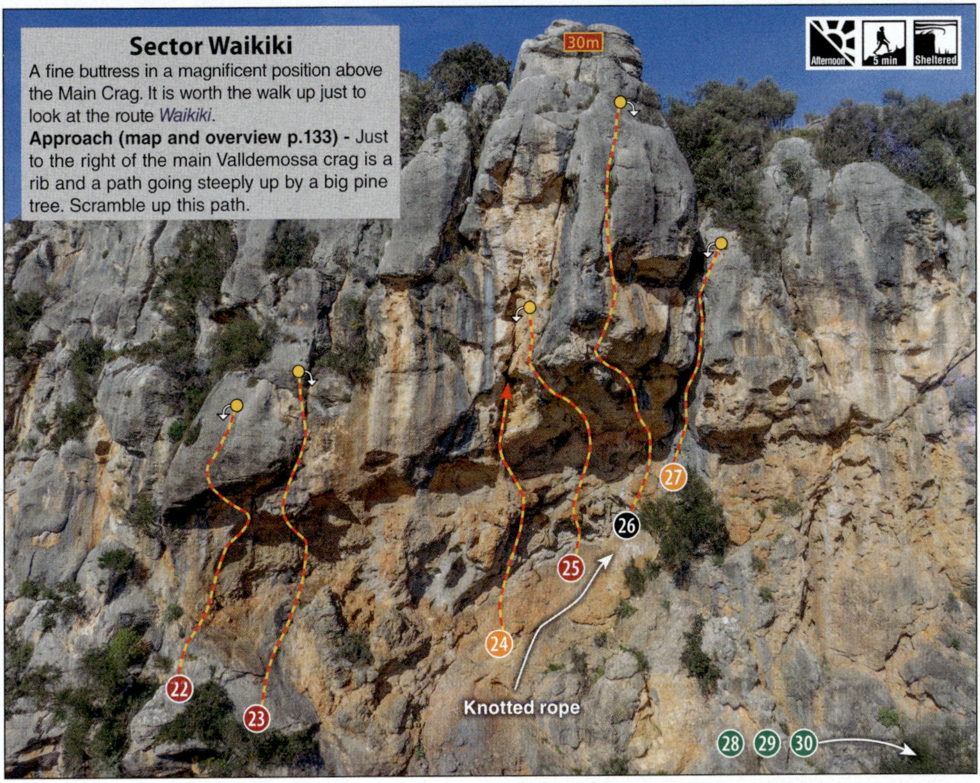

Roadside Buttress
This is the short wall back up the road from the parking that is easily missed when driving to the crag. Although the routes don't look too spectacular, they have some reasonable climbing. Please be very aware of cars speeding down the hill, since there isn't really anywhere to hide. The bolts go missing from this wall on occasion.
Approach (map and overview p.133) - The wall is further up the road you drove down to the crag.

31 Zurdo 6a
Up the short rib and wall above. The first hanger may be missing.

32 Rompededos .... 6a+
A touch scary at the top.

33 Pérfido encanto .... 6a+
The best of the routes on this buttress.

34 Triplet derecho 6b

35 Recto cresta 5c

36 Derecho castilla 6b
Fingery and technical near the top.

John McKenna grapples with the magnificent line of *Algo Salvaje* (6b+) - *p.146* - on the Paret Dels Coloms at Sa Gubia. Sa Gubia is the spiritual home of Mallorcan climbing that offers the visiting climber quality sport climbing throughout the grades. It also has a good number of multi-pitch routes including the classic *Albahida (Gubia Normal)* (4c) - *p.154* - up a beautiful spire just visible on the far right of this photo. Photo: Mike Hutton

Bunyola Area

Sa Gubia
Fraguel

Sa Gubia

The huge amphitheatre of Sa Gubia is the most extensive and varied crag in Mallorca. The climbing on the well developed sections of the crag will suit most tastes and styles, although it is lacking in the very highest grades. For the majority of climbers, Sa Gubia is a must-visit destination with a host of superb routes that range from slabby grade 4s to wildly steep grade 7s and a few 8s. It also has a number of excellent multi-pitch routes, some fully bolted, and others, like the essential *Albahida*, are semi-trad and require a small rack of gear.

Conditions
The different aspects of the various faces offer climbing in the sun or shade depending on the time of day. The right-hand side (looking in) gets the sun for most of the day, except for the bit tucked around the back, in the bay (Sector Isla Bonita and the *Sexo débil* wall). The Paret dels Coloms loses the sun in the early afternoon. It can be very windy in the gorge owing to the wind-tunnel effect. In the unusual event that it is raining, there may be one or two hard routes which stay dry for a while on Paret dels Coloms.

Gear
Virtually all the routes are fully bolted with good belays. The one notable exception is *Albahida*, which requires a small rack and some slings for threads. Most of the single-pitch routes can be climbed on a single 60m rope. For the longer routes, twin 50m ropes are preferable to enable abseil descents. Most of the bolts are good, although you may find the odd old one on some routes.

Approach
From Palma, take the Ma-11 north towards Sóller. Parking has become limited. There are two roadside spots, one before the roundabout turning towards Bunyola, and one just after the turning depending on where you approach from. The extensive restaurant parking is possible if you visit the restaurant. From the parking, walk along a narrow road - almost opposite the turning to Bunyola. Pass a gate, and another gate on the right which blocks off a track leading up to a large house. Keep going until a narrow path up a dry river bed is reached. Follow a good (but rocky) path up the river bed. A path eventually breaks out to the right entering trees near the crag. Branch off right up the hill to join a higher path which leads to the crag below Sector Silicona. All the main sectors can be reached from here.
For Paret dels Coloms, continue past Sector Excalibur, then locate a small path back left that leads down to the river and steeply up the other side. There are other paths further back that lead to the same point, but they can be awkward to find.
The approach to the upper routes on Cara Oeste, and also the descent from *Albahida*, is up a long twisty track about 1km up the road from the parking place by the restaurant. The walk up this track to the summit of Sa Gubia makes a great rest day walk, and also gives an opportunity to view the awesome Cara Oeste properly.

Descent from the Summit
A few routes including *Albahida*, reach the summit of the mountain. There are two descent options from here. There are also options to abseil back down described with the routes,
Descent 1 - From the summit, drop down the north side to a dirt road. This zig-zags down, past a farm, to the main road. There is a blocking gate that is often locked at 5pm here. Turn right and head back downhill to the car (1-2 hours).
Descent 2 - From the summit, drop down the north side but, before you reach the zig-zag track, walk leftwards under Cara Oeste. Keep well away from the face and drop steeply down the scree and scrub-covered slope between the main face and the thin ridge opposite. This is hard going and no real path, but relatively quick (1/2 - 1 hour from the summit).

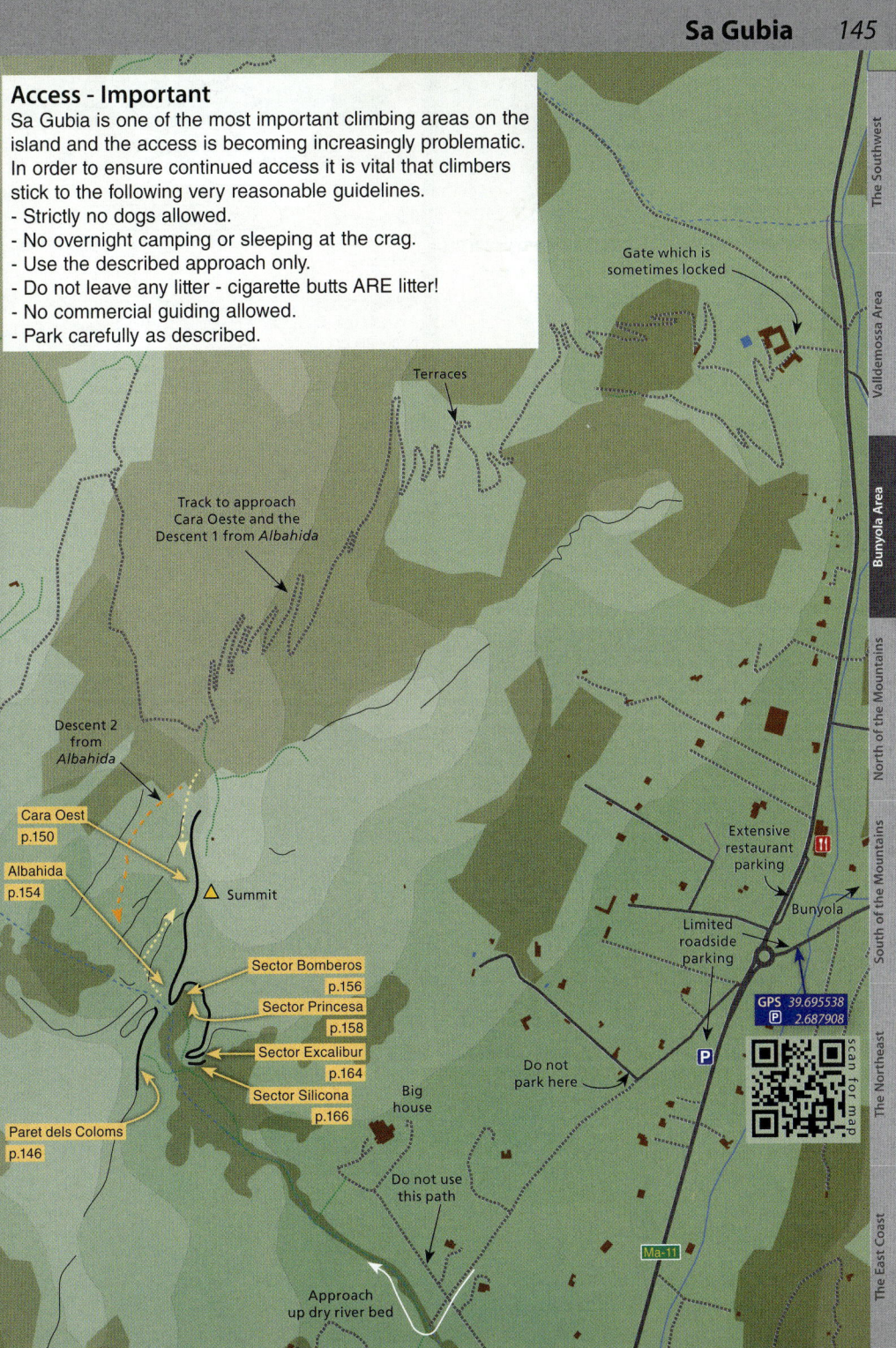

Sa Gubia — Paret dels Coloms

Paret dels Coloms

This is the massive wall on the left-hand side of the gorge at Sa Gubia. The best routes link up steep pocketed walls via long tufas and blobs.

Approach (map p.145, overview p.153) - Use the main approach to under Excalibur. Head down and left into the dry river bed and scramble up the other side. There are other paths but they are awkward to locate on a first visit.

1 Peur Impossible 7a
1) 4c. A reasonable pitch on its own at this grade.
2) 7a. Thin slab climbing weaving around the bulges.

2 Es poal 6b
An oddball up the left-hand edge of the cave with a point of aid.

3 Esto no es quinto superior ... 7a+
A line up the back of the bowl that has a high and hard crux.

4 Papidepau 7b
A long pitch right of the orange bowl.

5 Eternum 7c
Another long line breaking right out of *Papidepau*.

6 Hay Noray! 8a

7 Sal de arenal .... 6c+
A short-lived, but fine route up the wickedly steep tufas.

8 Tres menos cuarto ... 7b+
Desperate, reachy and technical.

9 Front 242 .... 7b+
An imaginatively-drilled route with an extremely blank, and hard, crux move.

10 Algo salvaje .... 6b+
A classic tick, linking some big blobs. There is a sit-down rest before the last bit. *Photo p.142.*

11 Piñón fijo 7c
The thin wall left of the two 'willies'. It feels a bit bold for a sport route, but comes highly recommended.

12 Si lo sé no vengo ..... 7a+
A superb, fingery climb which starts between the 'willies'. There is a top pitch (6a) but the gear is old. *Photo opposite.*

13 Perque triunfin els canalles .... 6c+
Climb the fingery wall right of the long, grey tufa-system.

Martin McKenna on *Si lo sé no vengo* (7a+) - *opposite* - at Paret dels Coloms, Sa Gubia. Photo: Mike Hutton

Sa Gubia — Paret dels Coloms

14 La Morgue .... 6b+
Seldom climbed.

15 Passenger Pigeon P1 .... 6c
The first pitch of a three-pitcher is popular. A full 35m.

16 Passenger Pigeon 6c
The full route sees little attention.
1) 6c, 2) 6c, 3) 5c.

17 Pesadilla final 6b
A long 35m pitch with good climbing.

18 La peladora 6c
The right-hand branch is very long - take care when lowering.

19 Combat Rock P1 .... 7a
The first pitch of a longer route has a great tufa then wall above.

20 Combat Rock 7a
The full route has four pitches. Descend *Passenger Pigeon*.
1) 6b+, 2) 6c, 3) 7a, 4) 6a.

21 Humi .... 6a+
Interesting climbing with a tricky crux bulge on sharp holds.

22 Mes rapit suc el vent 6a
A good companion to *Humi*.

23 Pellejo de tiburón 7a
Excellent technical climbing building to a fine finish.

24 Seis pelas P1 .... 6a
The first pitch of the original route of the face.

25 Seis pelas 7a
Extend the route for another much harder pitch. There may be a third pitch as well which is likely not to be as hard.

26 Decadencia corporal . 6c+
A brilliant pitch. The 7b+ second pitch has old bolts.

27 Comechochos .... 6a+
A fun little route where the grade depends totally on your leg length. It is a decent 5a to a lower-off at the base of the cave.

28 Punto G 6a
A great experience up the back of the cave. It shares the first couple of bolts of *Comechochos*.

29 Tao P1 .... 6b+
The right-hand rib of the cave has a hard move to the lower-off.

30 Tao .... 6c+
Extending this into the full route is very worthwhile.
1) 6b, 2) 6c+. The crack from the top of the cave.

31 Leather Face .... 7a+
Climb to a tree, step left into *Tao* and then move right onto the line which leads to a testing finish. The direct is a bit harder.

32 Pasteles de Isabel 7b
A stunning line up the tufa.
1) 7b. Reaching and leaving the tufa are the hard bits.
2) 6c+. Well worth doing.

33 Gay Power 7b
Technical face climbing on tiny holds.

34 Vol de nuit 6b
Good climbing up the easiest line on the wall right of the cave.

35 Tía melis 6a
An excellent route that crosses *Estricnina*.
1) 6a. The scoop-covered wall.
2) 6a. Climb rightwards and up from the belay.

The next routes start below an interesting pair of rock buttocks.

36 Estricnina 5c
A popular excursion which provides the easiest way up the wall.
1) 5c. Climb the wall past the buttocks. Many do just this pitch.
2) 5c. Traverse left below the belay of *Tía melis* then make a hard move up and left to the belay.
3) 5a. Climb up and rightwards across the wall to finish at the same belay as *Tía melis*.

37 Chungui chunguez 6c
A superb and direct second-pitch above the buttocks. Pitch 1 is as for *Estricnina*.

38 Danzomanía P1 .... 5c
Climb up rightwards to a prominent pillar. Climb up the pillar and gain a belay/lower-off.

39 Danzomanía 6b
The full route which almost reaches the top of the wall.
1) 5c. Climb up rightwards to a prominent pillar. Climb up this and belay.
2) 6b. Follow a mixture of old gear up the wall above.
3) 6a. Climb the wall to the left of a groove. This pitch is named *Pet espés*.

40 Guatón 6a
Another good route.
1) 5c. As for *Danzomanía P1*.
2) 6a. Step right and climb straight up the wall above.

Sa Gubia Cara Oeste

Cara Oeste

The west face of Sa Gubia ranks as one of the more impressive walls in Europe. It is around 100m tall at its highest point, overhangs for most of its length and is covered in some magnificent rock formations. To date, the wall has been developed by Yannick Courtes and Francois Thirion with several long, fully-bolted routes - an incredible achievement, especially when you consider the approach walk! Little is known about most of these routes beyond their name and pitch grades, although it is reasonable to assume that they will be brilliant and substantial challenges.

Approach (map p.145, overview p.153) - The upper section of the wall (routes 1 to 8) is best approached by walking up the *Albahida* descent route down the back of the mountain - see page 144 for a description and page 145 for a map. Once below the last section leading to the summit shelter, a vague path leads out under the face following some tiny red arrows and cairns.

❶ Bush rit et Massacre............... 7a+
❷ Interval training................... 7a+
❸ Gato negro........................ 7a+
❹ SOeScaladores en perdición..... 7c
The start is reached using a fixed rope.

❺ Lluvia providencial........... 7b
The start is reached by using the fixed rope to scramble down to a lower ledge. A short easy slab leads to a belay below the wall.
1) 7a+, 2) 7b. Grade and quality confirmed.

❻ Escaladores en la niebla ..... 6c+
From below *Lluvia providencial*, go along the ledge then make a 25m abseil to a lower ledge. Scramble up to reach the base of the route.
1) 6b, 2) 6c+, 3) 6b+, 4) 6c+. Grade and quality confirmed.

❼ Los colores de la caliza....... 7b
Starting down and right of *Escaladores...*, scramble up slabs to the base of the route. 1) 7b, 2) 7b, 3) 7a+, 4) 6c+ grade and route quality confirmed. The top pitch is run out.

❽ Le lapin en décomposition
.... 8a
The start is reached by a short traverse to a belay below the wall. 1) 6b, 2) 7b, 3) 7c/A0 or 8a, 4) 7a+. Grade and quality confirmed, though the 3rd pitch may well be **8a+**.

Approach to routes 9 and 10 - Walk under *Albahida* and follow the gully up until it opens out. Then scramble over rough terrain to the large spur leading out from the wall. Scramble up this to locate a cable which can be used to reach the base of the wall.

❾ Voyages dans l'eau de là 8a
The left-hand of the two lower routes.
1) 8a, 2) 7b+, 3) 8a, 4) 7a.

❿ Tres estrellas.................... 7c
The final route on the wall. The name suggests it may be worth three stars or one beer. 1) 5, 2) 7c, 3) 7c, 4) 7a

Paul Dearden on *Puta perro* (6a) - p.155 - at Sector Bomberos, Sa Gubia.
Photo: Mike Hutton

Sector Embrujada

The lower right-hand side of Cara Oeste has some long routes in the same style as *Albahida*. These routes see few ascents and the pitches and stances are approximate.

Approach (map p.145, overview p.153) - Walk under Sector Excalibur and keep heading straight on across to below the arete of *Albahida*. Continue around this to below the wall. There are some very short sections of via ferrata that are used to reach routes 1 to 3, which start higher up the gully.

❶ Gran Turismo............ 5c
1) 5b, 2) 4c, 3) 5c, 4) 5b, 5) 5c, 6) 5b.
Start below orange threads. A standard rack is required. The stances are bolted except the 4th.
FA. Derek Watson

❷ La Rosa dels Vents............. 7a
A long fully-bolted route of unknown quality.
1) 6a, 2) 6c, 3) 7a, 4) 6a+.

Sector Embrujada Sa Gubia 153

❸ Number 2 .... ☐ 7a+
A long fully-bolted route of unknown quality.
1) 6a+, 2) 7a+, 3) 6c+, 4) 6c+.

❹ Number 1 .... 🖉 ☐ 6b+
1) 5c, 2) 6a, 3) 6a+, 4) 6b+, 5) 6a, 6) 5a, 7) -.
A standard rack is required. The stances are bolted and there are some bolts on the harder sections. The original route of the face.
Descent - Abseil off (maximum 40m abseils).
FA. Lenon, Miquel Sintes

❺ Number 3 .... ☐ 6c
1) 6b, 2) 6b, 3) 6c.

❻ Embrujada .... 💥 ☐ 6b
An old route which has now been fully bolted.
1) 6a+. Start up a slab and climb direct past some rusted cables, through bulges crossing more broken rock.
2) 6a. Follow broken slabs up and slightly left to steeper ground, belay on the right of a large orange cave.
3) 6b. Head up the sustained wall to a ledge and tree shared with *Supernova*.
Descent - Continue up one of the other routes, or abseil off (requires doubled ropes).

❼ Sor-presa .... ☐ 6a+
A long single pitch.

❽ Supernova, Spits 'n Giggles .. 💥 ☐ 6a
A fully-bolted route up the left-hand side of the arete.
1) 6a. Head rightwards past a tree.
2) 5c. Climb the wall to a corner and belay above.
3) 5c. The wall direct to a belay.
4) 6a. Traverse left past a corner and climb a wall to a belay at a tree. A variation on the right is **7a**.
5) 5c. Climb up left and then back right and up to a belay.
6) 5c. A long pitch up walls and bulges to a belay on the arete.
7) 5c. Climb to the top.
Descent - Follow the descent as for *Albahida*.
FA. Joan Riera, Doog Menzies, Manfred Eckschlager, Martijn Gerards

Sector Albahida

The most striking of Sa Gubia's rock features is the dominant arete in the centre of the cliff - this is the line of the classic *Albahida* (*Gubia Normal*). The arete divides the massive faces of Cara Oeste and Sector Bomberos.
Approach (map p.145, overview p.153) - Walk under Sector Excalibur and keep heading straight on across to below the arete.

① Albahida (Gubia Normal). 4c

The most popular long route on the island is the spire-like ridge of *Albahida*. Climbing it is a full day's outing for most, including the long descent. The line of the route is vague since it wanders around the rib, however most of the stances have fixed gear - if in doubt, just follow the easiest line.
Gear - There is some old fixed gear but take a small rack consisting of medium wires and a few larger cams. Also take slings for the numerous threads high on the route.
Timings - Walk-in 30 mins; main ridge climbing 2 hours fast, 7 hours slow; upper ridge 30 mins to 1 hour; descent 1-2 hours. Total of 4 hours fast, or 10 hours slow.
Start at the base of the ridge by some red marks on the rock.
1) **3a**, 38m. Climb the ridge by the easiest line to a ledge.
2) **4b**, 28m. Move right then upwards with a hard move or two. Easier climbing leads back left around a rib to a recess.
3) **4b**, 26m. Climb over a small overlap to a scoop/ledge. Move right onto the rib which leads to a stance below orange rock.
4) **3b**, 30m. Climb up right past some loose blocks and then up a long flake/corner, past an odd bolt, to belay on a ledge.
5) **4c**, 28m. Climb direct past trees to a steepening. Make a few hard pulls, past some pegs, and onto the rib. This leads more easily to a scoop stance and belay on some natural threads.
6) **3b**, 55m. A long pitch. Follow the rib above, past numerous natural threads, heading for an orange bulge and a large stance.
7) **3c**, 45m. Move right to a corner, then climb up over a bulge onto an easy slab which leads to the top.
Gubia Variante - A right-hand start to the ridge can be made in three long pitches at about grade **5c** - see topo on next page.
Descent 1 - From the top of the climbing, scramble carefully up the ridge to the summit. Continue over the top and drop down the other side to reach a dirt road. This zig-zags down, past a farm, to the main road. There is a blocking gate that is often locked at 5pm here. See map on p.145. Turn right and head back downhill to the car (1-2 hours).
Descent 2 - Continue along the ridge and over the summit as for Descent 1. Before you reach the zig-zag track, walk leftwards under the Cara Oeste. Keep well away from the face and drop steeply down the scree and scrub-covered slope between the main face and the thin ridge opposite. This is hard going and no real path, but relatively quick (1/2 - 1 hour from the summit).
Descent 3 - Abseil down the last pitch. From here abseil down the right-hand (looking in) side of the ridge, down the line of *La ley del deseo*. Don't commit yourself to the first two abseils until you know where you are going. After that it is straightforward.

② Quan es fa fosc 5a

This excellent variation follows the steeper rib to the left of *Albahida*. The main three pitches are well bolted, but a few wires are needed for the first pitch unless you are happy soloing it.
1) **3a**. As for *Albahida*.
2) **5b**. Climb direct above the stance to a belay ledge.
3) **5b**. Move left and follow the line up a rib.
4) **5b**. One more pitch leads to an abseil point. Abseil off, or continue up into *Albahida*.

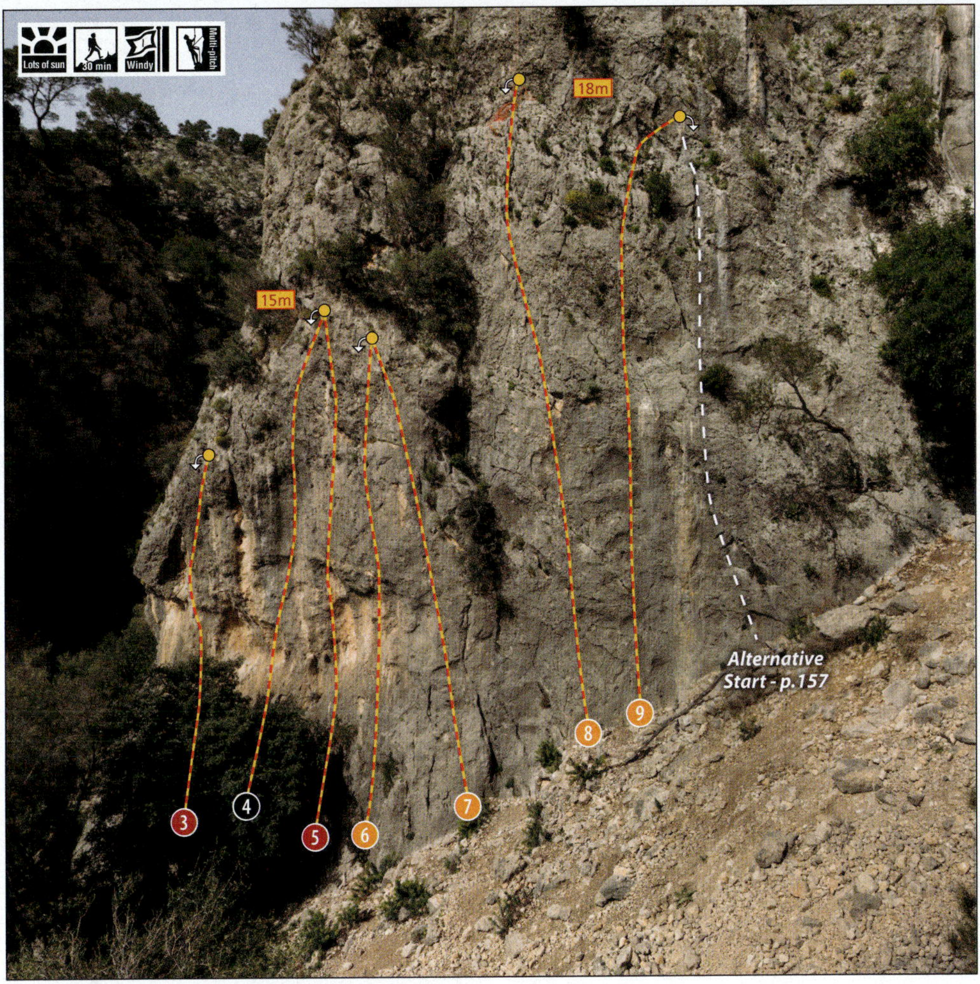

Bomberos - Lower Left

This very popular spot has a number of single-pitch routes and multi-pitch routes where the first pitch is worth doing on its own.
Approach (map p.145, overview p.153) - Walk under Sectors Silicona and Excalibur, and keep going across the bay to the far side.

3 Chitas marchitas........ 1 6b+
The leftmost complete line of bolts leading to a crack.

4 Charly danone....... 1 7a+
Technical climbing past a short tufa.

5 Jódete y baila.............. 6b+
Climb a line roughly up the centre of the wall.

6 Fill de ric........... 1 6a+
Follow the orange streaks to a fingery pull through the bulge.

7 Puta perro............. 1 6a
The right-hand edge of the slab. *Photo p.151.*

8 La ley del deseo P1.......... 2 6a
The first pitch of this classic long route is worth doing on its own, although leave it for those going all the way when busy.

9 The Master P1.............. 1 6a
Start just right of *La ley del deseo* from the flat area.

The Southwest
Valldemossa Area
Bunyola Area
North of the Mountains
South of the Mountains
The Northeast
The East Coast

Sector Bomberos   Sa Gubia   157

Sector Bomberos
The largest and most complex area at Sa Gubia is the huge bay which dominates the northern side of the gorge. From the base of the ridge of *Albahida*, the crag sweeps up and rightwards, forming a superb vertical wall of immaculate grey rock. This is home to many excellent multi-pitch sport routes, including the two full-height challenges of *La ley del deseo* and *Vía de los bomberos*.

Descents - For the two long routes, double 50m ropes are needed for abseiling. The rest of the routes can mostly be abseiled, or lowered down in stages on a 60m rope, but take great care since the pitches are longer than they appear.

Approach (map p.145, overview p.153) - Walk under Sectors Silicona and Excalibur, and keep going across the bay to the far side.

To the right of the small slab is a much longer wall of excellent compact grey rock that has superb, bolted multi-pitch climbs.

❶ La ley del deseo 6a
'The Law of Desire' follows the right-hand side of the main ridge at a very amenable grade. It is fully bolted and very popular. The main drawback is people abseiling down it while you are on your way up. For this reason, a helmet is advised.
1) 5c, 20m. Take the left-hand line of bolts, just right of a corner.
2) 5c, 20m. Continue in roughly the same line. This pitch can be combined with pitch one.
3) 4c, 25m. Continue up the line marked by silver dots, to a belay at the top of an open rib.
4) 5a, 35m. Continue to a well-positioned stance on a cleaned ledge. There is another belay 5m higher.
5) 4c, 40m. Move right and follow closely-spaced bolts up a wall on great holds. Pass the first tree stance and climb up another 15m to the next with twin bolts.
6) 6a, 40m. Make a hard start away from corner. There is a two-bolt hanging stance at 30m or continue (40m) to the stance at the start of pitch 7 on *Albahida*.
Descent - Finish up the last easy pitch of *Albahida* and walk down - see page 144. Alternatively, abseil off taking care to avoid parties climbing up below you.

❷ Sonrisa vertical 6a
Climb pitch 1 of *La ley del deseo*. From the belay, step right and climb directly up the wall above a small tree. Old bolts.

❸ The Master 6a
A worthwhile outing taking in some fine climbing and positions.
1) 5a. The line of bolts just right of *La ley del deseo* starting from the same flat area.
2) 6a. The left-hand line gives an excellent pitch.

❹ Polla boba 6a
1) 5a. As for *The Master*.
2) 6a. Move up slightly right to an awkward bulge.

❺ Méjico lindo .... 6a+
1) 5b. As for *The Master*.
2) 6a+. The right-hand line to the same lower-off.

❻ Alternative Start 5a
An easier start to the previous upper lines.

❼ Mongol Express .... 6b+
An excellent route that tackles the full height of the wall. An alternative easier start is possible up routes to the left.
1) 6b, 38m. The left-hand line to a scoop (possible belay). Continue between the two tufas. A good pitch on its own.
2) 5b, 20m. Easy broken ground leads to another belay.
3) 6a, 20m. A slightly steeper section.
4) 6b+, 20m. A steep technical wall leads to the top belay.
Descent - You can continue up *Albahida* (via three bolts) or abseil back down the route in three long abseils.

❽ Mongol Right 4c
The right-hand bolted line gives a short easy pitch.

❾ Oasis 6b
A huge single pitch between two tufas. Abseil off.

❿ Alan Bator .... 7a+
A hard alternative start to *Mongol Express*.

⓫ Bomberos Direct 6c
A direct version of pitch 1 of *Via de los Bomberos*. Aim for the chunky, white tufa. Tricky in its middle section.

⓬ Vía de los bomberos 6b
A tremendous route which takes the best line of unvegetated rock up the huge wall of the bay. The climbing is sustained but never desperate, and the views from the stances are excellent. Start at a clear area below a big white tufa in a hollow.
1) 6a, 30m. Take the right-hand line of bolts to the white tufa.
2) 6a+, 25m. Pull up right and climb the blunt rib.
3) 6b, 40m. A long pitch - take lots of quickdraws.
4) 6b, 40m. Steady climbing leads to a tricky section. Abseil off from here or try the next pitch.
5) 6b, 35m. A hard start then easy climbing to the ridge and a junction with *Albahida*. Follow this and walk down.
Descent - Abseil off on double 50m ropes from the top of P4.

⓭ Hambre eterna 6b
The last line on this section of the crag. Good thin climbing to half-height followed by easy but poor moves up the slab to a lower-off.

A multi-pitch route was bolted here called Salut i república. This area suffers from rockfall and the route is dangerous and shouldn't be climbed. Three routes in the high cave used the route for access and are also worth avoiding for this reason.

158 Sa Gubia — Sector Princesa

Sector Princesa

The huge rear wall of the bay is an immense and well-featured section of rock. At present it is home to just a handful of climbs, but two of them are mega-classics.

Approach (map p.145, overview p.153) - On the main approach, take the higher path under Sectors Silicona and Excalibur. Then head steeply upwards through the trees to the lower slabs of the *Sexo débil* area. *Princesa* is further around to the left.

Sector Princesa Sa Gubia

① Via Llum de Lluna 6b
Technical and sustained wall climbing on positive holds.
1) **6a+**. Climb the slab and holes over bulges to a shallow cave stance by a small tree.
2) **6a+**. After the initial moves to get established on the wall, continue through the vertical terrain on good holds.
3) **6a**. Slightly easier with a tricky move at mid-height.
4) **6b**. A cracking pitch with no particular difficulties.
5) **6b**. Continue up the easier slab (spaced bolts) to more powerful climbing and a memorable finish.
Descent - Abseil down the route in six 35m abseils. The rap rings are red, whilst the route's belays are green. Avoid the nest near the end of the fifth abseil.

② Negra Flor 6b
This route tackles the lower wall by two very long pitches on black bolts, before traversing across right to join *Princesa*. It then goes direct in two more long pitches to the summit.
1) 6b, 2) 6a, 3) 6b, 4) 6a.
Descent - Single 70m rope minimum. Abseil down the route then as for *Princesa*.

③ Slow Life .... 6a+
A long line which has the easiest climbing of the long multi-pitchers on this wall. It tackles the wide central scoop which has some vegetation connecting good quality rock.
1) 3a, 2) 6a, 3) 6a+, 4) 4a, 5) 4c, 6) 6a, 7) 5b.
Descent - Single 70m rope minimum. Abseil down the route.

④ Princesa 6b
An inspiring route that tackles the full length of the back wall of the bay. Start on the grey slabs below and left of the vast orange scoop in the back wall. Belay at the treeline or scramble up to where the wall steepens. The first bolt is an old one.
1) **6a**. Climb the wall to a stance below a steeper section of wall.
2) **6b**. Move leftwards past the steep section and continue to a stance. This used to go direct with one very hard move - **6c**.
3) **5c**. Climb to a stance on a ledge with trees.
4) **6a**. Climb straight past an overhang to a ledge (optional stance). Traverse right to a small stance below a corner.
5) **5c**. Traverse right for 8m then climb directly up the wall to the clifftop.
Descent - Single 70m rope minimum. Abseil from top of *Sol Solet* to the shared belay with *Princesa*. Continue down *Princesa* to a tree ledge stance. Continue down *Princesa* to the top of the second pitch. Two further abseils down *Princesa* to the ground.

⑤ Sol Solet .... 6b+
More adventurous than *Princesa*, and on great rock. There are various ways of combining pitches, including doing the whole thing in just three pitches with 60m ropes.
1) **6b+**. Climb the steep wall past an optional stance to a small ledge - a long pitch, the upper part of which has a line of bolts that lead left into the line of *Princesa* - do not go this way.
2) **6a**. Climb up left then back right to a poor sloping stance.
3) **6b+**. Move up and right via thin moves and tackle the overhang (try not to go too direct) and continue to a stance.
4) **6a**. Continue up on great rock to a shared stance with *Princesa*.
5) **6b+**. Tackle the overhang and enjoy the steep slabs to the top, passing another optional belay.
Descent - As for *Princesa*.

⑥ Sol Solet Right Start 6c
Two very long pitches that lead to an extra belay half way up *Sol Solet* P3. Finish up *Sol Solet* in another long single pitch making the whole thing just three massive pitches. 1) 6c, 2) 6c, 3) 6b+

⑦ Via Terra Lliure 6c
A trad-sport line through some impressive territory.
1) 6a, 2) 6b, 3) 6c, 4) 5c, 5) 5b (7b/A2 on the right).

⑧ Placa aspera .... 6a+
A lone, off-vertical wall pitch up the dark grey wall that lies beneath the big orange gash. Start approximately 20m to the right of *Princesa*. The bolts are difficult to spot. The climbing is both technical and sustained.

⑨ Tierra al reves .... 6a+
Spectacular climbing. Easy climbing leads up the orange scoop to a steepening. Delicate moves right gain buckets then a move across the steep section to a final hard pull. *Photo p.161*.

⑩ El Empalma Cantos .... ?
The left-hand line that breaks left after five bolts.

⑪ Diablo 8a
A spectacular and sustained route with impressive exposure! 40m.

⑫ Moca de pavo 7c
A marvellous route firing up the steep wall right of the elephant's backside tufa. Can be dirty. Scramble up easy rock to start.

⑬ Foracorda 8b
The continuation pitch to *Moca de pavo* is awesome.

⑭ Idem .... 7b+
Start up pitch 1 of *Sexo débil*.

⑮ De gorrones hasta los cojones
.... 8a
The continuation to *Idem*.

⑯ Steep Groove 7a
Direct up the steep groove above the pillar of *Sexo débil* with a short sharp pull into the groove.

⑰ Sexo débil .... 6b+
An amazing route that weaves its way up the shady right-hand side of the bay through some dramatic territory. Pitch 3 uses bolt-on holds to cross the bulging section. This gives access to the last two pitches which are superb. Start below the pillar of rock below the right-hand side of the cave.
1) **4a**. Climb to the base of the corner.
2) **6a+**. Pull up and right onto the wall, then climb to the ledge below an impressive bulging wall.
3) **6b+**. Traverse right, then heave up the tufas and 'bolt-ons' - reachy! These have worked loose over the years, making this pitch quite hard. A sling may be needed for aid.
4) **6b**. Make a superb, rising traverse leftwards, on immaculate rock and just enough holds, to a hanging belay.
5) **6b**. Traverse back right and up the open groove to the top.
Descent - Abseil down the route. On a single 60m, you will need to make three abseils via stances at the end of pitches 3 and 1.

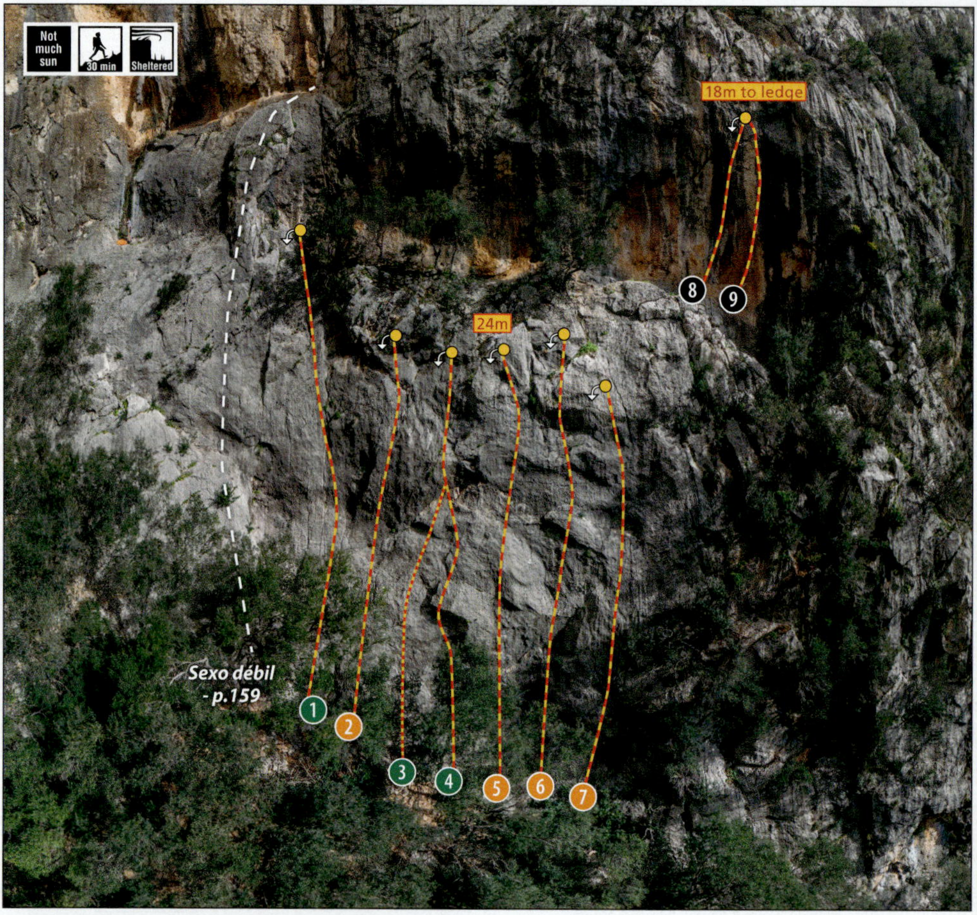

Sa Gubia — Sector Potaje Español

Sector Potaje Español

The slabby lower wall below *Sexo débil* has a fine set of easier routes, which are deservedly popular. Although they appear insignificant when compared to the vastness of the wall above, they are actually quite long, and have plenty of climbing. The sector is better sheltered than elsewhere, and is cooler in hot weather.

Approach (map p.145, overview p.153) - On the main approach, take the higher path, under Sector Silicona and Excalibur. Then head steeply upwards through the trees to the lower slabs.

❶ Easy Slab 4c
An easy slab leading to a crack. It is a long way from the top bolt to the lower-off.

❷ Es barbut 5a
Make a tricky move from the corner onto the slab. The lower-off is set well back.

❸ Cannabis 4c
A left-hand start to *Cannabis in vitro*.

❹ Cannabis in vitro 4c
Negotiate the protruding roof on its left-hand side.

❺ Potaje Español 5a
This pitch features a leaning wall at mid-height.

❻ El jardín de la abuela 5a
Climb the flake and wall.

❼ Tantum ergo 5b
The line furthest right has a tricky move to pass the fourth bolt.

The next two routes start from the ledge above the easy slabs. Do one of the previous routes to get to the ledge.

❽ Mipichica 7b
The left-hand bolted line up a very steep, bulging wall.

❾ Miju .... 7b+
The right-hand line.

John McKenna on *Tierra al reves* (6a+) - *p.159* - at Sector Princesa, Sa Gubia. Photo: Mike Hutton

Sa Gubia — Sector Isla Bonita

1 Caperucita roja.......... 6b
A short wall behind some trees past a square-cut roof.

2 Groove 6a
The curving groove.

3 Groove Right-hand.......... 6b

4 To kiski'm'toca 7a
Technical climbing to the left of the bolts.

5 Fina y segura........ 6b+
The left-hand side of the scoop - contorted movements.

6 Pringa mete el dedo 6b
Make fingery pulls to leave the right-hand side of the scoop.

7 La Isla Bonita Original....... 6b+
The original start requires a very fingery and technical move to gain the scoop which leads to the stance. Old bolts.

8 La Isla Bonita .... 6a+
1) **6a+**. The rib leads steeply up to a stance.
2) **5a**. Head up leftwards to below the impressive upper wall.
3) **6a+**. A delightful final pitch up the left-hand bolted line.
Descent - Abseil back down the route.

9 Climber Gay............ 5c
Start down the slope. Cracks and a corner lead to a stance. A good pitch. There is a seldom climbed **6b** extension above.

10 Franceses P1 .... 6a+
Climb a bulging scooped wall to a belay above a ledge.

11 Franceses............. 6c
The full route is good but unbalanced.
1) **6a+**, 2) **5b**. Plod up the fluted wall.
3) **6c**. The right-hand line is hard. Better to do *Isla Bonita P3*.
Descent - Abseil back down *Isla bonita*.

Sector Isla Bonita
A popular sector with some great routes. Some of the bolts and belays are old.
Approach (map p.145, overview p.165) - On the main approach take the higher path under Sector Silicona and continue around until you are under the huge arete of *Agárrate maldito*.

Sector Isla Bonita Sa Gubia

12 Phantasmagoria — 7b
Easy climbing leads to a short, hard section through the bulge.

13 Bongo bongo — 7a+
A dynamic move through the bulge. Climb left of the bolts above this on a crimpy finish.

14 Gigoló — 7b
A thoroughly desperate struggle up the crack out of *Why!*.

15 Why! — 6c
Trad climbing on bolts. There is a reachy move low down.

16 Cortocircuito — 6c
Superb climbing up the blunt arete with a hole. The start is probably the hardest move, but it remains tricky to the top.

17 Zaragüay — 6b
Gaining the crack is hard (from the right is a touch easier). The crack above succumbs to determined bridging in a fine position. Avoid squirming in the back if you can.

18 Agárrate maldito — 7c
A stunning extension up the arete but with old bolts.

Sector Excalibur — Sa Gubia

1 K.G.B. — 6c+
Begin at a lower level to the rest of the routes and climb a corner to reach a pocketed crack.

2 Na guarra — 6a
A good route up the wall left of the *Excalibur* groove, behind a small tilted block. Higher up, step right and bridge up the corner and crack to a lower-off.

3 Horrible belleza — 7a
A thin extension to *Na guarra*.

4 Excalibur — 6a
A fine line up the curving ramp and corner above. Excellent and varied climbing but don't expect a normal clip-up.
1) **6a**. Follow the curving ramp clipping some bolts on other routes. At its end, pull over the bulge and belay.
2) **6a**. The V-corner leads awkwardly to the top.
2a) **6b**. A poor right-hand finish is possible.

5 Ópera prima — 5c
Start as for *Excalibur*, but continue up the wall to a lower-off.

6 No haces más grado — 7b
Start as for *Trampera matinera*. Follow the old bolts up to a desperate wall and bulge.

7 Trampera matinera — 6b
Pull over some bulges onto a slab and the first bolt - very high! Follow the right-hand line of bolts above to the steepest part of the bulge. Pull blindly through this.

8 Bofetadas de placer — 7b+
Make very steep moves up the small tufas.

9 Charismatic — 6c+
Steep climbing on the left side of some holes.

10 Hot consuela — 6c+
Start up the side slab, then climb the short technical wall to reach good holds above. There has been a right-hand variation reported to this route at **6b+**.

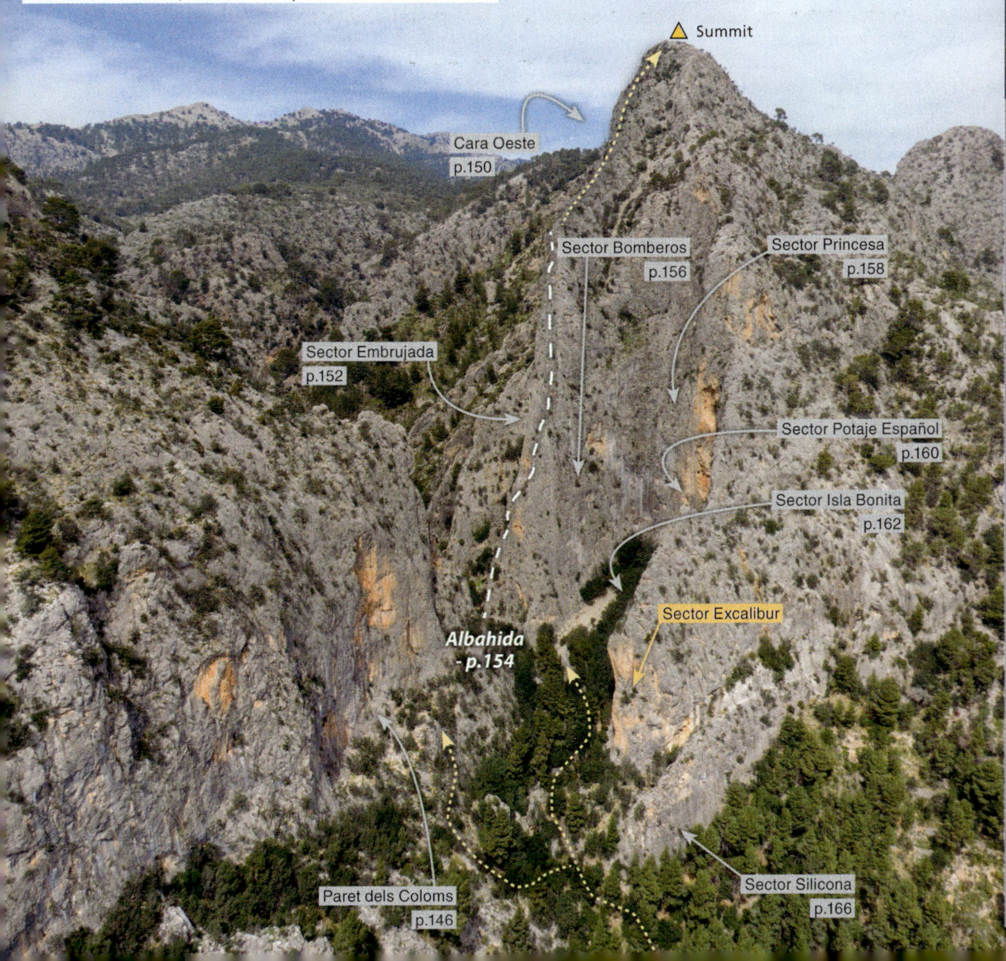

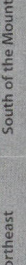

Sa Gubia — Sector Silicona

Sector Silicona

This popular sector is often the first section of Sa Gubia sampled by visiting climbers. The climbs are mostly slabby or gentle walls with some hard, technical moves. The lines are very easily located and have a pleasant setting with shade from tree cover at their base. However popularity means it can be a little polished in places.
Approach (map p.145, overview p.165) - The sector is situated just a few metres above the higher approach path at a clear area of ground amongst trees.

❶ The Hunter's Gun 4c
Climb a thin slab to a tricky bulge.

❷ Hawaii 5-0 .... 5a
The scratched slab up the left-hand edge of the wall is a good little pitch, although fairly polished.

❸ Silicona 6c
The thin slab starting between two bushes is a tough outing.

❹ Lulu .... 6b+
Start at the groove right of some bushes. Climb the wall and crack to a steep finish past an overlap.

❺ Proteina vegetal ...... 6a+
Climb the blank-looking slab to easier ground and continue to beneath the steeper upper wall. Pull up and left to finish at a niche and lower-off.

❻ Totom fa el que vol ... 6b
Start next to a stone wall at the base of the crag. Climb the steep slab then continue more easily to the upper wall. Make steep moves up and back left to the lower-off.

❼ Resaca .... 6a+
Start on top of the stone wall, below an open groove. Climb the straightforward groove to a hard finish over a small overhang. *Photo opposite.*

❽ Gran pis .... 6b+
A good and sustained pitch. Climb the lovely wall to a steep bulging finish moving up rightwards to the belay.

❾ Rustic pogo .... 6b+
An extremely hard move to leave the scoop in the middle of the wall, although the holds are positive.

❿ Route 9 .... 6a+
A steep upper section with some good pockets and jugs that are difficult to see from below.

⓫ Familia Iscariote 6a
Break right from *Route 9* to gain a fine finish.

⓬ Familia variante 6b
Start from ledges on the far right of the wall.

Wenzel Fröhlich on *Resaca* (6a+) - *opposite.* - on Sector Silicona at Sa Gubia. Photo: Alan James

Fraguel

| Grade Spread | 1 | 6 | 13 | 24 | 18 |

Fraguel is a stunning cliff that has some of the best hard sport climbing on the island, attracting climbers from all over the world. It is located in a beautiful wooded valley near the town of Bunyola, and is hidden from almost every direction, including the one used to approach the crag.

Approach
From the centre of Bunyola, drive towards Santa María. Turn left as you leave the village (this is 200m before a bar on the left). Follow the narrow road/track, gradually gaining height, through lots of hairpin bends. Just after the 5km marker, park the car carefully by a path on the right-hand side of the track - leave enough room for large forestry lorries to get past. Follow the path from the parking area for about 60m, to a small clearing (keep to the slight left-hand fork). Go left 15m after the fork, emerging immediately into an old charcoal pit (a grassy circle). Leave this on its opposite side and wander through the trees on a small path until near the edge of the cliff. Head leftwards (facing out) - (some cairns) to a short awkward groove with metal rungs in place which lead down to the crag base. The path leads back easily right (looking out) under the cliff to below the routes.

Conditions
The crag gets the sun until about 2 o'clock in the afternoon, which is a benefit in warm weather when it can offer pleasant afternoon shade. At cooler times, the crag can be extremely cold - even in April. This is especially true when there is any wind, since it howls down the gorge below the crag. If you're planning a long spell of belay duty, while your mate 'dogs' his or her 8a, take a big duvet jacket. Most of the harder routes will stay dry in moderate rain, but the tufas do start to seep after any prolonged rainfall. The easier routes at either end offer little shelter in the rain, but usually dry fairly quickly.

Sector Pink Panther p.170
Sector Goo Goo Mack p.171
Sector Football Fan p.172
Sector Bobo dodo p.173
Sector Rock Punk p.174
Sector Cous-cous p.176

Fraguel 169

Track from Bunyola

Metal rungs

Fraguel

The Southwest · *Valldemossa Area* · *Bunyola Area* · *North of the Mountains* · *South of the Mountains* · *The Northeast* · *The East Coast*

scan for map

GPS 39.698375
2.717178

Fraguel

Bunyola

Ma-2010

Ma-11

Ma-2020

Parking for Sa Gubia

Fraguel — Sector Pink Panther

Sector Pink Panther
The far left sector at Fraguel has a few of the better easier pitches at the crag, plus a number of sustained and fingery wall climbs.
Approach (map and overview p.169) - Continue to the far end of the crag, just beyond a step down in the terrace. The first routes start just beyond the tall, slender pillar.

There are some other pitches further left than those described, but these are rather poor and not well bolted.

1 Left Pillar 6a
The left-hand side of a small pillar to a shared lower-off.

2 Pastel de ochoce 6a
The right-hand line of the pillar on good rock.

3 Ochobe mas 6b
A gradually-steepening line to the ledge with large tree.

4 Vuit se mes 6a
Straightforward wall climbing on poor rock.

5 Ojo climico .... 6c+
1) 6c+. Difficulties gradually increase to a crux sequence just below the belay. Very thin and sustained climbing.
2) 6c. Continue in the same line.

6 666 .... 6c+
1) 6c+. A worthwhile pitch following the left line of bolts.
2) 6c+. Continue up the right-hand bolted line.

7 Tabasco .... 7a+
The left-hand side of the scoop on small holds.

8 Harissa 7b
The centre of the scoop has a tough move near the bottom.

9 Pink Panther .... 6a+
1) 6a. The corner gives one of the better easier pitches here.
2) 6a+. Excellent climbing and a lot easier than it looks.

10 El terrat 6b
A short left-hand finish to *Pink Panther*.

11 Caca de colores .... 7a+
The sheer wall right of the corner of *Pink Panther*.

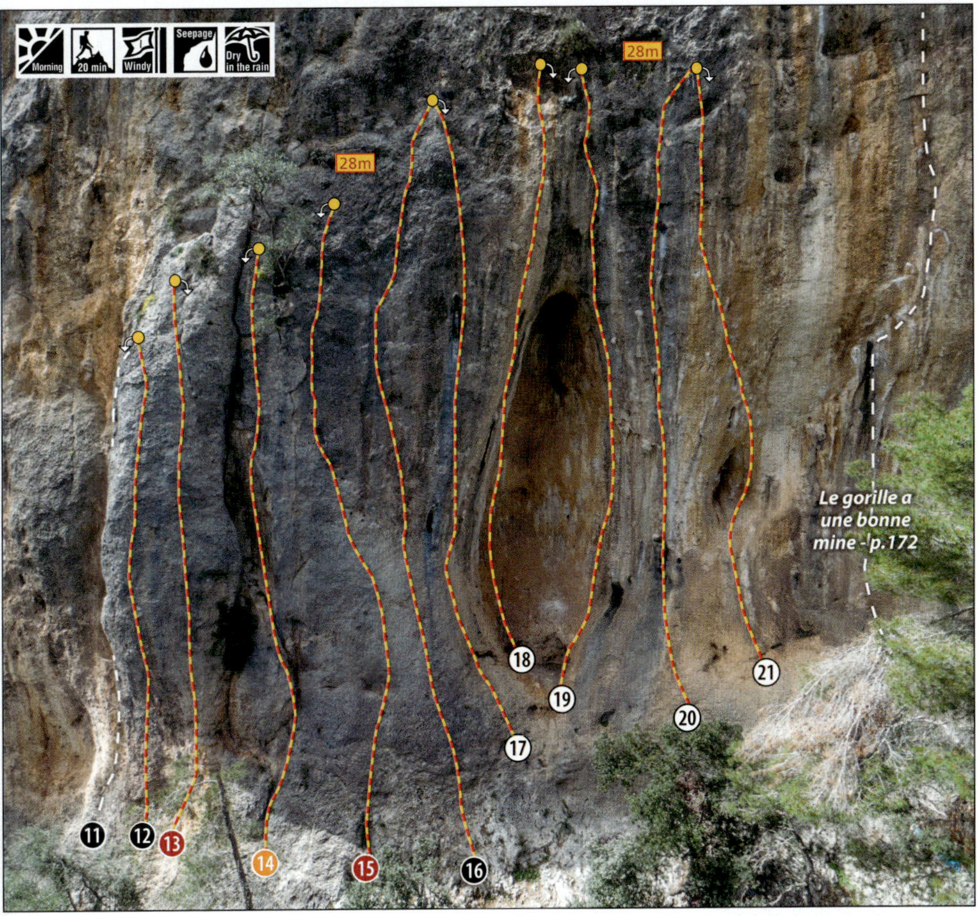

Sector Goo Goo Mack **Fraguel**

Le gorille a une bonne mine - p.172

⑫ Rosa de sanatorio.... 7b+
Climb just right of the blank-looking rounded rib of the tall pillar.

⑬ Fakir 6c
The right-hand line has a stopper move on sharp holds.

⑭ Flake and Groove 5c
An easy route up the flake and groove above. This line has suffered a rockfall and may be in an unstable state.

⑮ Psycho Killer .... 6c+
Good climbing, but a touch escapable higher up where the crux kicks in.

⑯ Jungle hop.............. 7a+
Superb, sustained and twice as pumpy as you'd think, considering that it looks like a slab!

Just right is a tall oval cave with two lines on its left-hand side.

⑰ Salpicón de menisco . 8a
The first of the mega hard, mega classic stamina tests.

Sector Goo Goo Mack

The routes to the left of the crag step are long, hard and impressive and centred on the huge orange depression and the smooth grey wall on its left.

Approach (map and overview p.169) - Walk towards the far end of the crag. Just beyond a step down in the terrace is a tall pillar. The first routes start just before this pillar below the huge orange depression.

⑱ Solo Sex 8a
Climbs from the back of the oval cave trending left to exit onto the headwall.

⑲ La otra linea .... 8b+
The line on the right-hand side of the oval cave.

⑳ Senglier 8b
Climb the grey streak/pillar just right of the oval cave.

㉑ Goo Goo Mack 8a
The line of bolts beginning in the small depression right of the oval cave. A fantastic route with sustained and hard climbing.

Fraguel — Sector Football Fan

Sector Football Fan
The best routes at the crag are on the two central sections. The left-hand side is home to some huge pitches, most of which are around 30m and 8a or above.
Approach (map and overview p.169) - The first lines start above the rock step.

❶ Le gorille a une bonne mine 7c
A classic pitch. Follow some steep tufa to a difficult move and a rest just above. Finish up the steep wall on sharp holds.

❷ Amnesia .... 8b+
The impressive wall with fixed quickdraws in place.

❸ Ca'n Bum 7c

❹ Football Fan 8a
One of the best and most popular 8a's on the island. A thin tufa gains a knee-bar at mid-height. The tufas run out on the upper wall, which is climbed on small holds.

❺ Shabada .... 8a+
The chunky tufas and steep headwall above the step in the crag base. From the tufas to the first lower-off is 7a+.

❻ Black hole .... 7b+

❼ Ramadán 8b
To the top of the tufa is 6a+ and worthwhile. The wall above gives a magnificent continuation.

Sector Bobo dodo **Fraguel** 173

Sector Bobo dodo

A stunning section of crag directly above the spot where most teams choose to gear up. All the routes are very sustained and far steeper than first appearances suggest. A few of the lines have intermediate lower-offs which allow the lower sections to be climbed as pitches in their own right.
Approach (map and overview p.169) - This is the widest section of ledge beneath the crag just before a short drop down a rock step.

⑧ **Big Men** .... 9a+
A major undertaking that is one of Mallorca's hardest pitches. *Photo p.28*.

⑨ **French Kiss** 8b
The pocketed wall past the triangular hole is a big and difficult pitch that might suit those averse to 'tufa yarding'.

⑩ **Terre d'adventure** 7c
The tufas left of the central cave give a fine hard pitch.

⑪ **Terre d'adventure plus** 8a
If the truncated version proved to be a path, then just keep going up the increasingly steep headwall.

⑫ **Fes lo que puguis** 7b
A fine but well-used route up the big tufas on the left-hand side of the cave. The start is difficult for the short and the upper section is pumpy for all.

⑬ **Miss Palma** .... 7b+
The super-steep groove past a couple of caves requires some contorted manoeuvres and a bit of lateral thinking.

⑭ **Bobo dodo (L1)** 7a
The tufa system just right of the central cave is a popular 7a to the first 'nowhere' lower-off.

⑮ **Bobo dodo (L2)** .... 7b+
To the second lower-off is an excellent and powerful 7b+.

⑯ **Bobo dodo** .... 8c+
The stunning full pitch to the top of the crag.

⑰ **Humanoide** .... 8a+
The full-height tufa system with the crux on the upper wall. To the first lower-off is 7c+.

Fraguel — Sector Rock Punk

Sector Rock Punk

The left-hand side of this section of the crag has some rather brutal pitches that contrast with the fingery and more popular wall climbs to the right.

Approach (map and overview p.169) - This area begins as soon as the narrow rock ledge that is used on the approach rounds the corner of crag.

1 No Name .... 8b+
A hard and bulging wall passing a small round hole midway.

2 Pantano boas .... 7c+
The well-defined and slippery lower tufa precedes more difficult climbing on the bulging wall above. *Photo opposite.*

3 Miguel and the test tube babies
.... 7c+
The bulging pocketed wall just right of a large hole.

4 Aloha from Hell...... 7c
The line of pockets up the wall to a bouldery crux above.

5 Glasnost............ 7b+
The infamous 'mono' on the mid-height steep bulging wall is always well chalked up.

6 Tête de pene ..... 7c+
Start up the same line of bolts as *Glasnost*, but branch out right.

7 El último vals................. 8a
Up the wall to the right of a cave, past a curving break.

8 Rock punk ...... 7c+
More tufa-pulling to a steep finish.

9 Cuencamelo..... 7c
Start behind the large, fallen tree. A superb, highly technical wall climb that never lets up.

10 On es l'avi.......... 7b+
One of the more popular routes which regularly spits people off from high up. A really good pitch.

Neus Colom on the tufa fin of *Pantano boas* (7c+) - *opposite* - at Fraguel. Photo: Pou Brothers

Fraguel — Sector Cous-cous

On es l'avi - p.174

Sector Cous-cous
The right-hand end of the crag has a selection of good routes that range from the thin and desperate to some relatively easier fayre in the upper 6th grades.

Approach (map and overview p.169) - The sector is the first clean wall of bolted rock encountered on the approach path

① **Pastanaga punyetera**
.... 8a
There are not so many tufas on this one.

② **Setebe el plumero**
.... 7b+
Sustained and technical climbing despite being split by two rests in holes.

③ **Gaucho** 8a
The left-hand line above a ledge with two trees.

④ **Cotorrot** .... 7c+
The right-hand line above the ledge.

Sector Cous-cous **Fraguel** 177

5 Cous-cous 6c
One of the best of the easier routes on the crag, although high in the grade. Start just to the left of a rounded rib. The climbing gradually steepens to a pocket-pulling finale.

6 Esto no es Calvià .... 6c+
The wall just to the right of the rib of *Cous-cous*.

7 Sementir .... 6b+
Start as for *Esto no es Calvià* and then branch right.

8 Comando rasta 6b
The slabby wall to the right gets gradually harder.

9 Hard Finish .... 6b+
Another one that packs it in at the top.

10 Peep show's barriga
.... 7c
A manufactured line up the bulge.

11 Marmade .... 7b+
There are some slightly bigger chipped holds on this one.

12 Tofol .... 6b+
A good little route climbing just to the left of a small bush.

13 Churro pino 6a
At last, something a bit easier. Don't be fooled - the bulge at the bottom is still hard.

14 Chris line 4c
This one really is easier, but it's not very good.

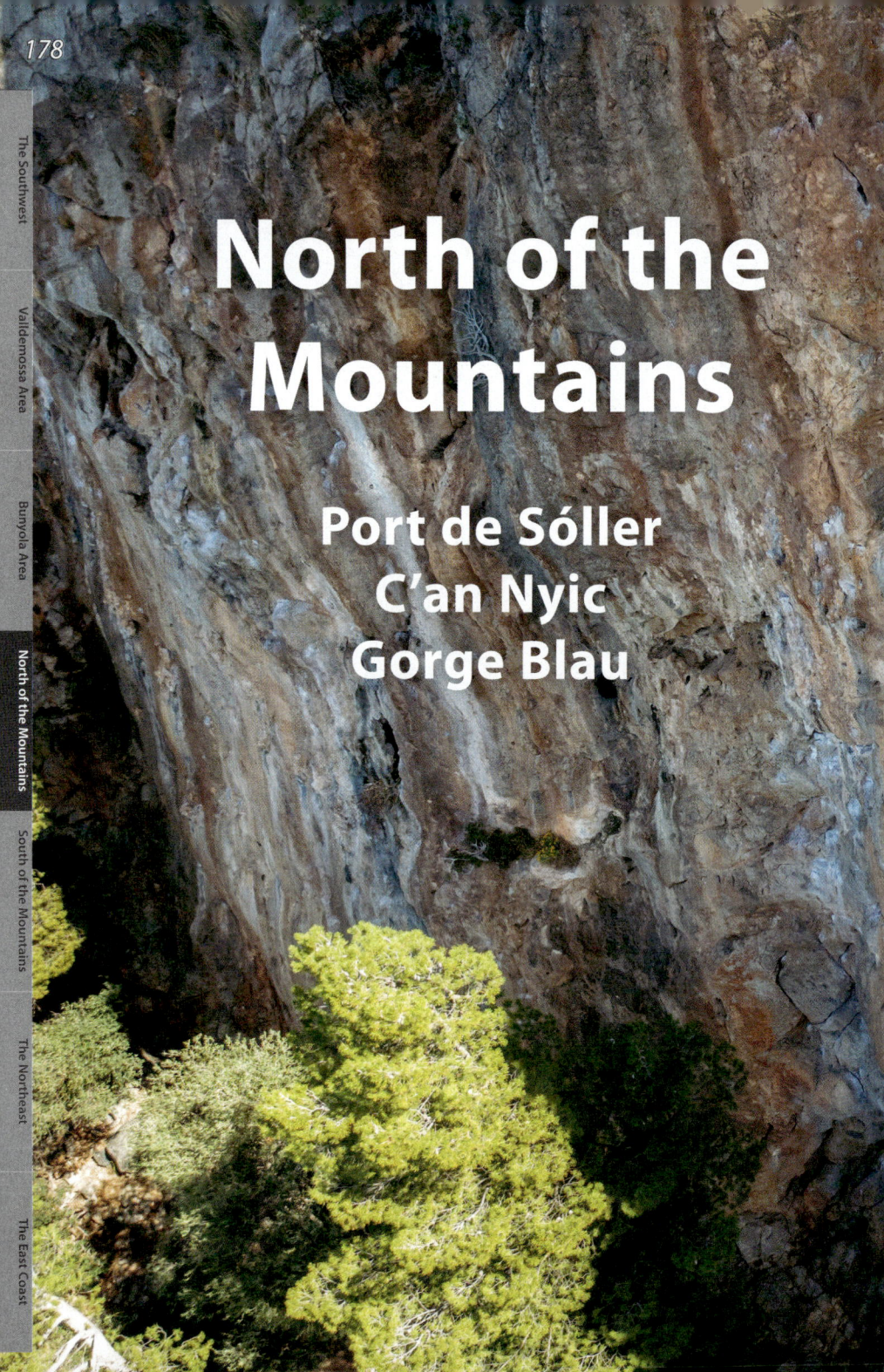

North of the Mountains

Port de Sóller
C'an Nyic
Gorge Blau

To the north of the crest of the Tramuntana mountains the land drops off steeply down to the sea and is the setting for three crags each with a very different character. Port de Sóller is a varied holiday climbing venue that will satisfy most tastes and abilities. Gorge Blau and C'an Nyic are perched high on the slopes of the mountain range and offer the chance of cool climbing during hot weather. Gorge Blau has a large number of hard routes whilst C'an Nyic is usually visited by climbers looking to bag the trio of brilliant grade 6s. All of the crags in this area have quick and easy access once the mountain roads have been negotiated! John McKenna enjoying the fine wall climbing on *Patito Feo* (6b) - *p.188* - at Port Sóller. Photo: Mike Hutton

Port de Sóller

The crag at Port de Sóller is set in a beautiful location looking out over the sea and harbour entrance, all framed by the backdrop of the Tramuntana mountains. The main feature of the crag is a huge central cave, which has some excellent testpieces for those operating in the higher grades. The walls to either side offer much more friendly-angled climbing, with some excellent mid-grade routes.

Access
Access was blocked off during the development of the hotel above the crag. The hotel is now finished and no access problems have been reported in recent times.

Conditions
The crag faces west and looks out over the sea, getting all the mid-afternoon and evening sun going, as well as a great view of any sunsets. The trees and general location give it shelter from wind, but can make it a suntrap in the afternoons. The cave routes will give dry climbing in the rain, but some of the tufas may seep after long spells of bad weather.

Port de Sóller   181

John McKenna getting to grips with the tufa blobs that give this Port Sóller classic its name *Blobland* (6c) - *p.186*. Photo: Mike Hutton

Port de Sóller

Approach

Drive to Port de Sóller through the toll tunnel on the Ma-11. Take the right-hand branch towards 'Centro' through another tunnel. At the roundabout, turn left and drive towards the town, then turn right and weave through streets to join a steep road going up hill towards 'Urb. Atalya'. Park by the Nautilus Bar. Walk down a track to the right (looking out) of the bar and along a path by some wire fencing where the crag comes into view. It is best to gain the base of the crag via a steep path below Sector Blobland (do not leave the path too early).

Linnea Qvarnstrom heading for the lower-off on the headwall of *Sun* (6c) - *p.188* - at Port de Sóller. Photo: Mark Glaister

Port de Sóller — Far Left Cave

Far Left Cave

The first routes are in a small cave 150m left of the main crag - a mini version of the main cave.

Approach (map and overview p.182) - From the path below *Blobland*, walk beneath the crag for 150m to the cave.

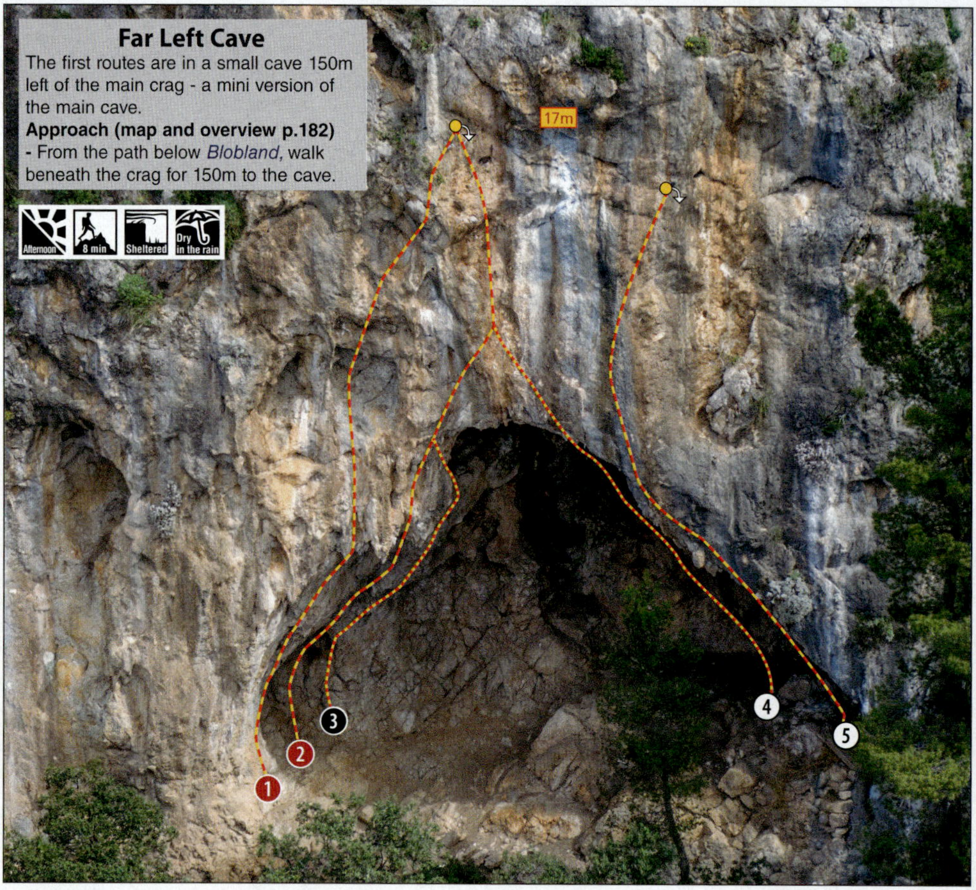

① Rufo .... 6c+
A strange route with a gap in the bolts.

② Rocko 7a
Start in the cave and swing out leftwards. Old bolts.

③ Rocko Right 7b
Good burly climbing and a technically interesting headwall.

④ Repowoman 8a
A hard and crimpy crux move just before half-height.

⑤ Repoman 8a
Slightly easier than *Repowoman* up the right edge.

Sector Nuevo

⑥ S'illeta .... 6b+
Neat climbing gradually increases in angle to a tufa finale.

⑦ Sa torre picada 6c
A tufa wall gains a stiff pull that leads to easier ground.

⑧ 25 de agosto .... 7a+
An excellent long line that finishes at the very top of the wall.

⑨ Quin berenar .... 7b+
A full-height line that is heavily drilled and glued.

⑩ Voramar .... 7a+
The right-hand side of the central wall to a thin ramp.

⑪ Sa roqueta 6c
A fine climb that follows a ramp and steep wall.

⑫ Crozzle Pillar Left 6c
The left-hand of two lines on the pillar right of Sector Nuevo. Climb the left-hand side past some suspect rock.

⑬ Crozzle Pillar Right 6b
The central line on the pillar weaves around at the start with some nice moves before a stopper finish on razors.

Sector Nuevo **Port de Sóller** 185

Sector Nuevo

A reasonable section of crag that features some sustained wall pitches, a couple of which are very long. Some of the holds are chipped and glued on the harder lines.
Approach (map and overview p.182) - From the path below *Blobland* walk leftwards a short distance to below the sector.

Port de Sóller — Sector Blobland

Sector Blobland
This is the left-hand side of the main area and features a pocketed wall with some overhangs high on its right, and a blob-covered headwall high on its left.

Approach (map and overview p.182) - The routes are directly above where the approach path meets the cliff.

❶ Dosis 7b
Start left of a big tree. A relatively short route that passes a couple of overhangs.

❷ La Machado 7c
A fine long route left of *Blobland*. Start right of the big tree.

❸ Blobland 6c
A stunning route up the long blob-covered wall. Climb the lower wall to some tricky and reachy moves leftwards. From the midway ledge, gaze in awe at the wall above. This proves to be easier than it looks, by simply connecting the blobs to a lower-off on the right. *Photo p.180*.

❹ Directland 7b
A fine direct version of *Blobland*. Where *Blobland* moves left, climb the crack to a rest and then move right and up the sustained wall.

❺ Blobland Right 6c
Another good route on this fine wall. Start up *Blobland* and move right. Climb up, generally on the right-hand side of the bolts, to a steep finish.

Sun - p.188

Port de Sóller

6 Bon vi .... 6a+
Good climbing with one technical move at the bottom and a steep finish.

7 Els salvatjes .... 6b+
More good climbing leading to a steep finish.

8 Els salvatjes Right .... 6c+
Climb easily to a steeper wall and then pull up some tufa into a hanging groove. Exit left to gain further tufas that lead to a lower-off.

Martin McKenna and his shadow on *El mar del amor* (6a) - *p.188* - at Port Sóller. Photo: Mike Hutton

Port de Sóller — Sector Sa Cova

Sector Sa Cova

The most important area of the crag is centred on the large cave, and the tall walls either side of it. The cave itself gives some steep and hard pitches, while the walls have slightly easier pitches in the grade 6 range. Virtually all of the routes are superb and very rarely out of condition.

Approach (map and overview p.182) - Walk right from where the main approach meets the cliff.

❶ Sun 6c
The bolts are to the right at the bottom. The upper part of the route is on orange tufa. *Photo p.183.*

❷ Sun Right-hand .... 6a+
A narrow line which features a low crux.

❸ El mar del amor 6a
Brilliant, varied climbing on huge holds. Pumpy at the top. *Photo p.187.*

❹ Patito feo 6b
Similar to its left-hand neighbour, but technically harder in its middle section. *Photo p.178.*

Take care when embarking on the next four lines, as a very large bees' nest has been seen at times near the route Virgin.

❺ Dit I fet .... 7a+
The left-hand edge of the cave is short but demanding.

❻ Virgin 8a
Extremely strenuous and sustained climbing up the edge of the cave to a lower-off at the top of the crag. Old bolts.

❼ Virgin Direct .... 7b+
A very good route that follows the steep and juggy underside of *Virgin* to join and finish up *Phantomas*. Old perma-draws.

❽ Phantomas 7b
Superb jug-pulling up the steep right edge of the cave and onwards across the roof to a tricky climax on the headwall.

❾ Ficalito 7c
From the 'rest' on the last route, power straight up the wall.

❿ Club super tres .... 7b+
Great climbing on tufa-covered rock with crux moves up the leaning pocketed wall.

⓫ Ja som five 7a
A superb sustained route. Easy climbing leads to a change in angle at half-height. A tricky reach/move gains the tufa covered headwall which is pumpy all the way to the finish.

⓬ Bubu mac .... 6b+
Start as for the previous route, but break rightwards up the wall. An early exit from the fixed krab gives a good **5c**.

⓭ Wall Left 6c
Excellent, intricate climbing leads to a depressingly hard fingery finish into a scoop.

⓮ Wall Right 6b
The wall gives increasingly intricate climbing to a final bulging section with a prickly crack.

C'an Nyic

Grade Spread - 1 6 4 2

C'an Nyic is a wall of excellent, vertical rock that stretches up the hillside high above the mountain village of Fornalutx. Although there aren't many routes, they are mostly high quality and the three mid-grade routes make a superb trio that are amongst the best of their grade on the island. The striking mountain scenery also adds to the general appeal.

Approach
From Sóller, follow signs for Pollença and Lluc. At the first proper tunnel (10km from Sóller) park in a lay-by. A faint path leads leftwards (looking in) up the steep slope below the cliff towards the crag.

Conditions
C'an Nyic is a mountain crag, hence it can be windy and cold. It makes a pleasant venue when it is hot, since it only receives the late afternoon sun. There is some slight seepage after heavy rain.

C'an Nyic

1 Bernadí Company .... 6c+
Across the gully on a prow down and left is a tricky pitch up the pillar - sharp rock at times.

2 Nycinyatos 5a
An unspectacular route up the rib.

3 Borinot 6c
The blank groove is awkward. There is a small forgotten project to the right.

4 Ho passam pillo 7a
Hard and thin climbing up the bulging wall.

5 Bona nyic 6b
Superb climbing up the wall and bulges above the flake. It keeps going all the way to the lower-off.

6 Molins de paper ..... 6b+
Equally as good as its neighbours. Pumpy, not too technical and with some reachy moves.

7 Tutup 6c
A magnificent wall climb that features a perplexing start which requires a bit of lateral thinking.

8 Na faresta .... 7b+
A superb route. The start is sometimes wet and the holds are often dirty.

9 S'Horabaixa 7c

The path leading up the slope to the main crag passes under a lot of just about climbable rock. Hardly any of this has been developed but there are four listed hard routes. There is little evidence that any of these have seen ascents in recent years.

10 Agent Orange ... 8a+
Past a stone wall is a faint, left-facing groove. This gives a hard and sustained pitch.

11 Impossible .... ?
An impossible looking line of tiny holds and chipped pockets.

12 Thin Seam 7c
The thin seam above the stone wall.

13 Max Cady 7c
Climb the orange streak just uphill from a cable lying on the ground.

Gorg Blau

| Grade Spread | 1 | 4 | 17 | 27 | 18 |

Set high up in the mountains on the long and winding Ma-10 north coast road, Gorg Blau is best considered as a warm weather venue to escape from the heat. The gorge itself is a narrowing valley lined with black and red-streaked limestone cliffs on each side. Most of the routes consist of long, vertical or slightly overhanging pitches, sometimes following tufas and almost always on high quality rock. There are a few easier routes, but in reality Gorg Blau is only of any real interest to those operating at 6b and above.

Dam wall

Sector des Cable p.196

Sector Plaques p.194

Sector Es Torrente p.197

Access

As of March 2023, there is a prominent 'Climbing forbidden' sign at the bottom of the crag, from the Ayuntamiento de Palma. Local climbers have confirmed that this is not robustly enforced, and some do still climb here, but the prohibition prevents re-equipping and there are now many lines with badly rusted bolts. On some lines with good bolts, you may still find rusty bolts at the anchor - beware.

Gorg Blau 193

Approach

The gorge is situated at the top of the approach road to Sa Calobra on the Ma-10, to the north of the mountains. This can be reached from either Sóller or Pollença depending on where you are staying. Once on the road, continue until you reach a turning for Sa Calobra, by a large, arched viaduct - about 20km from Sóller and 30km from Pollença. Turn onto the Sa Calobra road and immediately park on the left in a lay-by, opposite the cafe/shop - do not park by the cafe/shop. On the opposite side of the road is a bridge and a fenced off entrance. Drop down to the left of the fence and then scramble up again to the track on the other side of the fence. The track leads to the gorge in a couple of minutes from where the crags are easily viewed.

Conditions

Gorg Blau seeps badly and is a very chilly spot in the cooler months. If there is little seepage on the mountain crags and no wind, then it could be worth a look, but remember to pack your duvet. If it is raining, it will offer some dry climbing if the seepage hasn't set in. When it is hot, the gorge will offer cool climbing with shade always available on one side or the other, although in the height of summer it is probably too hot, even here.

Gorg Blau — Sector Plaques

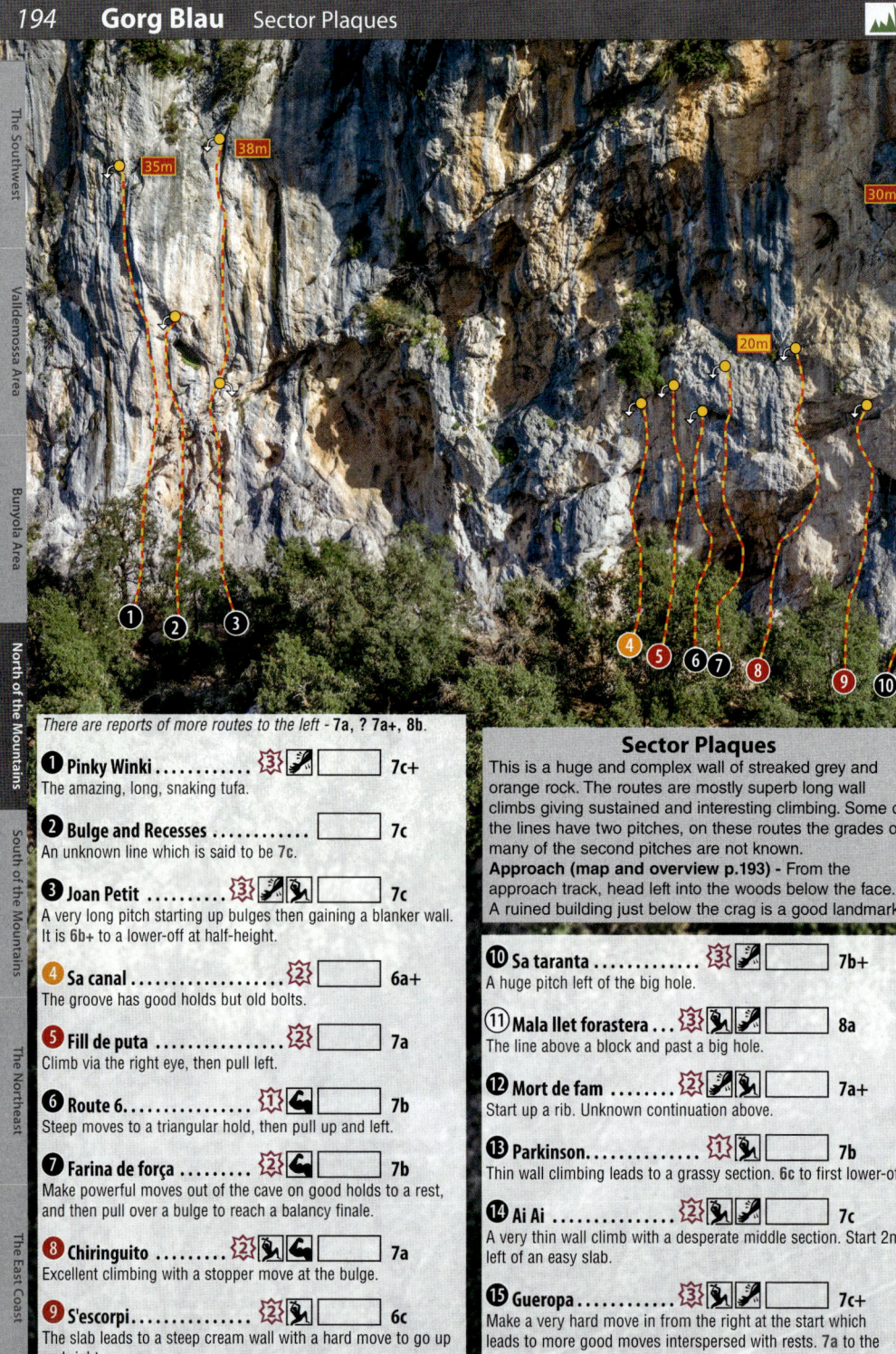

There are reports of more routes to the left - **7a, ? 7a+, 8b**.

① Pinky Winki .... **7c+**
The amazing, long, snaking tufa.

② Bulge and Recesses **7c**
An unknown line which is said to be **7c**.

③ Joan Petit **7c**
A very long pitch starting up bulges then gaining a blanker wall. It is **6b+** to a lower-off at half-height.

④ Sa canal .... **6a+**
The groove has good holds but old bolts.

⑤ Fill de puta **7a**
Climb via the right eye, then pull left.

⑥ Route 6 .... **7b**
Steep moves to a triangular hold, then pull up and left.

⑦ Farina de força **7b**
Make powerful moves out of the cave on good holds to a rest, and then pull over a bulge to reach a balancy finale.

⑧ Chiringuito **7a**
Excellent climbing with a stopper move at the bulge.

⑨ S'escorpi **6c**
The slab leads to a steep cream wall with a hard move to go up and right.

Sector Plaques
This is a huge and complex wall of streaked grey and orange rock. The routes are mostly superb long wall climbs giving sustained and interesting climbing. Some of the lines have two pitches, on these routes the grades of many of the second pitches are not known.
Approach (map and overview p.193) - From the approach track, head left into the woods below the face. A ruined building just below the crag is a good landmark.

⑩ Sa taranta .... **7b+**
A huge pitch left of the big hole.

⑪ Mala llet forastera **8a**
The line above a block and past a big hole.

⑫ Mort de fam .... **7a+**
Start up a rib. Unknown continuation above.

⑬ Parkinson **7b**
Thin wall climbing leads to a grassy section. **6c** to first lower-off.

⑭ Ai Ai **7c**
A very thin wall climb with a desperate middle section. Start 2m left of an easy slab.

⑮ Gueropa .... **7c+**
Make a very hard move in from the right at the start which leads to more good moves interspersed with rests. **7a** to the mid-height lower-off.

Sector Plaques — Gorg Blau

16 Short Slab 4a
One bolt to a lower-off. Don't come here for this one.

17 Airbus .... 7a+
A thin wall leads to a bulge.

18 Ximo 7a
Climb direct to the left-hand side of a high overhang. 6b to the first lower-off.

19 Xama .... 7a+
Easy rock leads to a wall below a large, square roof. It is 6b to the first lower-off. Old bolts.

20 Springfield .... 7c+
A long pitch right of a tufa. 6c to the first lower-off.

21 Marge Simpson 7a
A featureless wall behind the ruin. Unknown second pitch.

22 Bart Simpson .... 8a+
The blank wall behind the ruin. Said to be 6b+ to the first lower-off but that looks doubtful.

23 New 7a 7a

24 Lisa Simpson .... 6b+
Direct up the wall to the left of an open groove. Brilliant!

25 Easy Open Groove .... 6b+
The open groove is 6a+ to the first lower-off.

26 Zampabollos Left .... 6b+
Share a bolt with *Easy Open Groove*.

27 Zampabollos 7a

Gorg Blau — Sector des Cable

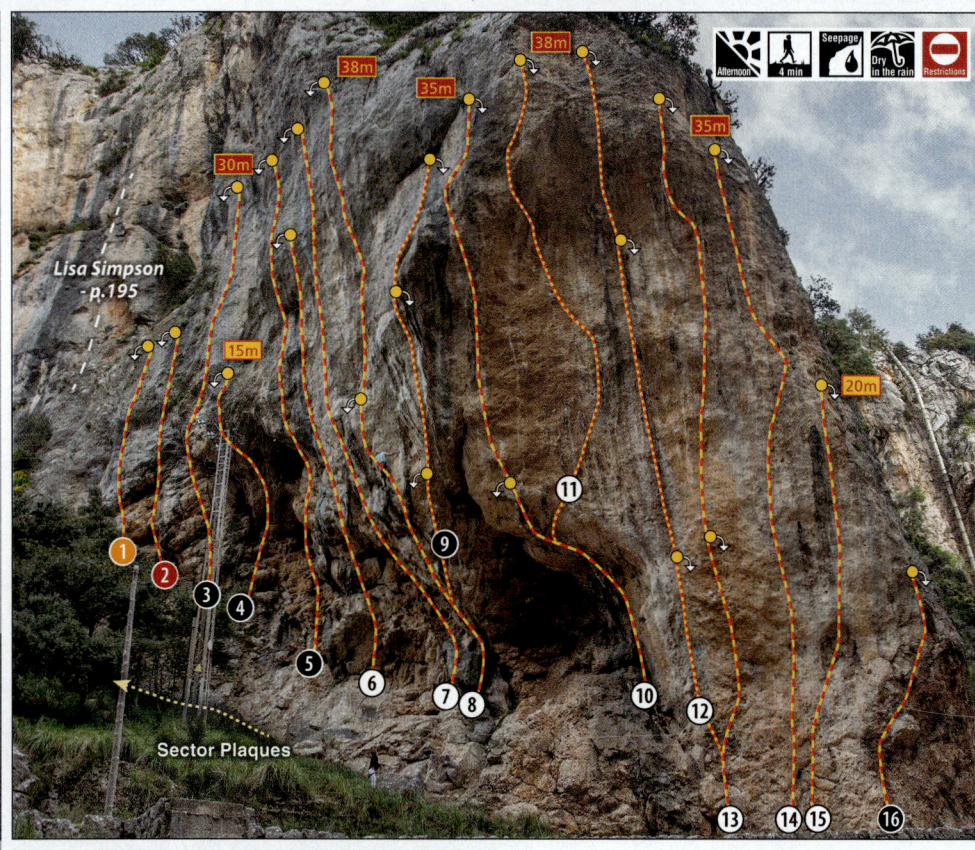

Sector des Cable

A neck-craning piece of rock with some cables that run low across the face and it can be noisy when the dam's turbines are running. Currently there is a sign saying climbing is forbidden.

① **Cuevana** 6a

② **Cuevana Right** .... 6c+
Left of the cave. A hard crux!

③ **Cantos picados** .... 7a+
Juggy overhang climbing leads to a tough tall wall of crimps.

④ **Grado residual** 7c
Steep climbing out of the cave.

⑤ **Reunió de granots** .... 7c+

⑥ **Sportacus** .... 8a+

⑦ **Foracorda Junior** .... 8a+

⑧ **Chill Out** .... 8a+
A long single pitch. To the mid-height lower-off is a good 7a.

⑨ **Gorg Blau** .... 7c+
The pitches are 7a, 7b+, and 7c+.

⑩ **La misión** .... 8b+
A steep first section (7c).

⑪ **Totes.com** .... 8b+
Start up *La misión* but head off up the long wall in a huge pitch.

⑫ **Sa fosca** 8c
The super central tufa line. To the three different lower-offs the grades are - 7a, 7c+, 8c.

⑬ **No Badis** 8b
The red wall to the first lower-off is a good 7a.

⑭ **Long Beach** .... 8a+
A massive single pitch.

⑮ **Petita Aixa** 8a

⑯ **Los tres mosqueteros** .... 7b+
A short pitch crossing the cable.

Sector Es Torrente — Gorg Blau

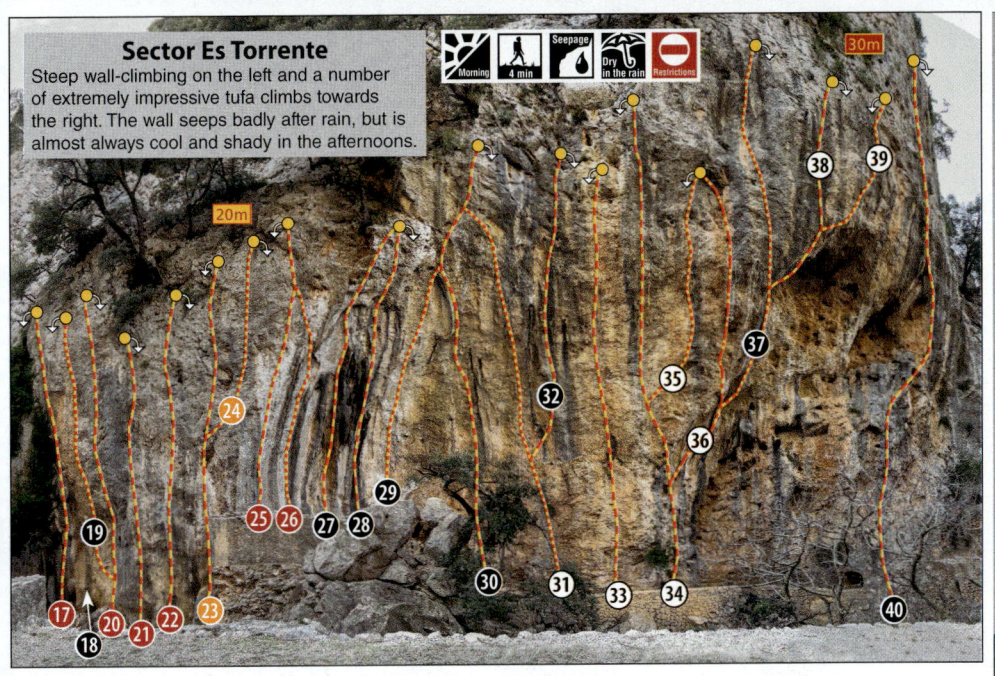

Sector Es Torrente
Steep wall-climbing on the left and a number of extremely impressive tufa climbs towards the right. The wall seeps badly after rain, but is almost always cool and shady in the afternoons.

17 Aixo es L'Habana — 6b+
A good pitch up the tufa and flake-crack.

18 Aixo Right — 7b+
Possible new line.

19 Estreny els dits — 7b
The blank wall is technical with a high crux.

20 Lola's — 6c+

21 Not Lola's — 6b+
Good fingery wall climbing to a lower-off below a tree.

22 Only for Women — 6b+
The tufa and wall above.

23 Luisa en la repisa — 5b
Climb up the metal rungs and the wall above.

24 Luisa me avisa — 6a

25 The arete — 7a
The arete. Borrows bits from the next line *Sa primera*.

26 Sa primera — 6c+
The tufas just right of the arete.

27 Muscleman — 7a+
The tufas from the ledge. May be **7b**.

28 La noche me confunde — 7b+

29 Lo más — 7c+
Work up right to join the next route.

30 Ni quibo ni bloco — 7c+
This is the first line from the lower ledge.

31 Na taca — 8a
The second line of bolts on this section.

32 Sa festa — 7c
The superb central line.

33 Natiu — 8a+
A very blank wall.

34 S'Entreforc — 8b+
Desperate climbing up the steepening blank bulge.

35 Entrepa — ?

36 Mr. Magu — 8a+
A series of bulges left of a tufa line.

37 Karakorum — 7c
This stunning climb follows the right-leading tufas.

38 Big Boy — 8a+

39 Sóliva — 8b
The rightward finish to *Karakorum* is very steep.

40 Far Right 7b — 7b

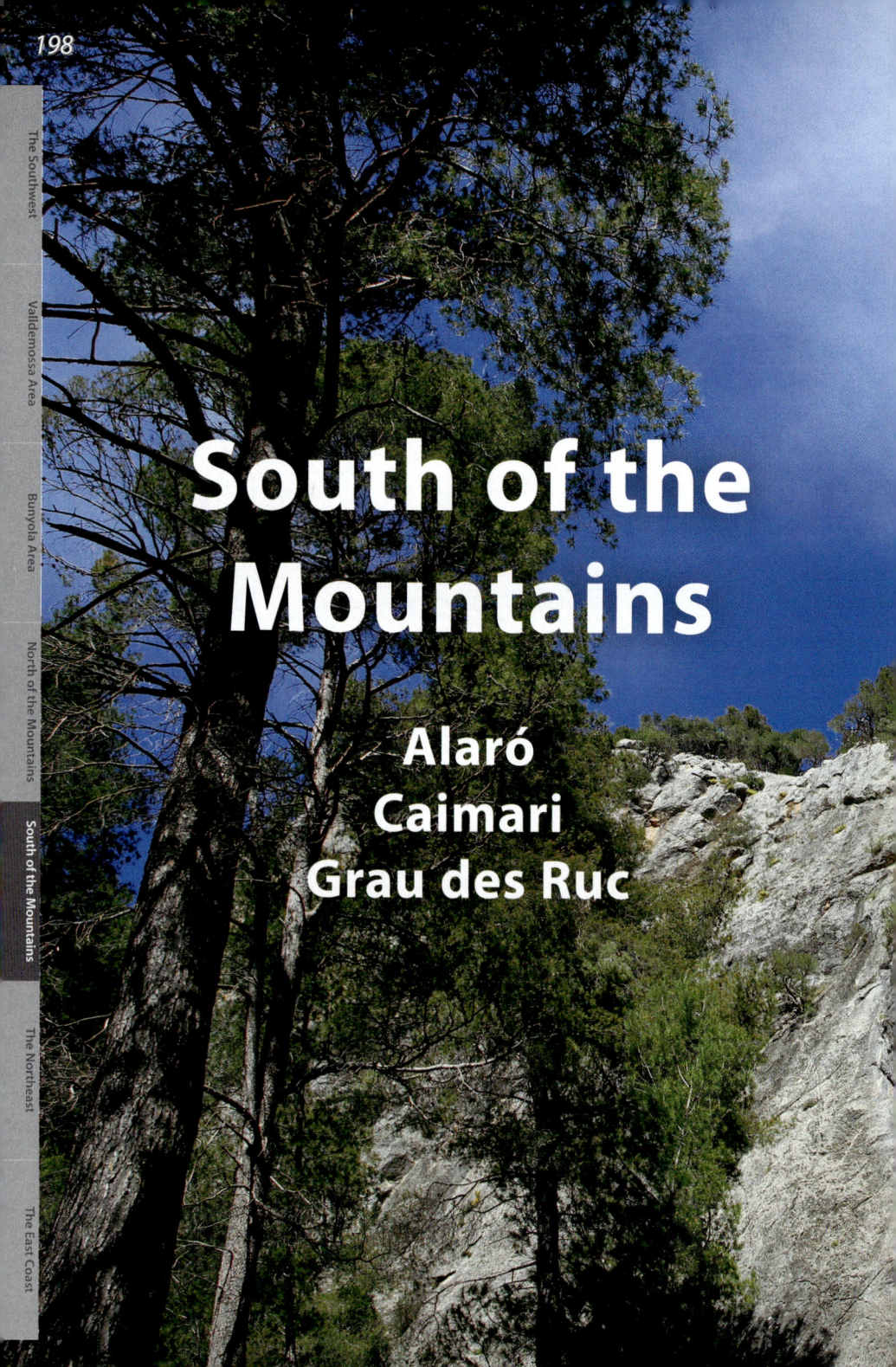

South of the Mountains

Alaró
Caimari
Grau des Ruc

When travelling along the main road between Palma and Pollença the massive bulk of Alaró sits proud of the main mountain range and is home to one of the most famous pitches in Europe - *Buf* (7a) - *p.207* - at its Sector Chorreras. Caimari lies at the foot of a long valley that winds up into the mountains. It is a magnificent destination that is a collection of crags, some very hard, and others with a plethora of lower and mid-grade routes. Grau des Ruc is located further up the Caimari valley and is very much a crag for the climber operating in the higher grades.
Here Mark Glaister is finishing *Relaja la Raja L1* (6b) - *p.220* - at Comuna de Caimari, Caimari. Photo: Mike Hutton

Alaró

Grade Spread | 3 | 16 | 20 | 31 | 6

The elongated hulk of Alaró dominates the view towards the mountains when travelling along the main road that crosses the interior of Mallorca. The small number of existing climbable routes are mostly brilliant and on wonderful rock formations. Sector Chorreras offers 30m pitches up immaculate tufa systems ranging from the pencil-thin to tree-trunk-like. Just to the right, some incredible looking higher grade lines that take the wall above the older slab routes have been established. The other two sectors are not quite as spectacular, but still have some major routes. These include some easier ones on Paret de sa Porta, and some multi-pitch routes on Sector del Medio. The restaurant Es Verger is a fantastic spot for a beer or to sample its famous lamb dish.

Conditions

The Castillo d'Alaró is high and exposed, hence it can be windy and cold. Most of the crags receive the sun at around midday although Sector del Medio stays in the shade for longer. It is worth remembering that tufas are formed by drainage streaks, which means that the face is usually wet after rain. The bolts on Paret de sa Porta are showing their age although some of the lines have been re-equipped in recent times.

Alaró

Approach
Drive into Alaró and pick up signs for 'Castillo d'Alaró'. It is possible to avoid the complex centre if you turn right on entering the town, but if you miss this, there are other options. Once on the road up the hill it soon turns into a twisting dirt track. Eventually the track arrives at the restaurant Es Verger. Park here, or, if this is full, at some pull-ins further down the road. For the detailed approaches see the individual sector descriptions. It is also possible to drive on further up the track and park at the top, although this isn't advised as the gate by the restaurant is sometimes shut in the evenings and the track is very rough.

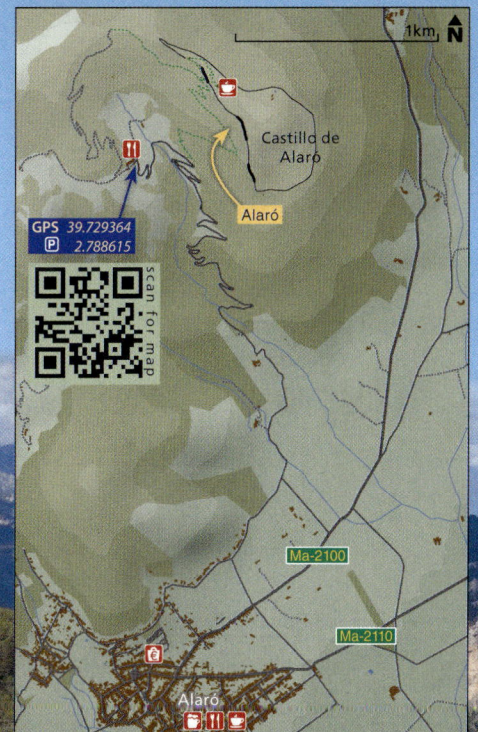

GPS 39.729364
2.788615

Cafe/Hostel

Mouth-shaped feature easily seen from the car park

Sector del Medio p.204

Hop over wall here for Sector Chorreras

Sector Chorreras p.206

One-way section

Access
There have been problems with access in the past, particularly on the Paret de sa Porta crags directly below the castle. The best advice is to use only the described approaches and to leave if asked to. No problems have been reported in recent times and there is even a copy of the Rockfax guidebook pages in the cafe/hostel. There is a bird restriction in place at Sector Chorreras - no climbing 1st March to 30th June.

Alaró — Paret de sa Porta

Paret de sa Porta

The wall at the left-hand end of the main face is small compared to those further right, but it still manages to give some superb long pitches. The crag busy symbol is for walkers not climbers. Many of the harder lines have old bolts.

Approach (map and overview p.201) - From the restaurant, walk (or drive) up the rough road to a higher car park. A short walk reaches the Paret de sa Porta.

❶ **Glue-ins** .... 7b+
Short and steep past two pockets. Glue-in bolts.

❷ **A** 7b
The steep pocketed wall behind the bushes. Hard to onsight but the difficulties are only short.

❸ **B** 7a
Superb climbing up the tufa with a long reach at the crux.

❹ **C** 6c
There is a drilled mono on the crux but it is possible to do it without just to the right at **6b**. Old and missing bolts.

❺ **D** 6a
Steep, juggy climbing but the hard bits are escapable. If the direct line is followed the route goes up to **6b**.

❻ **Still a Project?** 7b
The left-hand of two bolt-lines.

❼ **Esteban** .... 7b+
The wall is superb and has a puzzling crux sequence.

❽ **¿Amigos para siempre?** .... 7c+
Wonderful, technical and sustained!

❾ **Foam Party** 7c
A hard and brilliant line to the left of the tall orange cave.

❿ **¡Muérete ya!** 7c
The right-hand side of the cave is a very good pitch.

⓫ **Zatropeck** 7c
The line of tufa behind a curious plinth at the base of the crag.

⓬ **Old Bolts** 7b
A line of old bolts.

⓭ **Aferra el tul** 6c
Something a bit easier - at least as far as the last bulge, then it has a bit of a sting in the tail although it is only one move.

⓮ **Mata guiris** .... 7a+
A superb and testing route which has a hard crux followed by a long arete on cheese-grater rock. It is a pleasant **5c** to the twin ring lower-off.

Path to the cafe

Paret de sa Porta **Alaró** 203

15 No res .... 7a+
Similar climbing but slightly easier than *Mata guiris* and also **5c** to the half-height lower-off.

16 Sobrassada 6a
A nice route up the short wall to a lower-off on a ledge.

17 Frit 5a
Good climbing and low in the grade.

18 Bulge By-pass .... 6a+
A fine, long pitch with a hard finish over a bulge that can be bypassed on the right at **6a**.

19 Snowboard 5c
Climb the slab directly above the path.

20 Fido-dido 6a
Just to the right of *Snowboard*, climb over a bulge.

The next routes are further right, above a bend in the path. Sometimes the first bolts disappear on these routes.

21 Vagon roll 4c
The left-hand side of the slab. Poor lower-off.

22 Las mallas de cristo 5a
The line right of *Vagon roll*. Start up a flake behind the tree.

23 Tiddler 5c
A shorter line up the white streak.

24 Hola qué tal 6a
An old two-pitch route marked by a line of tin hangers on very old bolts.

25 Far right line 6a
The line furthest to the right has only five bolts in its entire length but has a good finish. Take care on the lower section.

Alaró — Sector del Medio

Sector del Medio

This excellent area is situated to the right of the huge 'mouth' in the middle of the west face. It gets the sun later in the afternoon than the other two main areas.

Approach (map and overview p.201) - From the restaurant, walk back down the road and pick up a signed path on the left that leads up the slope towards the crag and eventually joins up with a diagonal path next to a wall. At a hairpin bend head up and slightly leftwards under the huge wall. The routes are about 75m up through the trees.

1 Pitopausico 6c
A two-pitch line that starts 50m left of the first line shown on the topo. The first bolt is located at the top of an easy-angled rib at 10m. 1) 6c, 2) ?.

2 Triquinosis 6c
Start at a slab left of a small bush close to the start of *Idiot Ballroom*. 1) 6c, 2) 6c.

3 Idiot Ballroom .... 7b+
Start below a short diagonal crack. A very appealing but tough looking line. 1) 6c+, 2) 7b+.

4 Blobs 'n' Bushes .... 7b+
Start below two shallow blobs and a bush at 6m.
1) 7a, 2) 7b+.

5 Sa curta 5c
A line that climbs to the left corner of 'the mouth'. Start at a tree on a ledge.

6 Sa figuereta .... 6b+
Climb to the right-hand corner of 'the mouth'. Good technical climbing on sharp holds.

7 Left Line 6a
Fingery wall climbing. Finish rightwards.

8 Right Line .... 6b+
A very technical and sustained line that does ease off a bit near the finish.

9 Wall 'n' Crack .... 6b+
Climb the steep crack and wall to the first belay of *S'acabat*.

10 S'acabat .... 6c+
A brilliant three-pitch route which reaches the top of the wall.
1) 6c. Pull out of the cave and climb to a belay in an orange recess.
2) 6c. Exit right from the recess onto a crozzly wall.
3) 6c+. A wide groove leads to the top.
Descent - Abseil off.

11 Lute 7a
Gain the tufa blob then head right and up the thin wall.

12 Superchorrera access 6a
The access pitch for the next routes has a hollow feel and is bolted for 7b climbers!

Sector del Medio — Alaró

13 Superchorrera — 7b
Struggle up the inner thighs of this elegant route.

14 XTR — 7b+
Start from the right-hand cave and head for the crack.

15 Therapy — 7b
Start from the right-hand cave. Pull right from the tufas onto the thin wall.

16 Magnum — 7a+
A stunning, long route.
1) 7a+. Climb up tufas and the white wall above to a hanging belay in the cave. Technical in its middle section.
2) 6c. The magnificent diagonal crack to a large ledge.
3) 6b. Step back left and head for the short hanging corner high on the wall.
Descent - Abseil off.

Mouth-shaped feature easily seen from the parking

Alaró — Sector Chorreras

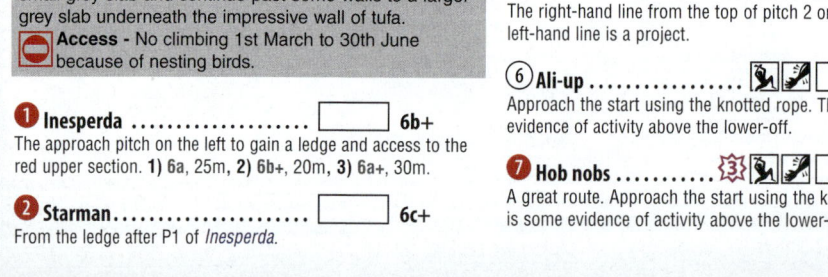

Sector Chorreras

The right-hand side of the west face of Alaró is a massive wall laced with tufas, home to some of the best climbs on the Island. It seeps badly after rainfall.

Approach (map and overview p.201) - From the restaurant, walk back down the road and pick up a good, signed path on the left that leads up the slope towards the crag and eventually meets a diagonal path next to a wall. At a hairpin bend in the path, jump down over the wall and continue rightwards under the face. Pass a small grey slab and continue past some walls to a larger grey slab underneath the impressive wall of tufa.

Access - No climbing 1st March to 30th June because of nesting birds.

❶ Inesperda .... 6b+
The approach pitch on the left to gain a ledge and access to the red upper section. **1)** 6a, 25m, **2)** 6b+, 20m, **3)** 6a+, 30m.

❷ Starman .... 6c+
From the ledge after P1 of *Inesperda*.

❸ Tangerine Dream .... 7a+
Right of *Starman*.

❹ Orion .... 6c+
Good climbing with a reachy move on the first pitch.
1) 6c+. As mentioned above there is a long move on this pitch.
2) 6a+. To a big ledge. Walk leftwards.
3) 6b+. From the left end of the ledge.

❺ Sirius .... 6b+
The right-hand line from the top of pitch 2 on *Orion*. The left-hand line is a project.

❻ Ali-up 8a
Approach the start using the knotted rope. There is some evidence of activity above the lower-off.

❼ Hob nobs 7a
A great route. Approach the start using the knotted rope. There is some evidence of activity above the lower-off.

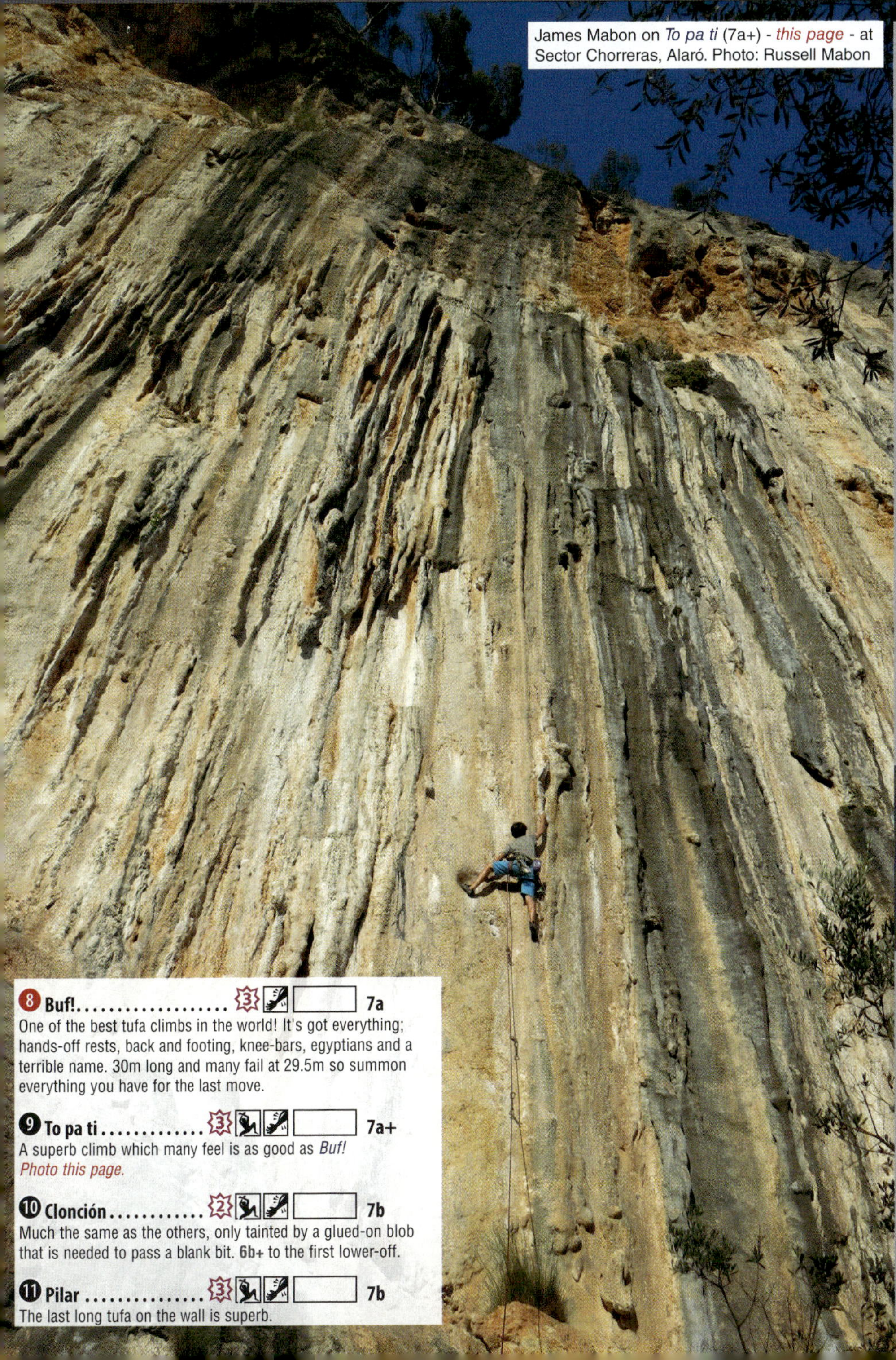

Alaró 207

James Mabon on *To pa ti* (7a+) - *this page* - at Sector Chorreras, Alaró. Photo: Russell Mabon

8 Buf! 7a
One of the best tufa climbs in the world! It's got everything; hands-off rests, back and footing, knee-bars, egyptians and a terrible name. 30m long and many fail at 29.5m so summon everything you have for the last move.

9 To pa ti .... 7a+
A superb climb which many feel is as good as *Buf!* Photo this page.

10 Cloncion 7b
Much the same as the others, only tainted by a glued-on blob that is needed to pass a blank bit. **6b+** to the first lower-off.

11 Pilar 7b
The last long tufa on the wall is superb.

Sector Chorreras **Alaró**

The next routes are on a slabby apron 60m down to the right.

12 Dig for Gold .... 6c+
Start left of the large tree. 1) 6b, 30m, 2) 6c+, 25m.

13 Oh My God .... 7b+

14 Lone Ranger 7b
Start up *Oh My God*, break right then back to a shared belay.
1) 6c+, 40m, 2) 7b, 15m.

15 Slab 1 .... 6c
The fingery slab left of the bulge.

16 Lluvia dorado .... 6b+
Climb the bulge directly.

17 Miko Moko 6c
The right-hand side of the bulge past a small loose flake. It is possible to escape rightwards at 6a+.

18 Ramon me ha hecho el avion .... 6a+
The slab to the right past the same loose flake.

19 Pincha uvas 5c
The crack is delightful. Move right near the top to finish.

20 Kiko .... 6a+
An excellent, sustained and enjoyable high-angled slab climb.

21 Grey Slab Left 4c
The left-hand line.

22 Grey Slab Right 4c
The right-hand line.

Continuing above the lower-offs of the slab routes are some recent much harder lines. All are said to be excellent.

23 Claro de Luna 7c

24 Influjos Solares 7c

25 Buitres Negros 8a

26 Corvus 8b

27 Pinchas uvas Extension .... 7b+

28 Paris Conexión .... ?
This is a project.

29 Flashback Samurai .... 7c+

30 Poker Face .... 7b+
This is the route on this upper wall which gets ascents.

31 Escamas de Dragon 7c

The final two routes listed are a further 100m to the right.

32 Xavier 7b
The left-hand line.

33 Luna 7c
The right-hand line is worth seeking out.

Puig Major (1445m) highest point on Mallorca

It's not always sunny and warm in Mallorca's Mountains! This photo was taken just after the 100 year snowstorm that hit the island in late February 2023. The main casualties were the trees in the mountains that collapsed under the weight of the wet snow. The roads were closed for weeks and paths in the mountains took a year or so to be reinstated. Photo: Mark Glaister

Caimari

Grade Spread | 1 | 34 | 56 | 39 | 21

The area known as Caimari refers to four individual crags scattered along a narrow valley just north of the town of Caimari itself. Sector Cueva is a super-steep cave and bulging wall with a fine set of very hard routes. The other crags are a complete contrast and have many more routes at friendlier grades. Hairpin Wall consists of a tall buttress with some good easier routes and only a minute stroll from the car. The other two cliffs - Muro de Caimari and Comuna de Caimari - are adjacent to each other and composed of excellent rock. Both have routes with plenty of variety, most being fingery walls or long lines of discontinuous tufa. Also the bases are shrouded by trees giving useful shade in warmer weather.

Conditions
The cave is a useful venue when it's too hot or too wet for some of the island's other crags. Hairpin Wall, Muro de Caimari and Comuna de Caimari are more exposed, but are relatively sheltered from strong winds, and get the afternoon sun.

Martin McKenna high up on the tough moves to leave the tufa of *Relaja la Raja* (7a) - *p.220* - at Comuna de Caimari, Caimari. Photo: Mike Hutton

212 Caimari

- Comuna de Caimari p.214
- Hairpin Wall p.222
- Muro de Caimari p.224
- Sector Cueva p.226
- Grau des Ruc p.228

Ma-2130

1km N

GPS 39.776130 / 2.897737
Caimari

GPS 39.772742 / 2.898893

Caimari

Ma-2130

Park here for Sector Cueva

Caimari

The Southwest | Valldemossa Area | Bunyola Area | North of the Mountains | South of the Mountains | The Northeast | The East Coast

Caimari

Approach
The village of Caimari is to the north of Inca, on the Ma-2130, which crosses the mountains to join the Ma-10 north coast road. From Inca follow signs for 'Selva' and then 'Caimari'.

Sector Cueva - Park on the far side of Caimari and continue up the road on foot. After 200m pass a sign for 'Lluc 10km' and a 7km post. Take the second track on the left after this - the crag is on the left after 200m. If the first spot is full, it is also possible to use the parking for Hairpin Wall and walk back down the road. DO NOT try and park under the crag since the track is someone's gated driveway and the crag is on private property - access could easily be banned.

Hairpin Wall - Continue past the turning to Sector Cueva and park on the first hairpin bend. Walk along a track to the crag.

Muro de Caimari - Just around the bend from Hairpin Wall are some small pull-ins on the right and left. If these are occupied park at the Hairpin Wall parking. Walk up the road to the next bend and cross a fence using a stile next to a gate. A small path leads up and left to the crag. Head up to the wall first before going left to avoid the bushes.

Comuna de Caimari - Either park as for Muro de Caimari or continue around the next hairpin bend and park - various small pull-ins. The crag almost reaches the road and a path runs up leftwards below it.

Mark Glaister on *Lucas* (6b) - *p.225* - at Muro de Caimari, Caimari. Photo: Mike Hutton

Caimari
Comuna de Caimari - Sector Adalt

Comuna de Caimari - Sector Adalt
The farthest section of the cliff is less continuous, more open and much quieter than further right. A wide range of grades, route length and styles is on offer and it is worth walking the extra distance up the hill especially if you are in a group of mixed ability.

Approach (map and overview p.212) - Walk up the path below the cliff until an easy-angled short slab. The sectors are spread out on either side of this.

1 Via d'Juli 7a
The tufa line on the far left. A hard start to a rest.

2 Via d'Johny 7a
The orange and grey wall passing two large horizontal pockets.

3 Pijama .... 7b+

4 Higiene cerebral 7a

5 Te mastico pere no te trago ..... 6b+

6 Kalandraka .... 6b+

7 Es padri .... 6b+

8 Agujetas perpetuas ..... 6c+
Climb the grey fingery wall to a ledge.

9 Victorinox .... 6a+
Crimpy and positive with side-pulls and cracks galore.

10 EMI .... 6b+
Climb the pillar on the right of the buttress.

11 EMI Right 5c
The far right of this section of wall.

Comuna de Caimari - Sector Adalt **Caimari**

An isolated slab has a couple of easy routes up cracks.

12 Imserso Left 5c

13 Imserso 5c

14 Rib Left 5c
The rib on the left-hand side of the hollow.

15 Rib Right 6a
Start up *Rib Left* and then branch out right.

16 Scoop Left .... 6b+
The orange scoop/cut-away on the left side of the hollow.

17 Scoop Direct .... 7a+
The line of tiny finger pockets at the back of the hollow.

18 Las uñas de Dori . 7a
The grey and streaked orange line. High in the grade.

19 Ziga zaga 6c
A short steep pitch on the right wall of the scoop.

20 DJ'S Club............... 5c
The long off-vertical rib to the right of the hollow.

21 Pena Negra 6a
Climb the wall just to the right of a tree and orange scar.

22 La Gaditana..... 6b+
Finish direct over the bulge.

Caimari
Comuna de Caimari - Sector Adalt

23 Easy Slab 3c

24 Far Far Left Slab 5a
Sling on a tree to lower off.

25 Far Left Slab 5a

26 Middle of Slab 5b

27 Las Margaritas ...... 6b+
A multi-pitch line with pitches of **5b**, **6b+**, **6b+**. Abseil off.

28 Right Side Slab 5c
The slab right of a bush.

29 Via des vombers 5c
The narrowing slab on the left-hand side of the wall.

30 La Princesa del Pueblo... 6a+
Start up through a gap in small trees and go left.

31 El lute .... 6a+
The bolted line right of *La Princesa del Pueblo*.

32 !Mis Vecinos son Yonquis! 7a+
A groove and slab lead to a bulge and tricky grey wall. Finish up the orange wall above.

33 Yonquis de la Broca .. 6c+
Start by a large flake and head left of the tree at 10m.

34 Day of the Reflection. 6b
Start up *Yonquis de la Broca* and then take the right-hand line

35 Doctor Feel Good 6b
The long wall to a lower-off above the high overhang.

36 Smooth Criminal..... 6b+
A very long pitch (40m) 19 quickdraws required.

Jeremy Wilson on *Las bolas del chino* (7a) - *p.219* - at Sector Es Raconet, Comuna de Caimari, Caimari. Photo: Mark Glaister

The Southwest
Valldemossa Area
Bunyola Area
North of the Mountains
South of the Mountains
The Northeast
The East Coast

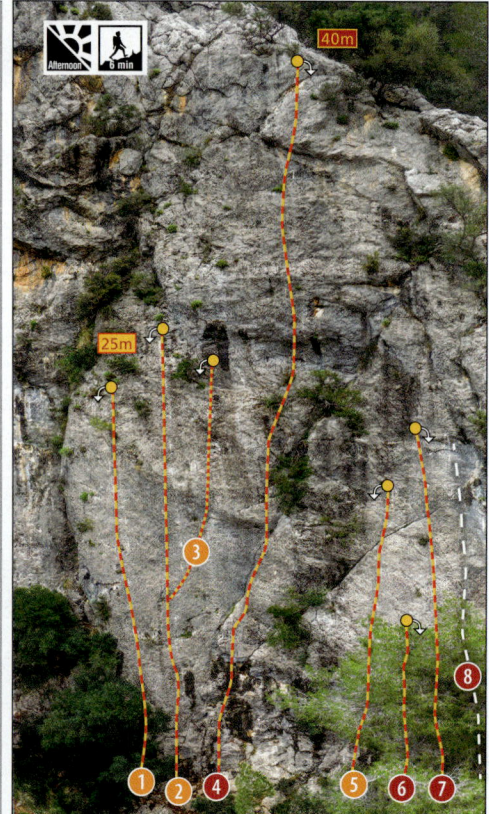

Comuna de Caimari - Sector Es Raconet

The central section of the cliff has some superb routes and offers the best and most popular climbing at Comuna de Caimari. On the left is a vertical water-worn wall that is home to some long and fingery lines that incorporate the odd section of tufa. To the right is a large wall that becomes overhanging in its upper reaches and has a number of spectacular hard pitches. The lower part of the wall has some fine and popular easier pitches.

Approach (map and overview p.212) - The normal approach path arrives under the route *Jarribaras*. The wall continues up and leftwards from here.

1 Xorixapes .... 2 stars **6a+**
The first line passing a flake and a couple of small bushes.

2 Rellquies del passat .... 3 stars **6a+**
The line just to the right of *Xorixapes* has a steep section but is straightforward above and below this. *Photo opposite.*

3 Bolt Whisperer .... 2 stars **6a**
Start up *Rellquies del Passat* and break right.

4 Gran Lubina .... 1 star **6b**
A long pitch that requires a 40m rope and care when lowering.

5 Con el puno por debajo .. 2 stars **6a**
Pleasantly sustained climbing.

6 Enanismo emocional . 1 star **6b**
A shorter route to a pocket and lower-off.

7 Mucky .... 2 stars **6b+**
Long line passing the large pocket on its right.

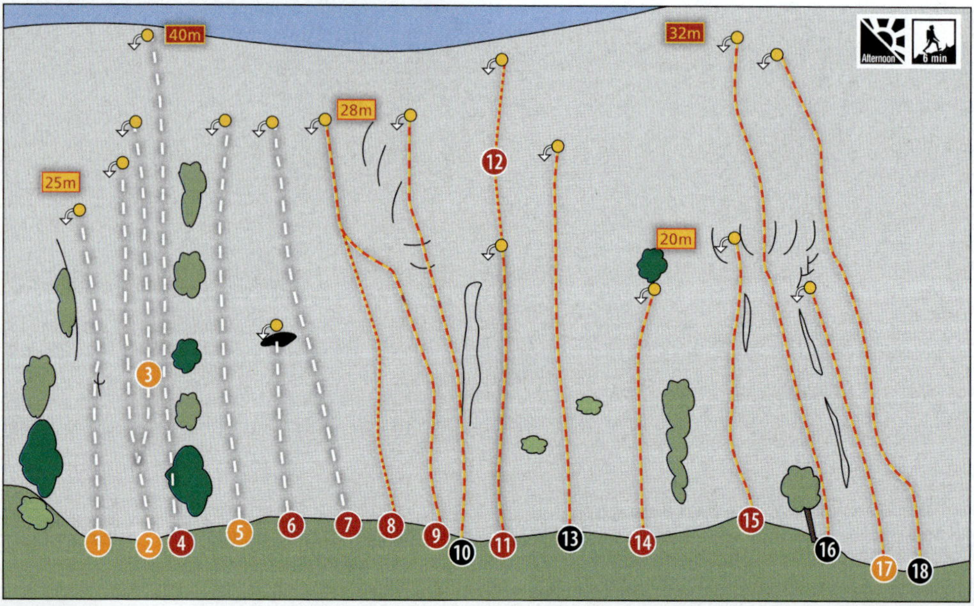

Caimari

8 Cachinochalgo Left... 7a
A big pitch that passes a 'potato-like' feature low down. Fine and fingery climbing.

9 Cachinochalgo....... 6c+
Steep and thin wall climbing just to the left of some bushes. Join and finish up *Cachinochalgo Left*.

10 Jeremy .... 7a+
The crack/flared corner and bulges above.

11 Las bolas del chino L1 ... 6b+
A great line up the wall between tufas.

12 Las bolas del chino... 7a
The full route is superb. *Photo p.217*.

13 Depinyolvermell..... 7b
Can be wet. Follow the grey-streaked wall and tufa.

14 Hippipunklperriklautico
.... 6c+
Steep fingery wall climbing left of some bushes.

15 Via morito 6c
A lovely pitch that follows the slab and tufa left of the *Sweetie the Pooh* tufa.

16 Sweetie the Pooh 7b
A fantastic line up the central tufa and headwall.

17 Corrich .... 6a+
Good pitch with a difficult start and tricky finish.

18 Right of Corrich.............. 7c+
Massive pitch up wall right of *Corrich* and long headwall above.

Charlotte Macdonald enjoying the fine sustained wall climbing encountered on *Rellquies del Passat* (6a+) - *opposite* - at Comuna de Caimari, Caimari.
Photo: Mark Glaister

Caimari
Comuna de Caimari - Sector Es Raconet

19 Relaja la Raja L1 ..... 6b
Climb leftwards up grey rock to a steepening where the difficulties start. *Photo p.198.*

20 Relaja la Raja 7a
The continuation is a magnificent 40m pitch. *Photo p.210.*

21 La matate chorrea 6a
Excellent climbing left of an inverted yellow triangle.

22 Rompesuelos 5c
A good pitch right of the inverted yellow triangle.

23 Pa Torrat 6a
Fine climbing leads to a steep pull to finish over a tufa bulge.

24 Jarribaras L1 .... 6a
Climb between two trees to a steeper section where a quick pull gains the first belay.

25 Jarribaras Left-hand 6c

26 Jarribaras 7b
Continue up the steep headwall. (40m)

27 Canibalismo vaginal L1 .. 6a
A nice slab to a bulge, then harder climbing on some large features. Move left and back right to gain the belay.

28 Canibalismo vaginal .... 7b+
The superb continuation crack has one desperate move.

29 Canibalismo variant .. 8a
Break right out of the lower section of *Canibalismo vaginal*.

30 Los lunaticos .... 8a+
Sustained and technical climbing direct up the steep headwall.

31 On Line 7b
Break right out of *Los lunaticos*.

32 Billie Boy 7b
A big pitch up the right-hand side of the wall. (33m).

33 The Freaky 7b
Climb left of the short, blunt tufa. (36m).

34 Mi darmata .... 6b+
Fine climbing just right of the short blunt tufa. (24m)

Comuna de Caimari - Sector Placa Rotja — **Caimari** — 221

1 Frijolito .... 7a+

2 Black Line .... 7a+
Two pitches. It is 7a+ to the first lower-off and 7a above.

3 Cocolino .... 7a+
Break right out of pitch 2 of *Black Line*. 33m to the ground.

4 Saca las uñas nini .... 7a+
An intense grey wall.

5 La madura me ma pone dura . 7a
The left-hand side of the open scoop.

6 Choni chapa 7a
Break right out of *La madura me ma pone dura* up the centre of an open scoop. Poor rock.

Comuna de Caimari - Sector Placa Rotja

The tallest and most impressive section of Comuna de Caimari is the large red scoops at the right-hand side of the crag. It is not as popular as further left.
Approach (map and overview p.212) - Walk up the approach path and scramble up ledges on the right to reach the base of the red wall.

7 Tecnoverborrea .... 7b+
Tackle the long open scoop. Easy to a desperate finish.

8 Pensamiento infinito 8a
Climb up to the steep hanging arete.

9 Ca'n Furiós 7b
The smooth red wall right of the big scoop. Painful crux move.

10 Parabolt treu banya ..... 6b+
A steepening groove on the right-hand side of the red wall.

11 Milu .... 7b+
The grey rib right of the groove.

12 Trundling .... 7a+
A big pitch up the right-hand side of the wall.

Down by the road are two more long routes on a grey pillar.

13 Demencia clitorania 6c
The left-hand line above the road.

14 Espolon Timy .... 6b+
The right-hand line above the road.

Hairpin Wall

This little crag was one of the first areas to be developed although it has now been surpassed in quality by those further up the hillside. The small set of routes should prove entertaining to mid-grade climbers.

Approach (map and overview p.212) - Drive up the road from the town of Caimari and park at a good parking spot on the left at a bend. The crag is 100m along the track which leads off from this parking area.

1 Curving Groove 5b
The slab left of a curving groove has a tricky move between bolts 2 and 3. The route is bizarrely bolted.

2 Central 5c
The nicely bolted central line is the best of this first trio.

3 Right 5a
The easiest of the three, but still strenuous.

4 Cristo en pel, taronges navel . 7a
An upper pitch, starting from the lower-off of *Right*.

5 The Hard One 7a
Steep and technical climbing. The first bolt is high, but the climbing to reach it is easy.

6 The Blob 6c
The easy slab leads to a steepening. Use the blob to get onto the upper wall.

7 The Blob Right-hand 6b
Start as for the previous route, then climb direct to join the finish of the next route. Not much independent climbing.

8 The Blob Indirect 6a
The less steep line right of the central bulging section.

9 Pocket .... 6a+
Start up blocky rock then continue via a pocket.

10 Pocket Right 6a
Start in the same place but move right after the second bolt to the centre of the slab. Old bolts.

11 Poor .... 6b+
Up the slope to the right of the buttress is a poor route with a high first bolt.

Caimari

Iker Pou on *Master Hit* (8b+) - *p.226* - Sector Cueva, Caimari. Photo: Pou Brothers Collection

Caimari — Muro de Caimari

Muro de Caimari
A smallish crag of compact vertical rock with some tufa formations towards the left-hand end. It is a shady crag for much of the day and has trees close to the base but will provide little shelter in wet weather.

Approach (map and overview p.212) - From the parking, walk up the road and cross over a stile next to a gate at the bend. Head left up the hill on a faint path to beneath the wall.

1 Nosferatu............ 6c
Classy climbing up blobs, walls and overlaps to a steep finish.

2 Paparazzi........... 7a
The right-hand side of the massive tufa trunk has a hard move to leave the tufa. Old bolts low down.

3 Tránsfuga........... 6b+
The wall just right of the tufa trunk. Tough on the skin.

4 Suquet............. 6b
Climb the wall and small pillar just right of a lone, low bolt. There are a number of difficult sections.

Muro de Caimari **Caimari** 225

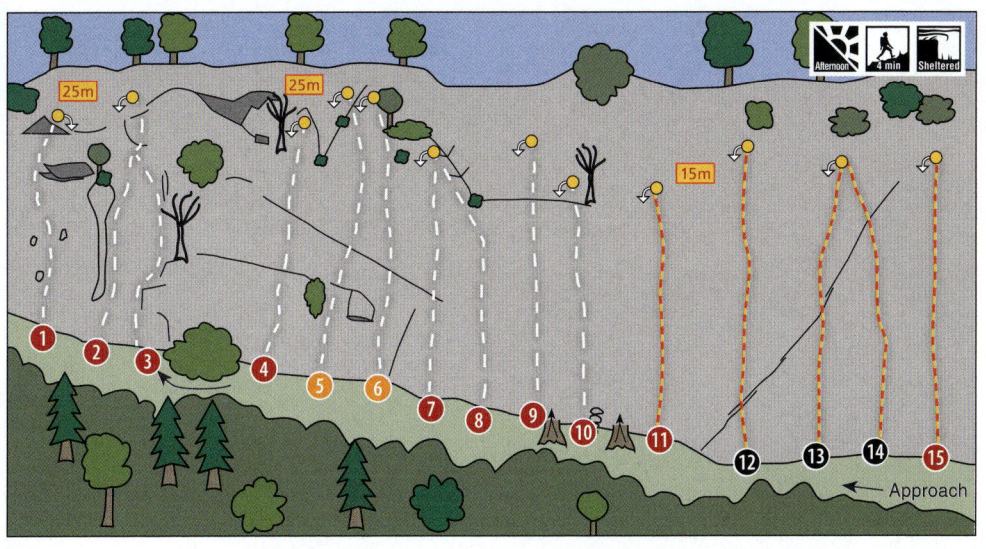

5 A la fresca 6a
A good pitch that wanders up the broken wall just right of a bush on dimpled rock.

6 Mantis 6a
Interesting climbing up the clean wall with a tricky bulge.

7 Lucas 6b
The crozzly wall gives a sustained and technical pitch. *Photo p.213.*

8 Mescalina 6b
The crozzly wall to the same lower-off as *Lucas*.

9 El calvario del enano . 6c
The steep wall behind a tree.

10 Dos bidedos y un destino
.... 6c+
The wall above a small pile of stones.

11 Arrufa es cul 7a
Climb the wall past a low flat tufa feature.

12 Sacrilegio .... 7a+
The blank fingery wall.

13 Capitan gotera ...... 7a+
No really hard moves but very little respite.

14 Doctor maligno ...... 7a+
The wall has some painful holds.

15 Mini yo 6c
Climb up past a depression.

There are two routes above where the path arrives at the crag.

16 El sonido de la gaita.. 6b+
The line just right of a mid-height tree. Can be dry if there is seepage elsewhere.

17 Vive dios............ 6b
Unlikely but good climbing on pockets.

Caimari — Sector Cueva

Sector Cueva

A very impressive cave and bulging wall that has a concentration of excellent routes in the upper grades. The crag is a good place to head for in poor weather.

Approach (map and overview p.212) - Park on the far side of Caimari and continue up the road on foot - DO NOT try and park at the crag. After 200m pass a sign for 'Lluc 10km' and a 7km post. Take the second track on the left after this - the crag is on the left after 200m. It is also possible to use the parking for Hairpin Wall and walk back down the road.

The first five routes are off to the left off the topo.

1 Grade 5 .... 5a

2 Less Purchase 6b
The slabby line on the far left-hand side of the crag.

3 Septaplua .... 7a+

4 Petit poi 6c
Climb the hanging groove. Quite technical.

5 7b+ Route .... 7b+

6 Ball de bot .... 7a+
Hard at the bottom, with an awkward crux.

7 Empire State 8b
As you delve further into the cave things start getting a bit harder. The start is close to *Ball de bot*.

8 Project No More .... 8b+
This project has now been climbed.

9 Peu deret .... 8b+
The left-hand finish to *Commando Madrid*.

10 Commando Madrid 8b
Head for the large hole high up in the cave. Unbelievable!

11 Odissy .... 8c+
Emerge from the back of the cave. To the first lower-off is 8b.

12 American Express 8c
Starts just left of the right-hand side of the cave. To the intermediate lower-off is 7b.

13 Master Hit .... 8b+
The right-hand side of the cave has another ultra-steep pitch. It is 7c+ to the lip lower-off. *Photo p.223.*

14 M & M's 8b
A fine pitch starting down and right of the cave.

15 Colgao 7b
A superb route split by a rest ledge on the right. The upper section involves swinging around on the blobs getting pumped, prior to the final hard moves.

Sector Cueva **Caimari**

⑯ Penjat **7b**
The right-hand line from the rest on *Colgao*.

⑰ Agárrate Ruiz de la Prada .... **7c+**
Up the steep wall and much easier overhanging corner above.

⑱ A vista de pájaro ..... **8a+**
A sustained line just left of the small cave.

⑲ Guiris Left .... **8b+**

⑳ Guiris go Home **8c**
Climb through the small cave onto the blank headwall.

㉑ 8a Route **8a**

㉒ Motorhead **8a**
Just to the right of a small cave. A bouldery start.

㉓ Motorvisión Full .... **?**
A very hard route above the boulder problem *Motorvision*.

㉔ Terrorvision **8a**
Another bouldery start.

㉕ Die Toten Hosen .. **7c**
Climb past some pockets and a tufa to a move right at the top. Easier for the tall. A seepage line so it is sometimes wet.

㉖ Bota Petit **8a**
This one usually requires a dyno. Staple bolts.

㉗ Penthouse .... **7c+**

㉘ Playboy **8a**
A right-hand start to *Penthouse*. *Photo p.5.*

㉙ Hoodoo Gurus .... **7b+**
The big protruding tufa. A popular objective.

㉚ Txapuz Board .... **7c+**
There is a right-hand start up and left into the tufa - 8a.

㉛ Picados **8a**
A right-hand start to *Txapuz Board*. Also called 'Natural Line'.

Bouldering

The right-hand side of the crag gives some excellent all-weather bouldering which mostly consists of the starts of the routes.

㉜ Motorhead Start Left-hand ..... **f7B+**

㉝ Motorhead Start Right-hand .... **f7B+**

㉞ Motorvisión .... **f7B+**
The wall between *Motorhead* and *Terrorvision*.

㉟ Terrorvisión Start **f7C**

㊱ Die Toten Hosen Start .... **f6C+**

㊲ Bota petit Start .... **f6C+**

㊳ Penthouse Start **f7A**
From sitting, pull left into *Penthouse*.

㊴ Pent gurus **f7A**
A sit start to black cave between *Penthouse* and *Hoodoo Gurus*.

Grau des Ruc

| Grade Spread | - | 1 | 9 | 35 | 11 |

This set of crags is situated up the Lluc road from Selva and Caimari. The main attraction is the superb north-facing wall of Grau des Ruc which offers some brilliant steep climbs in the 6c to 8a and above range. It does have an awkward approach but the effort is more than rewarded when you get to the crag. Additionally there are two other less interesting sectors; one roadside wall which looks good but it is only partially developed and suffers from road noise; and one very steep cave with a few hard routes only.

Approach
The crags are reached by following the Ma-2130 from Inca towards Lluc. Drive through Selva and follow the road through Caimari and past the crags. Continue for around 6km to a large cutting on a bend (this is around 200m after the 12km post on the roadside). Park just after the cutting underneath Bella Donna - Aparcamiento.
Es Salt - Walk back towards the cutting and find a steep via ferrata on the left. Go down this and follow a very vague path down and around to the cave.
Grau des Ruc - Walk back down the road through the cutting and turn immediately left after the cutting where there is a small cairn visible. Follow these cairns steeply downwards over sharp rock for 15 mins to a steep down-climb with ropes and metal rungs which leads to the large crag.

Conditions
The crags face north or northeast and give plenty of shade when it is hot. The sun lingers longer on Bella Donna Aparcamiento and Grau des Ruc Dreta. There may be some seepage after rain but this is unlikely to be too bad. Grau des Ruc and Es Salt will give dry climbing in the rain.

Bella Donna Aparcamiento and Es Salt — Grau des Ruc

Bella Donna Aparcamiento
The wall above the road has some good rock but appears to be only partially developed. The road is also much busier than you might expect.

1. Coliflor women 6c
2. Realidad paralela 7b
3. Pasos de rellero ..... 7c+
4. Es salt 7b
5. Baixem una estrella 6b
   Start up a long tufa.
6. Decota decotador 7c
7. Tulipán 7a
8. Quint 6a

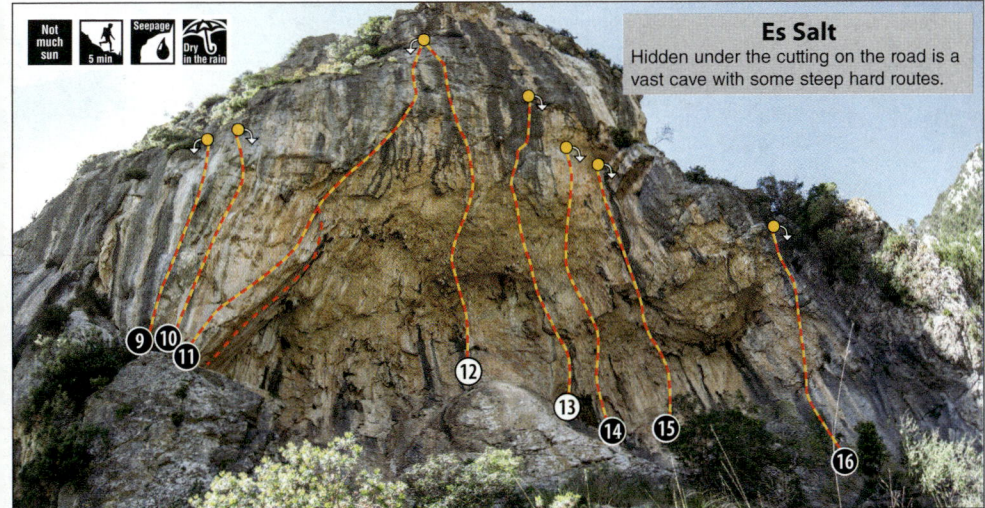

Es Salt
Hidden under the cutting on the road is a vast cave with some steep hard routes.

9. Superferret .... 7a+
10. Kilometre 13 .... 7b+
11. De malas a peor .... 7b+
12. Hotel glamour 8b
13. El fari aparca .... 8a+
14. Papi chulo 7c
15. Santa Bush 7b
16. Poda d'altura .... 7a+

Grau des Ruc — Sector Esquerra

Sector Esquerra

The best wall in this area has some superb routes in the 6c to very hard range. It faces due north, is well sheltered from the wind and stays dry in the rain.

Approach (map and overview p.228) - Walk back down the road through the cutting and turn immediately left after the cutting where there is a small cairn visible. Follow cairns steeply downwards over sharp rock for 15 mins until a steep down-climb with ropes and metal rungs leads to the large crag. Sector Esquerra is the wall to the right (looking out) of the approach.

❶ Porcona 6c
A short route on the left edge of the wall.

❷ El fingidor d'orgasmes 6c
Climb orange rock past some flakes.

❸ Las grupis .... 6c+
Tackle the wall direct past a prominent underlap.

❹ Na curta 7a
A shorter line past a crozzly section to a grey streak.

❺ Aixi es maten .... 7a+
The thin yellow wall past a small bush.

❻ Decision hit .... 7a+
The edge of the cave, then up past V-notch.

❼ Gold Single Traverse 8a
Climb the left edge of the cave to a tufa rail leading all the way to the right side of the cave.

❽ Precisión milimétrica 7c
Climb direct through the left-hand side of the cave.

❾ Vida fácil .... 7c+
The right-hand side of the cave.

❿ Agresió física 7c
Work rightwards out of the cave.

⓫ Tira que ve peix ..... 7b+
Climb left of the grey streak.

⓬ R-line .... 7a+
Straight up past twin drooping tufas.

⓭ Bingo 7c
The long thin wall.

⓮ Siracusa mon amour .... 6c+
Climb straight up past a brown tufa and two overlaps.

⓯ Zaratrusta ...... 7c+
A long line up blobs to a bulging headwall.

⓰ Ariestocrata ...... 8a+
Start up a large blob and continue to the headwall.

Sector Esquerra — Grau des Ruc

⑰ **Qui tub retub....** 8a+
Left of the hanging tufas with a bush to the massive headwall.

⑱ **Ingravito** .... ?
May be 8a or a project.

⑲ **Calladita estás más guapa**
.... 8a
Climb a thin tufa to the big headwall. There are some rests on the pillar but it is still very pumpy.

⑳ **Efecto mariposa .** 8a
Start left of a low bulge then move up onto the steep headwall.

㉑ **El justciero..........** 7c
Two tufas lead onto the upper wall.

㉒ **Moscos fora ....** 7c
A long tufa system to a short headwall.

㉓ **Te matarás..........** 7c
Break right from *Moscos fora*. The direct start is a project.

㉔ **Es grau des ruc ......** 7b+
The right-leaning tufas to a thin wall.

㉕ **Skiasical........** 7c+
Start up a short fat tufa.

㉖ **Coquito ergo sum ....** 8a
Above the step up on the approach. A wall leads to a bulge. May still be a project.

㉗ **Remate final ....** 7b+
Break right from *Coquito ergo sum*.

㉘ **Tramontana.........** 7b
Just left of the approach staples.

Grau des Ruc Sector Dreta

Approach from via ferrata

Sector Dreta
The right-hand wall (looking in) has some excellent rock formations and a few superb tufa climbs. It faces southeast and gets the sun in the morning for a while. It is more likely to seep after rain.

Approach (map and overview p.228) - Walk back down the road through the cutting and turn immediately left after the cutting where there is a small cairn visible. Follow cairns steeply downwards over sharp rock for 15 mins until a steep down-climb with ropes and metal rungs leads to the large crag. This is the wall to the left (looking out) of the approach via ferrata.

❶ **El somriure de la bruixa..** 7a+
A featured wall to a sharp grey wall.

❷ **Capiacua** .... 7a+
The centre of the heavily featured wall.

❸ **Let's deux** .... 7a+
Tufas to a grey wall.

❹ **No country for plafoneros** 7b
Climb the steep bulge to a hanging tufa.

Sector Dreta **Grau des Ruc** 233

5 Tia aina .... 7c+
A long leftwards-leaning line. Start up tufa then head diagonally left towards a beak at the crag top.

6 Project Colateral............... ?
Direct finish to *Tia aina*.

7 Sobrasada power 8a
A short tufa past a thin wall to a blob.

8 A golpe de gas.......... 7c
The red wall left of the long tufa.

9 Perdiuota............... 7a
A brilliant long tufa line.

10 Escalfament 7b
A steady line of tufas leading to a hard grey bulge.

11 Rallito 7b
Climb up tufas onto a grey wall.

12 Tongo mongui.......... 7a+
Break out right from *Rallito*.

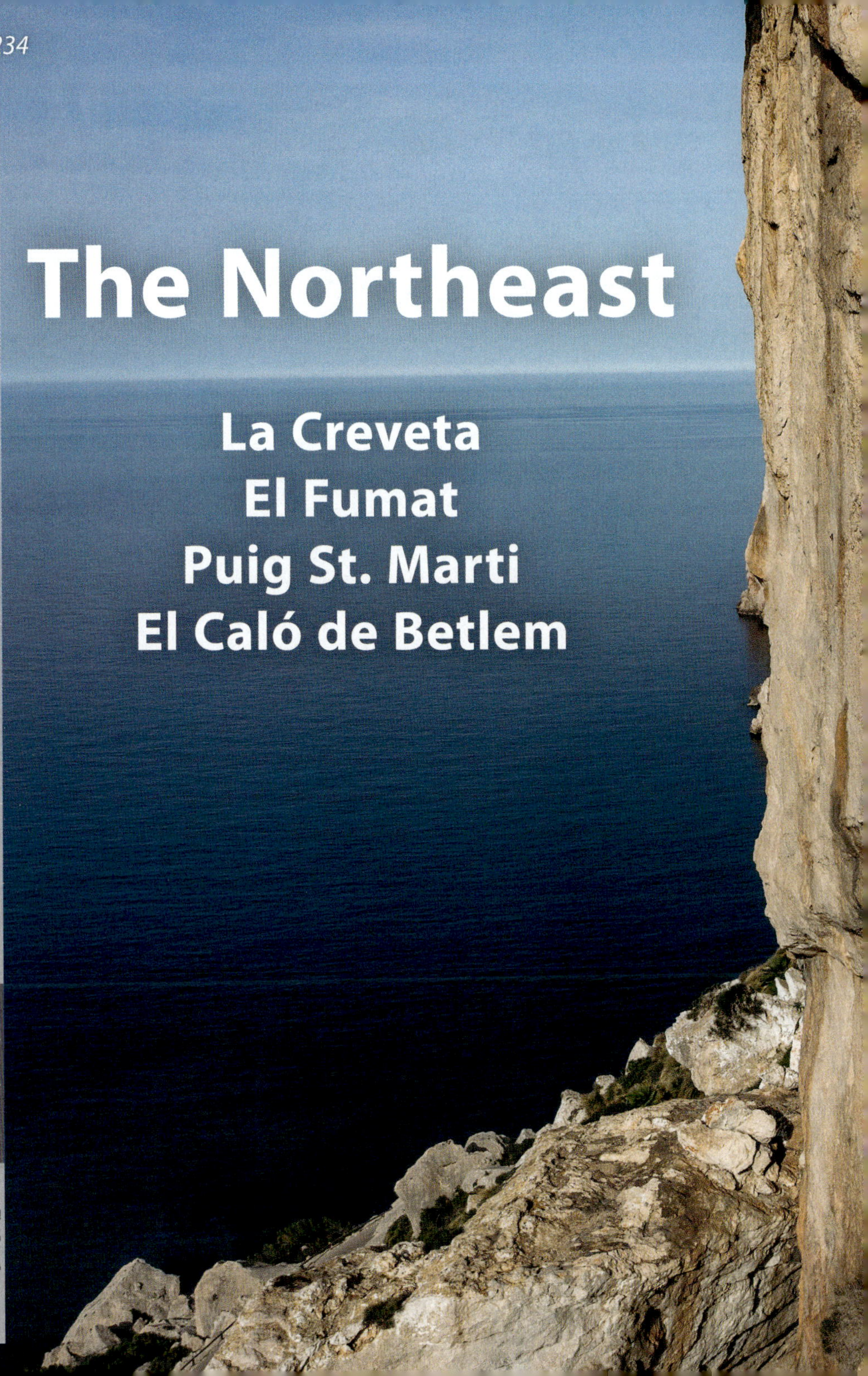

The Northeast

La Creveta
El Fumat
Puig St. Marti
El Caló de Betlem

The spurs of land that form the perimeters of Pollença and Alcúdia bay are incredibly scenic and provide the backdrop to four compact crags which will be of most interest to climbers looking for lower-to-mid grade routes in gorgeous surroundings. In the photo John McKenna is making his way up the steep bit of *Mercury* (6b+) - *p.245* - at El Fumat. Photo: Mike Hutton

La Creveta

| Grade Spread | 2 | 13 | 13 | - | - |

La Creveta is one of the older crags on the island and historically was extremely popular offering a great range of slab and wall climbs in the lower and mid grades. It is still worth a visit for the great set of easier slab routes on the left of the main wall and the brilliant *Records de Bunyola* which is one of the best 6bs on the island. These have all been rebolted with modern bolts and good lower-offs. The rest of the routes on the main wall have old bolts at the time of writing. They still see occasional ascents but most climbers are likely to be put off by the rusty hangers. Hopefully these may be rebolted sometime. Two other sectors - North Wall and Gringo North - are now banned for climbers due to environmental issues and this might also cause problems for re-bolting on the main wall.

Approach
Leave Port de Pollença towards Cap Formentor. The road winds uphill for 5km, eventually arriving at a viewing area with plentiful parking - 'Mirador es Colomer'. Walk back from the parking area, down a vague track next to an old pipeline. After 200m at an old post and large cairn, break out rightwards up the hillside along a cairned path towards the second of two cols in the ridge. Cross the col and scramble down leftwards under the cliff face to eventually arrive at the Main Wall.

Access
No climbing on the two buttresses passed on the approach and be careful on the Main Wall routes with rusty bolts.

La Creveta

Alan James starting out on the brilliant face climbing encountered on *Récords de Bunyola* (6b) - *p.239* - at Creveta. Photo: Mark Glaister

Conditions
The buttresses are located high above a valley to the north of Port de Pollença. This exposed position means that it can suffer from high winds and offers little shelter from any bad weather. The crag faces west and receives all the afternoon sun going.

La Creveta — Main Wall

Main Wall

The left-hand side of the Main Wall has some excellent long slabs that have tricky starts.

Approach (map and overview p.236) - From the approach walls continue below the crag-line before dropping down slightly to the base of the Main Wall.

1 The Boulder Route 5c
A technical start that is harder for the short.

The next routes are on the main face, starting almost in the gully behind the semi-detached flake.

2 Nordkap 6a
Start up *Lord of the Rings* and step left to gain the upper section which is a bit run out. The direct start is a desperate **6b+**.

3 Lord of the Rings 4c
A thin start with a high first bolt. Superb climbing above.

4 Coordina coordinator 5a
A delightful and long route. A hard lower section leads to a fine finish. Take plenty of quickdraws.

5 Curset 5a
A lovely route, with consistently straightforward climbing but slightly spaced bolts by modern standards.

6 Baba 5a
The prominent flake-line/groove.

Right of the groove is a short, triangular slab.

7 Camisasque 5c
The left-hand side of the slab is hard at the bottom. There is some loose rock just before the lower-off. *Photo p.31.*

8 Krilin 6b
Climb the tiny slab past a hard move to a lower-off. It is also possible to continue and join up with *Hyperion*.

9 Hyperion 6a
The right-hand side of the slab and the wall above (not the bolts on the right). There is a reachy move to gain the second bolt. Take care with the rock at the top.

10 Hyperion derecho .... 6a+
Climb the line to the right of the upper section of *Hyperion*. The traverse right is the awkward bit.

The next two routes start from a ledge behind the prickly bushes. This is best reached from the right. The gap in the middle of the bushes is only used when you lower off.

11 Els corderos atacan de nuevo
.... 6b+
The wall with a niche has a stopper section with a worrying ledge not too far below. Old bolts.

12 Jerita 6c
The steep and blank wall. Old bolts.

Main Wall **La Creveta** *239*

The next route starts just right of some large bushes.

13 Hussein 6c
Fingery wall climbing with a distinct crux move. Old bolts.

14 Terapia de grupo 6c
Direct up the wall on tiny, razor-sharp holds. Old bolts.

15 Ca magre, puces .... 6a+
Up the open black scoop roughly in the centre of the wall.

16 Ja me pagaràs 6c
Fingery climbing up the right-hand side of the scoop. Old bolts.

17 Lastrolophithicus .... 6c+
Tricky climbing up the slightly bulging wall. Old bolts.

At the right-hand end of the wall is a tall grey slab with a cave.

18 150 Sipis 6b
Sustained climbing up the wall just right of the large flake, gaining a flake/crack near the top. Old bolts.

19 Rècords de Bunyola 6b
The classic of the crag. Climb the blank wall right of the large flake with some tough moves at the overlap. *Photo p.237*.

20 El Sant Crist .... 6a+
Climb to the cave and pull out rightwards across the lip, then back left. Old bolts.

21 Som-hi 6a
A devious climb which avoids the first bulge by a sly traverse left and then back right. Old bolts.

22 Ball o'en banyeta verda.. 6b
More thin wall-climbing. Move left at the top to tackle the bulge. Ignore the rusty lower-off to the right. Old bolts.

23 Somni bucolic 6b
The last route on this part of the wall is particularly tricky for the short. Leaving the ledge is the crux. Old bolts.

The far right-hand end has some routes above a jumble of blocky ledges. Scramble across to the starts.

24 Glückspilz 4c
A hard start and slightly spaced old bolts.

25 Black Streak .... 6a+
Good climbing up the crozzly black streak. Old bolts.

26 Leuchtturm .... 6b+
A fingery route left of the ragged crack.

27 Just Married .... 6b+
Reachy climbing up and right of the crack. Old bolts.

28 Angsthase 5c
The crozzly wall up and left of a big flake. Missing bolts.

Photo: Mike Hutton

El Fumat

El Fumat is a huge northwest-facing mountain crag, perched high above the road on the Formentor peninsula. The crag has a small set of single-pitch routes on its lower walls, which are positively dwarfed by the bulk of the mountain itself. This place has incredible potential, although only a small selection of routes have been developed and some of these have old bolts at the time of writing.
Sector Duke is the main attraction with a handful of quality pitches including four brilliant grade 6s which have good bolts. Sector Free Tibet is characterised by a long mid-height roof with some tough pitches with distinct cruxes but sadly these routes are not climbable at present as the bolts are old.

Conditions
El Fumat is exposed to the elements, so is best avoided in windy or rainy conditions. The rock is different from much of the limestone on the island and can be slippery and soapy in the wrong conditions. The sun hits the crag late in the afternoon, making it a pleasant evening venue.

El Fumat 241

Mike Hutton on *Rafael Borras* (6b) - *p.245* - at El Fumat. This route is one of four stunning grade 6s on a very impressive crag located midway along the Formentor peninsular. Photo: Alan James

El Fumat

Approach
From Port de Pollença, follow the road towards Cap Formentor. At the 13km post, turn off to a parking area on the left, which has a path leading down to a rocky beach. From the far end of the parking area, cross back over the road and follow a very vague path up the hillside towards the crag.

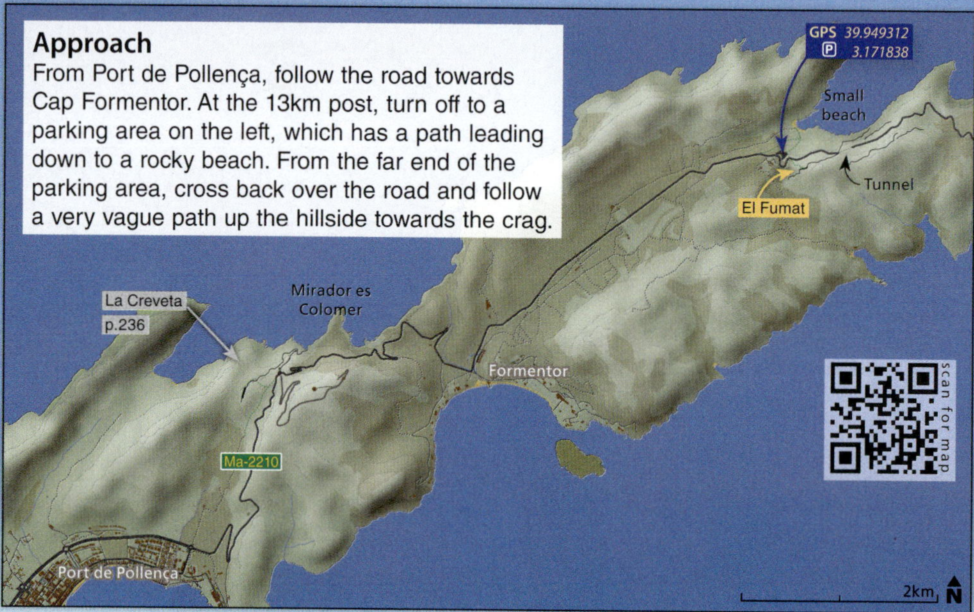

GPS 39.949312 / 3.171838

El Fumat 243

Alan James on *Ziritone* (6a+) - *p.244* - at El Fumat. Photo: Mike Hutton

El Fumat — Sector Duke

Sector Duke
An impressive crag. Whilst its surface appears to be very smooth, there are many cracks, and holds materialise from nowhere on the steeper bits. The black lichen in the deeper cracks is very slippery in damp conditions.

Approach (map and overview p.242) - The first routes are on the huge left-hand face, which is accessed by a path through the boulders and vegetation at the base of the crag.

1 Ziritone .... 6a+
Climb the crack, then move left to follow tufa lumps on the edge of a groove. A great pitch and a good starter but it can be wet on the tufa. *Photo p.243.*

2 Apendre tort 7a
The thin crack and technical wall give excellent climbing, which really kicks in above half-height. Old bolts in the upper half, but the line can be top-roped from the lower-off of *Duke*.

3 Duke 6b
A magnificent trip up the centre of the crag. Climb the thin crack (tricky) and pull through a pumpy section at mid-height to gain and finish up an open groove. A long pitch that should only be attempted when dry.

Sector Free Tibet **El Fumat** 245

④ Duquesa................ 7b
A breathtaking three-pitch extension to *Duke* that follows a line to the left of the vast black wall.
1) **7a+**, 30m, 2) **7b**, 25m, 3) **6a+**, to the top.
Descent - The route is too steep to abseil so you must walk down to the right (looking in). You can abseil down *Uudos* which tops out about 50m to the right but the line is difficult to find.

⑤ Mercury .... 6b+
The thin slab ends at the steep midway overhang. Carefully pick a line through this section (crossed hands!) and climb the steep pillar above. *Photo p.234.*

⑥ Rafael Borrás 6b
Move up the right side of the main slab and then climb the steep groove strenuously to a surprising finish. *Photo p.241.*

⑦ Na palonia................ 5c
Climb just to the left of the bolts.

⑧ Colorado............... 6a
Climb the crack.

⑨ Old Bolts 5c

Sector Free Tibet
The main feature of Sector Free Tibet is the long narrow roof. The next routes all cross this with the roof providing the crux move on every route. At the time of writing most of the bolts on all these routes are old.

⑩ Popeye .... 7c+
The tufa is said to be brilliant.

⑪ Hostal Paraiso.......... 7b
The crack in the wall leads to a weakness in the roof.

⑫ Citroën 7b
A very thin wall leads to a hard roof.

⑬ Free Tibet 7a
A short wall leads to hard roof.

⑭ En Miquel está fumat ... 6c
Follow staples to the roof. Cross it to old bolts on the headwall.

⑮ Ghandi .... 6b+
Climb the wall between tufas to a reachy roof.

⑯ Obelix............... 6c+
Use the tufa boss and a layaway to get over the roof.

⑰ Obi Wan 6b
The roof is easier here than most of its neighbours to the left. Above is a crozzly wall.

⑱ El martell de Thor....... 6c
Climb over the bulge to get on a thin wall.

⑲ Vívora.................. 6b
Pull over the low bulge onto the wall.

⑳ Uudos................. 6a+
This route has three pitches and leads all the way to the top. The start is just before a fence.
1) **3a**, 10m, 2) **6a**, 30m, 3) **6a+**, 30m.

Puig St. Marti

| Grade Spread | 6 | 12 | 1 | - | - |

A nice little crag with a good west-facing wall and a great spread of low-to-mid grade routes. The rock is well weathered and the routes on the West Face give fine climbing. The first bolts have a habit of going missing but it isn't a big problem since the lower moves are usually fairly easy - take care and a clip-stick could be handy.

Conditions
The main crag faces west and gets afternoon sun. It will catch the wind and gives no shelter in the rain. The North Buttress offers some shade if it is hot.

Puig St. Marti 247

Puig St. Marti
- South Peak

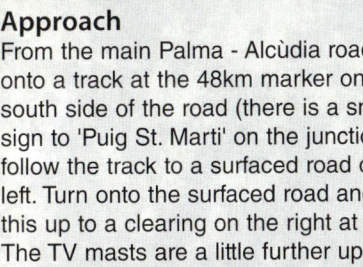

Approach
From the main Palma - Alcùdia road, turn onto a track at the 48km marker on the south side of the road (there is a small sign to 'Puig St. Marti' on the junction) and follow the track to a surfaced road on the left. Turn onto the surfaced road and follow this up to a clearing on the right at a col. The TV masts are a little further up, at the summit. A path leads to the crags in about 2 minutes.

Puig St. Marti — North Buttress

North Buttress
Shady, short and not very significant, but the rock is okay, and the view is spectacular. Some of the bolts are old.

Approach (map and overview p.247) - Walk up to the West Face then head left.

1 Rata pinyada 5c
A steep start gains a diagonal crack.

2 Chispita 6a
A steeper right-hand start to *Rata pinyada*.

3 Sostre del murero .... 6a+
Step onto the wall above a cave, then tackle the roof.

4 Respect the Rock 5c
A good pitch.

5 Blancanieves 6a
The right-hand side of an open scoop.

6 Tramontana fuerza 5c
The left-hand side of a blunt arete.

7 Pa los abuelos 4a
A slabby sidewall.

8 Tufolandia 6a
Powerful pulls past a fin and out of the cave. Old bolts.

9 Langostino .... 6b+
A very steep, pocketed crack.

There may be a 6a+ to the right.

Puig St. Marti 249

Bridget Glaister on *La Mosca* (4c) - *p.250* - at Puig St. Marti. This is an excellent venue for ticking off some quality easier climbs in a fabulous hilltop location. Photo: Mark Glaister

Puig St. Marti — West Face

West Face
A lovely wall with great rock, a superb outlook and some very worthwhile lower-grade pitches. The first bolts are sometimes missing but it isn't a big problem since the moves are usually easy.

Approach (map and overview p.247) - Walk straight up the hillside to the crag.

① New 3c 3c
A short line on the far left-hand side of the West Face.

② Tio listo 5c
Climb the wall past a mid-height bulge.

③ Atila 6a
A right-hand variation on the first route.

Past a tree is a small bay with three more routes. The first bolts on these are sometimes missing but the lower moves are easy.

④ Alzheimer 5a
The left-hand side of the wall right of a wide crack.

⑤ La mosca 4c
A fine pitch. The central line is tricky at mid-height.
Photo p.249.

⑥ 100 duros 4c
Excellent rock and climbing to a slightly harder finish.

West Face Puig St. Marti

50m further right are three more routes. The first bolts are sometimes missing on the lower sections.

7 Stone Lion 4b
Start 5m left of *Pedorretas*. Climb the slab and bulges on good holds.

8 Pedorretas 4c
A series of gentle bulges connected by good moves.

9 7 vidas y una más 5a
Start via bulges and finish up a slab. Not well bolted.

10 New lower-off 5c
Easy climbing to a high first bolt (take care with the rock).

El Caló de Betlem

Grade Spread - 5 14 7 1

This charming little venue sits at the eastern tip of the island, near the villa settlement of Betlem, on the way to Cap de Ferrutx. The two main buttresses offer a variety of climbing styles on excellent rock, all set in a stunning location. El Caló de Betlem boasts a collection of good mid-grade routes and is an ideal spot to catch the last rays of daylight. The central dome-shaped wall features two outstanding technical climbs, while the flanking walls present steeper, contrasting pitches. Sector Subte will mainly appeal to those who crave intensely steep, explosive climbing and are eager for a dose of steep tufa action. Though somewhat off the beaten path, the crags are easy to reach and serve as a perfect stop-off on the way back from Cala Magraner or Cala Bota. Rebolting is taking place but a good number of the lines have old bolts.

Conditions

The mountains on Cap de Ferrutx are isolated from the rest of Mallorca and often experience very different weather conditions. It can be rainy or cloudy in the mountains and yet the sun will still be shining on Betlem. Both crags face roughly northwest and get the late afternoon and evening sun, although the right-hand side of El Caló de Betlem faces southwest and gets plenty of sun. Despite the general aspect El Caló de Betlem is not a very cool crag when the sun is blazing down.

Charlotte Macdonald on *Facil* (6a) - *p.258* - at El Caló de Betlem. Most visit this waterside collection of well-weathered walls to climb the classic steep slab *Es pasto (Dog Walker)* (6b+) - *p.256* - although there are also a good number of other worthwhile grade 6s at the crag to fill a day. Photo: Mark Glaister

El Caló de Betlem

El Caló de Betlem

Approach

Head towards Artà on the eastern side of the island. Take a minor turning towards 'Colonia de Sant Pere'. Follow the road for 5km to a sharp left turning to Sant Pere. Continue straight on to the villa settlement of Betlem. Drive straight through Betlem to roadside parking just before the end of the road (parking at the very end is private). Walk to the end of the road and follow a wide track for 10 minutes to Sector Subte, and a further 5 minutes to El Caló de Betlem.

GPS 39.754475 / 3.320253

East Face **El Caló de Betlem** 255

East Face
This is a very pleasant location with pine trees at the base and the Mediterranean down below. The routes give fingery climbing up walls and slabs of around 20m.
Approach - Scramble up the left-hand side of the crag.

❶ Sostre 7a
Located on a buttress just left of the East Face. Steep in its upper section.

❷ Joan 90 .... 6a+
The left-hand side of the slab and groove above. The name is on the rock to the left of the actual bolt-line.

❸ Wall Left 6b
Excellent climbing on superb rock with a high crux.

❹ Wall Right .... 6b+
Good climbing but slightly spoilt by being too close to the crack. Harder than its left-hand neighbour. Older bolts.

❺ Fisura 5c
A fine line with good climbing up the crack. The bolts are to the right at the start. Older bolts.

❻ Wilow .... 6a+
A very good sustained and fingery wall climb. Climb just right of the crack-line of *Fisura*. *Photo p.257.*

❼ Juanma .... 7a+
A clean line with thin moves to reach a hole.

The line on the right is a project.

El Caló de Betlem — Sector Es pasto

Sector Es pasto

The main sector for climbing at El Caló de Betlem is on the clean grey dome of rock, with a man and dog scratched at its base. This bit of 'artwork' has now been given a modern twist with the addition of a new scratching which looks a bit like a ship sailing past the old Wembley Stadium.

Approach (map and overview p.254) - This is the section where the rock reaches the track.

1 Canal Rocks .... 6c+
Thin moves on drilled pockets gain a runnel and lower-off above.

2 La curta 7a
A sharp, crozzly wall with a thin stopper move.

3 Es pasto (Dog Walker)  6b+
The best route on the crag tackles the central slab, starting just to the left of the scratchings. The climbing is superb and sustained from start to finish. The route was for many years known as *Dog Walker*, named after the scratching at the base.

4 Tequila Forever ...... 7a+
A superb, technical slab route. The main difficulties are in the first half and involve the use of some tiny sharp holds.

The blunt right arete is an extremely hard longtime project.

Mark Glaister making the most of the daylight on the fingery face climbing encountered on *Wilow* (6a+) - *p.255* - at El Caló de Betlem.
Photo: Charlotte Macdonald

El Caló de Betlem — West Face

1 Xupamela 6b
Start up the slim corner-crack and then take the wall (hard) and overlap above. Use a long extender on the bolt at the lip.

2 Facil 6a
Technical climbing up the groove. Move up the blunt rib right of the slim corner and step right to a peg in the base of the groove. Climb the sustained groove/corner to the top. *Photo p.253.*

3 Crozzly Wall 6b
The crozzly wall left of a the *Facil* upper groove. Start up the wall just right of the blunt rib of *Facil*. Slightly escapable.

4 Almudaina 6a
The awkward, short, blocky rib. Harder if climbed direct.

5 Moro .... 8a+
Drilled pockets at the start followed by a thin flake above.

6 Left-slanting Crack ...... 6b+
Climb the left-slanting crack. A short-lived crux.

7 El nostro projecte 6c
An excellent pitch, at first steep and then fingery and technical on the final wall.

8 Tot picat 7b
Head directly up the wall from just above the start of the slanting groove of *El nostro projecte*.

9 Murto 6c
The line of orange bolts that sports the crux towards the top.

West Face
The West Face has a number of secluded routes that are well worth a look. All the lines are steep at the bottom and have fingery crux moves.
Approach (map and overview p.254) - Walk up to the right from the track.

Afternoon · 15 min · Sheltered

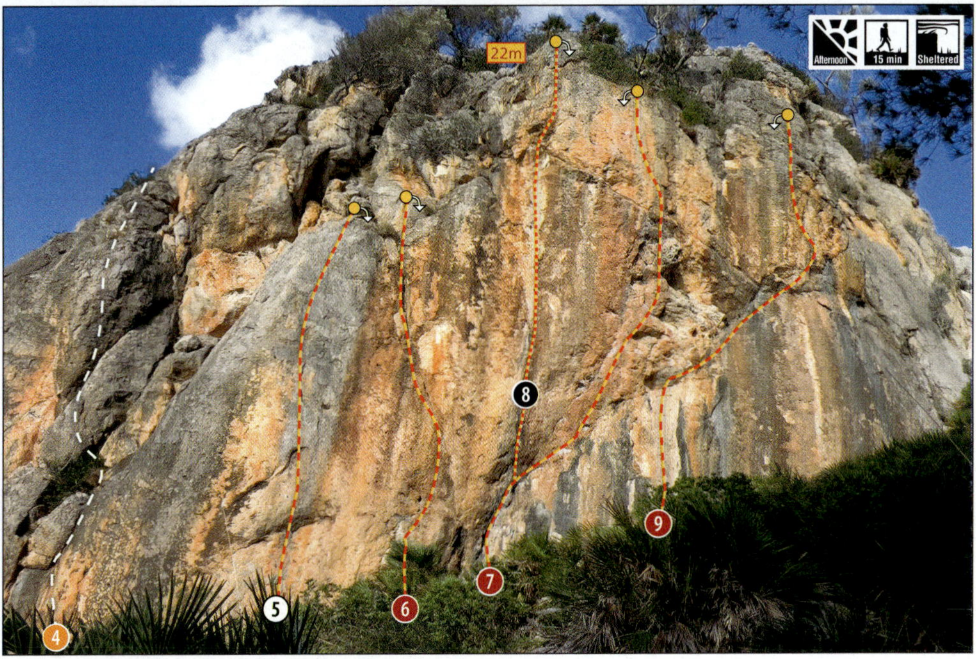

Sector Subte — El Caló de Betlem

Sector Subte
This small sector has a set of steep, blobby routes with powerful moves and some strange holds.
Approach (map and overview p.254) - Walk along the track for 10 minutes until the crag appears on the right.

⑩ Horilous 7c
On the left-hand side of the crag.

⑪ Pin 6b
Harder for the short (**6b+**). Climb steep ground and make a long reach from a sidepull to a concealed slot.

⑫ Pon .... 7b+
The often chalked-up line goes right and is hard. There is an easier left-hand version (**7a+**). The local grade is **6c+**.

⑬ Tot Disney 7a
Up the hanging tufa making use of a block to start.

⑭ Yogui 7b
This is the local grade. Almost certainly much harder.

⑮ Bubu .... 7a+
The back of the scoop. May well be harder than **7a+**.

⑯ Bordillo 7a
Climb out of the right-hand side of the cave.

The East Coast
Son Servera
Sa Mola de Felanitx
Cala Magraner
Cala Bota
Torre d'en Beu
Tijuana

A climber completing the final moves of *Sa des plastics* (7b+) - *p.309* - at Tijuana. The climbers to the right are on *Tarta Lemon* (6b+). Tijuana is the toughest of a number of seaside crags spread out along the east coast, each having plenty of routes to attract teams of all abilities. Away from the sea and beaches the inland Sa Mola de Felanitx escarpment is a prime spot for ticking off many grade 4s, 5s and 6s. Photo: Mark Glaister

Son Servera

Conditions
The crag is a sheltered west-facing suntrap. A good winter venue and also somewhere to consider in light rain, although the tufas will drip eventually.

A crag typical of many of the smaller hard crags in Mallorca - good routes, on good rock with the odd chipped hold. The setting is pleasantly secluded, the approach easy and it is worth stopping by if you are leading in the upper 7s and 8s.

Approach
Turn off the main Artà to Manacor road towards Son Servera. Drive through the town following signs to Cala Millor. On leaving you come to a roundabout with a Honda garage and petrol station. Turn right here, following signs to 'Polignon Industrial'. After about 500m, turn left onto Carrer de Joan Alcover signed to 'Petopen Promon'. Drive up here towards the Pikolo distribution warehouse and park to its left in a large car park. The crag is on the hillside above you. Avoid going up the track that appears to head straight for the crag. Instead, find another big track from the back corner of the parking which starts at a complex junction with wooden posts. Continue up this track for 175m to an easy-to-miss track on the left. Pace this out to be sure. This small path leads directly up to the crag.

Son Servera

❶ Pasqualín 6a
The pillar on the far left-hand side of the cliff. Climb the lower wall passing a ledge and finish up a steep face.

❷ Reset 6c
Climb the steep pillar on sharp rock.

❸ Beirut 7c
The technical crack out of the cave. Eases higher up.

❹ No vull ser com tu 7c
Chipped pockets up the blank wall.

❺ Musaka .... ?
An old project that has a new set of glue-in bolts so may have now been completed.

❻ Be good 8a
Pockets lead to a broken tufa.

❼ Fido Dido 7b
An excellent pitch worth seeking out. Climb the pocketed wall then branch left. Staple bolts.

❽ Google .... 7c+
The right-hand finish to *Fido Dido* is much more technical. Staple bolts.

❾ Kudota 8a
Climb blobs up rightwards to chipped slots past a blank section.

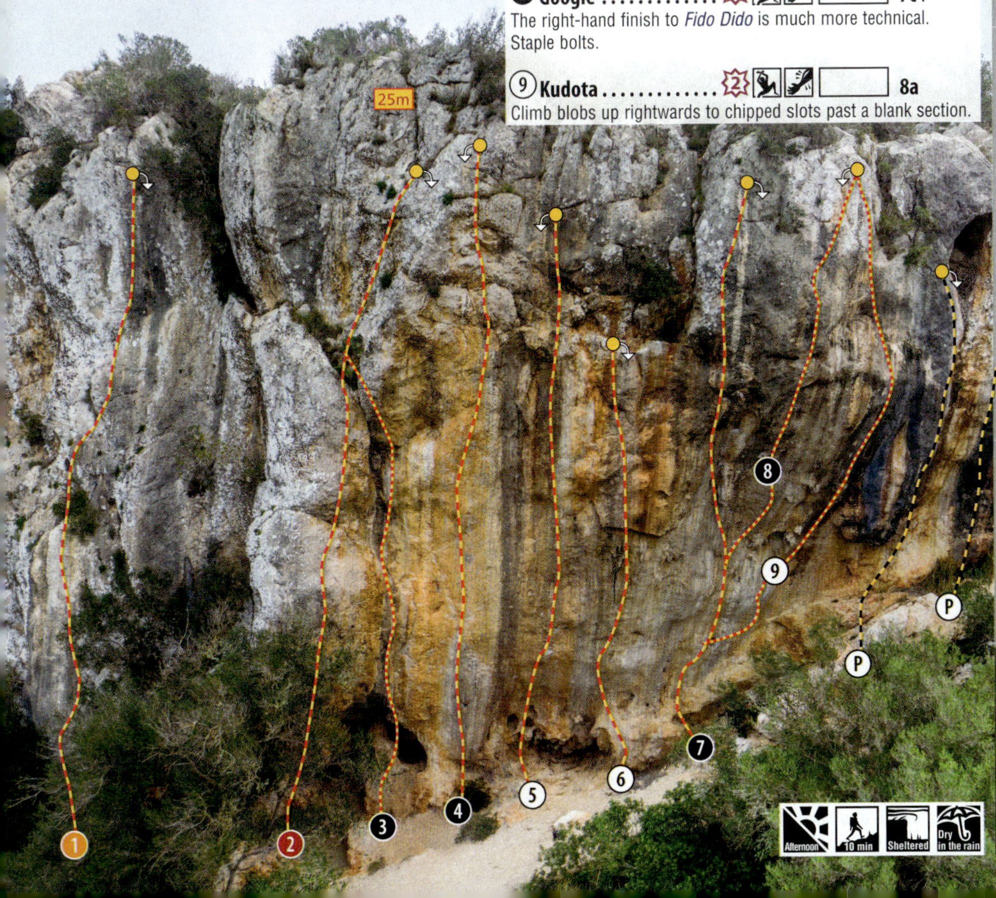

Alan James on *Medizincentrum Santanyi* (6a) - *p.270* - at Sa Mola de Felanitx. The crag is composed of a heavily eroded white limestone that has left the escarpment covered in a myriad of cracks, holes and corners which ensures the climbs have plenty of character. Photo: Mike Hutton

Sa Mola de Felanitx

Sa Mola de Felanitx is a long line of white limestone that overlooks the town of Felanitx. The crag has been climbed on for many years but in more recent times it has received a complete overhaul and now possesses around 50 very good, well-bolted routes with many in the lower grades. The rock formations offer some fascinating climbing on white walls and sculpted rock often with honeycomb pocket features of all shapes and sizes. The crag environment is extremely pleasant, the cliff base being clean, flat and partially shaded by trees. It is now one of the better low-grade climbing venues on the island. Thanks to the late Armin Helbach and his wife Kerstin for their efforts in turning this into a very pleasant crag.

Conditions
The crag is east-facing and gets the morning sun. It is relatively sheltered from the wind and may stay dry if it is raining in the mountains.

Sa Mola de Felanitx

Approach

Drive to Felanitx on the Ma-14. Go around the town on the ring road and you will see the small low crag to the west, perched above an old bodega. At the roundabout closest to the bodega, turn off and park on some waste ground by the roundabout on the opposite side of the road to the bodega. Walk up the track left of the buildings, then turn right and weave through the ruins to find a small path along a wall. Walk along here, then go through an arch and up some steps. Weave through the terraces above until you eventually arrive at the crag. **There have been break-ins to cars parked for this crag.**

Sa Mola de Felanitx

John McKenna making his way up the cracks and grooves of the lower section of *Die Toten Hosen* (6a) - *p.271* - at Sa Mola de Felanitx. Photo: Mike Hutton

Sa Mola de Felanitx

Sa Mola de Felanitx
The orange and white rock has been well developed to give some superb routes offering a variety of climbing styles on good rock formations.

Regular Route - As a fun diversion it is worth soloing up the easy rock between routes *Traverse to the left!!!* and *Cruila fi* where easy ledges lead upwards to a fascinating trench on the summit. This leads right along the top of the crag to the far end where you can walk easily back down to the base.

Approach (map and overview p.266) - Walk up the track left of the buildings, then turn right and weave through the ruins to find a small path along a wall. Walk along here, then go through an arch and up some steps. Weave through the terraces above until you eventually arrive at the crag.

❶ **Frankenjura** 5c
The leftmost line on the crag.

❷ **It's Tricky** 7a
A boulder problem start (*f7A*) then move right to *Xisco vell*.

❸ **Xisco vell** .... 6a+
Start up the thin crack and then join *It's Tricky* to finish.

❹ **Ufff jajajajaja** .... 6a+
Right of *Xisco vell*.

❺ **First Strike** 4c
4m left of *Monika*. Start at the small orange wall.

❻ **Monika** 5b
A nice face climb.

❼ **JoJo** 6a
The wall through a cave to a pumpy finish.

❽ **Old Route to the Root** ... 6b
Climb the orange face to the horizontal tree root at the top.

Sa Mola de Felanitx

9 Catalina Cisna 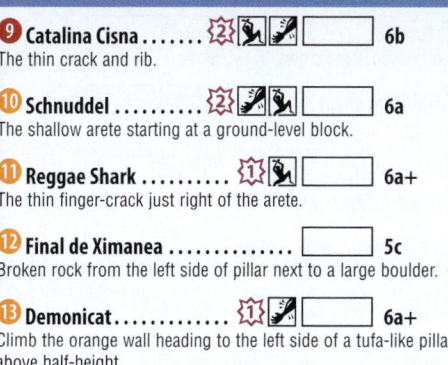 6b
The thin crack and rib.

10 Schnuddel 6a
The shallow arete starting at a ground-level block.

11 Reggae Shark 6a+
The thin finger-crack just right of the arete.

12 Final de Ximanea 5c
Broken rock from the left side of pillar next to a large boulder.

13 Demonicat 6a+
Climb the orange wall heading to the left side of a tufa-like pillar above half-height.

14 Puta Mares 5c
As for *Demonicat* but break right up the wall and then a tufa.

15 Abelles mortals  6a
The long crack-line with a large flake midway. There is a occasionally a bees' nest in the flake.

16 Dias como estas 6b
Start up a sandy hollow to reach technical moves high up.

17 Xisco jove 6a+
Climb the white rib behind a standing block, then go up rightwards to finish over a bulge and up the wall.

18 Traverse to the left!!! 4c
Up the gully/crack and then left via a long traverse crossing *Xisco jove*.

19 Cruila fi 5b
Ascend the front of the block and then up the corner above. Perhaps best done in two pitches belaying at a tree midway.

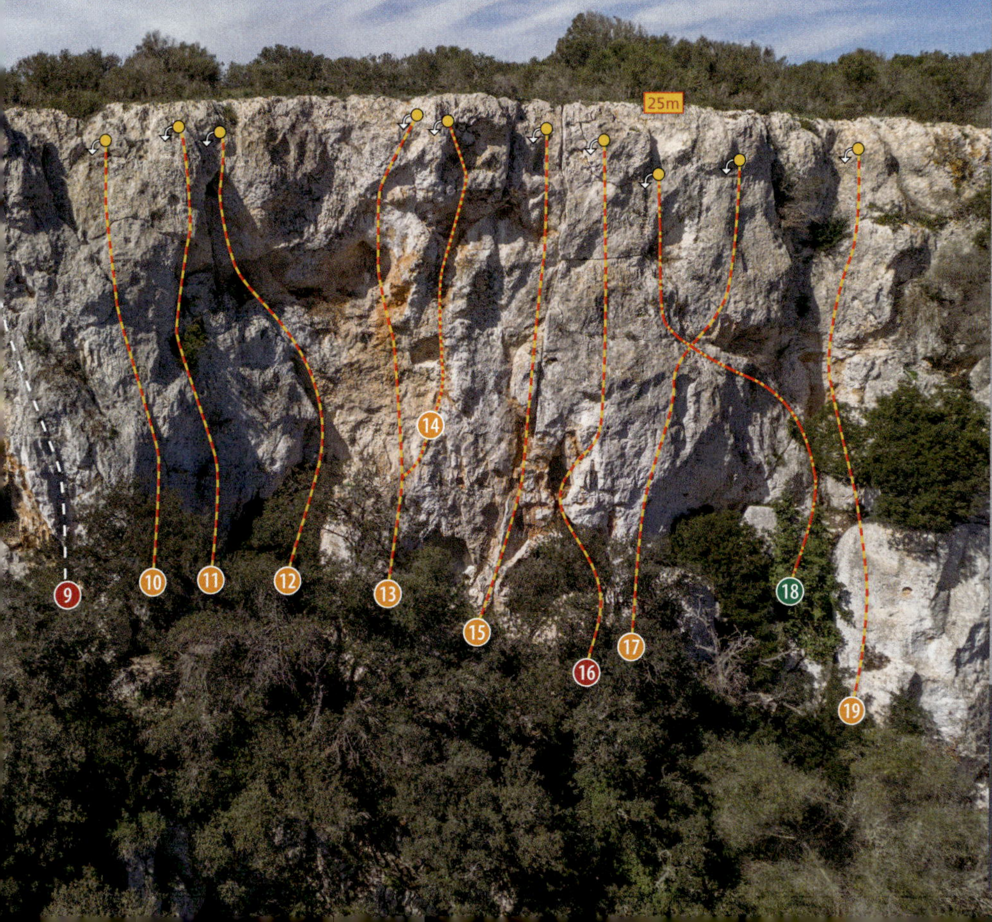

Sa Mola de Felanitx

20 Escoleta 5a
A short pitch up the small open corner/grooves on a big block.

21 Trad Dream 5c
Climb the left-hand groove and its continuation.

22 Papallona 5c
Start up *Trad Dream* then head up the big red corner. A fine line. *Photo p.19.*

23 Alternative Start .... 6a+
The little corner to join and finish up *Trad Dream* (or others).

24 Que chulo 6c
Steep moves up the eroded hollow to a blind move before heading up the groove in the prow. Approaching the upper groove from the *Alternative Start* gives a good **6a+**.

25 Ettringen .... 6a+
Climb the wall left of a crack.

26 Türlich Türlich .... 6a+
The wall right of the crack, passing a midway lower-off.

27 Tom 6a
Pass a ledge. Can be done in two pitches.

28 Un final difícil 6a
The corner just left of the wall.

29 Wave Scalpel .... 6a+
A red-stained groove/slim corner.

30 Medizincentrum Santanyi 6a
Move up the left edge, then make a hard pull through the middle pillar of the depression. Unclip the first bolt to reduce rope drag. *Photo p.264.*

31 3D 6b
Ascend the right edge of the depression, then pull out and make a hard move before finishing direct. Unclip the second bolt to reduce rope drag.

32 Left Loop .... 6a+
Variation on the route *Na Llarga* looping out left above the third bolt.

33 Na Llarga 6b
Climb the vertical pocketed wall to a small niche. Then follow a juggy flake and finish via the left line of bolts up a scoop.

34 Sa figuera .... 1 star ☐ 6a
Move up the steep wall on pockets to gain a diagonal crack. Take the crack and flake to finish up the right-hand line of bolts.

35 Na curta .... ☐ 6a+
Move up to a short crack and thin wall to a lower-off below an overhang. A short pitch.

36 The Roof .... ☐ 6c
An extension to *Na curta* out over the roof. Left is vegetated, right is close to the next route.

37 My Princess .... 2 stars ☐ 7a
The fine looking white wall finishing up an easy corner.

38 Die toten hosen .... 2 stars ☐ 6a
The left-facing red crack/groove to the upper white wall. The dangling chain is to avoid putting a bolt in a thin rock shield. *Photo p.267.*

39 Glory Hole .... 1 star ☐ 6b+
A shallow white rib on pockets and edges.

40 Sa fisura .... 2 stars ☐ 6a
The boot-sized long crack to a high overhang. Finish on the right.

41 Se mes dificil .... 1 star ☐ 6b
The blank-looking wall starting from a ledge.

42 Es crui .... 1 star ☐ 5c
The corner and crack in its left wall, past a rock scar that used to have a large loose flake. The bolts are also on the left wall.

43 Sa rampa .... 1 star ☐ 4b
The easy-angled corner just right of *Es crui*.

44 Primer plato .... 2 stars ☐ 4b
The easy-angled slabby rib/wall right of the corner.

45 Sa cova .... ☐ 5c
Follow jugs steeply to a flake-crack on a slab. Climb this to a rib and finish up it.

46 Darrera sa pared .... ☐ 5b
Ascend a wide cracked column and pull around into a scoop.

47 4++ .... 1 star ☐ 4c
Move up and right into a scoop. The last line on the crag.

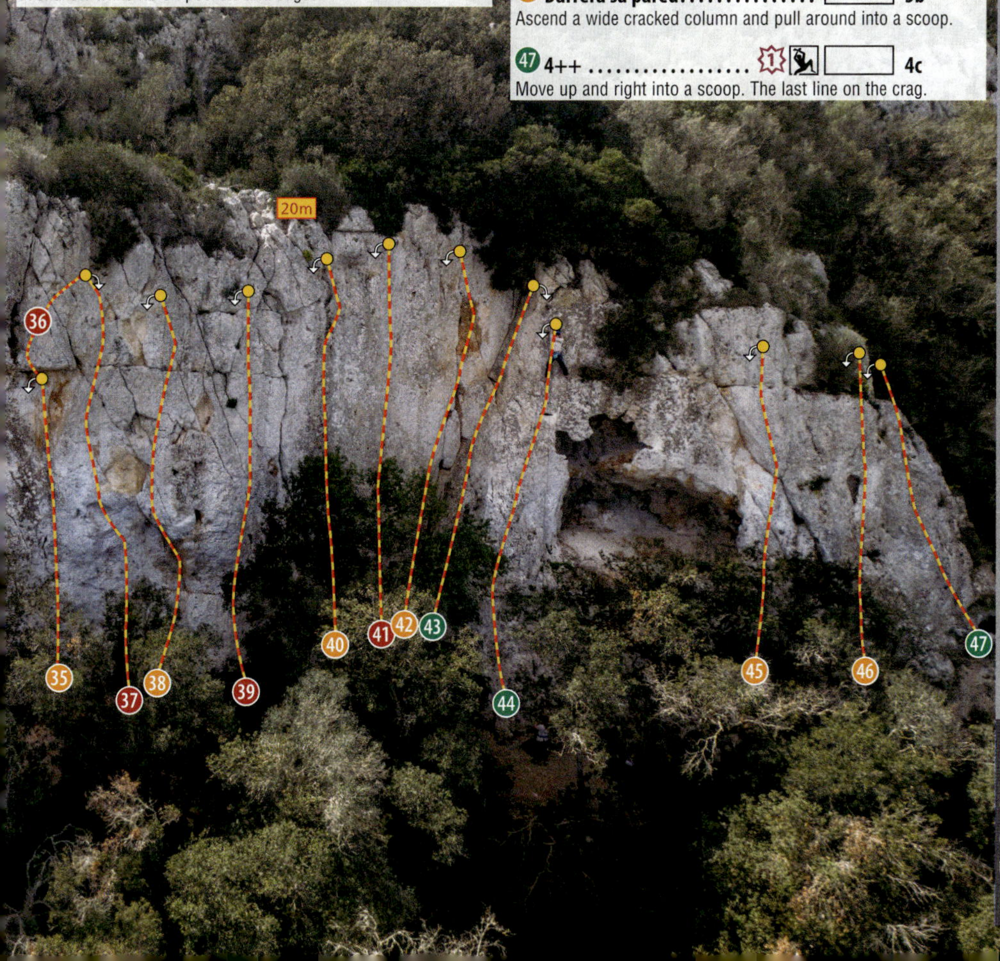

Cala Magraner

Cala Magraner is located in a lovely beachside position on the southeast coast amidst some of the tourist hotspots, and climbing here can take on a real holiday atmosphere. The climbs for the most part are technical wall climbs, usually encompassing tricky fingery cruxes, although there are a couple of steeper sections. There are some pleasant, easy slabs for beginners, and loads in the middle grades. The swimming is excellent.

Conditions

The main area is a south-facing, sheltered suntrap, which is great if visiting in January and everywhere else is freezing, but it can get unbearably hot in the warmer months. The steep cave offers one of the few hard climbing venues on the island that gets a lot of sun. It should also be remembered that the east coast is often dry when it is raining in the mountains.

Ralph Frause climbing *Nautilus* (6a) - *p.280* - at Sector Xorics, Cala Magraner. Cala Magraner fulfils the brief of what most visitors will want out of a holiday sport crag - its combination of beach, swimming and array of good climbs is unlikely to disappoint. Photo: Mike Hutton

Cala Magraner

Approach
Drive to Manacor and pick up signs for 'Calas de Mallorca' and follow them southwards out of the town. Continue for about 8km to arrive at a 'T' junction. Turn right and after two bends there is a rickety stile on the left of the road and lay-bys on both sides. Park here if there is room, otherwise continue past the dry river-bed to a larger lay-by. Back at the rickety stile, follow a well-marked path down the line of an old stone wall, crossing the wall once. Eventually the dry river-bed is reached. Follow this until the first cave appears on the left. The rest of the crags are further down the dry river-bed.

There have been break-ins to cars parked for this crag.

Ulli Seeher on the intricate wall climbing to be found on *Sa nyoscla* (6a) - *p.279* - at Sector Pipiricot, Cala Magraner. Photo: Mike Hutton

Cala Magraner — Sector Cueva

Sector Cueva

The first sign of climbing encountered on the approach is a large cave that has some good hard routes although the grades should be treated with caution. The bolts are mostly quite old.

Approach (map and overview p.274) - This is the large breaking-wave formation, on the left of the dry valley, as you near the sea.

❶ Un tio conflictiu ..... 7a+
The short left-hand side of the cave.

❷ Wall and Bulge .... 7c+
The blank wall and bulge.

❸ Nameless .... 7c+
One extremely hard move but otherwise reasonable.

❹ Imagine 7c
A powerful section at the overhang.

❺ TNT 8a
Much more sustained than its neighbours, but no move harder than on either *Nameless* or *Imagine*.

❻ Dingo .... 7a+
Superb climbing up the central line starting to the right of the low circular cave.

❼ Tufa Big .... 7b+
An impressive direct line above the big tufa.

❽ Sand Bag .... 7b+
The right-hand finish to *Tufa Big* has a surprise on the lip of the overhang. This line is confirmed at the grade and is not 7a+.

❾ Project .... ?
The independent line through the overhang is given 7a+ in the local topo, but if it has been climbed, it is a lot harder than that.

❿ Delicatessan .... ?
The left-hand line at the overhang.

⓫ Delicatessan Right-hand. 7b
Use tufas to gain the wall and slopey pockets.

⓬ Right-hand Roof 1 .... 7a+
Climb to the sloping ledge and then direct through the overhang.

⓭ Right-hand Roof 2 .... 7b
Head up to the sloping ledge and then traverse right before moving through the overhang.

Lots of sun | 25 min | Sheltered | Dry in the rain

John McKenna on the steep start to *Cave Left* (7a+) - *p.279* - at Sector Pipiricot, Cala Magraner. Photo: Mike Hutton

Cala Magraner — Sector Sense Voler

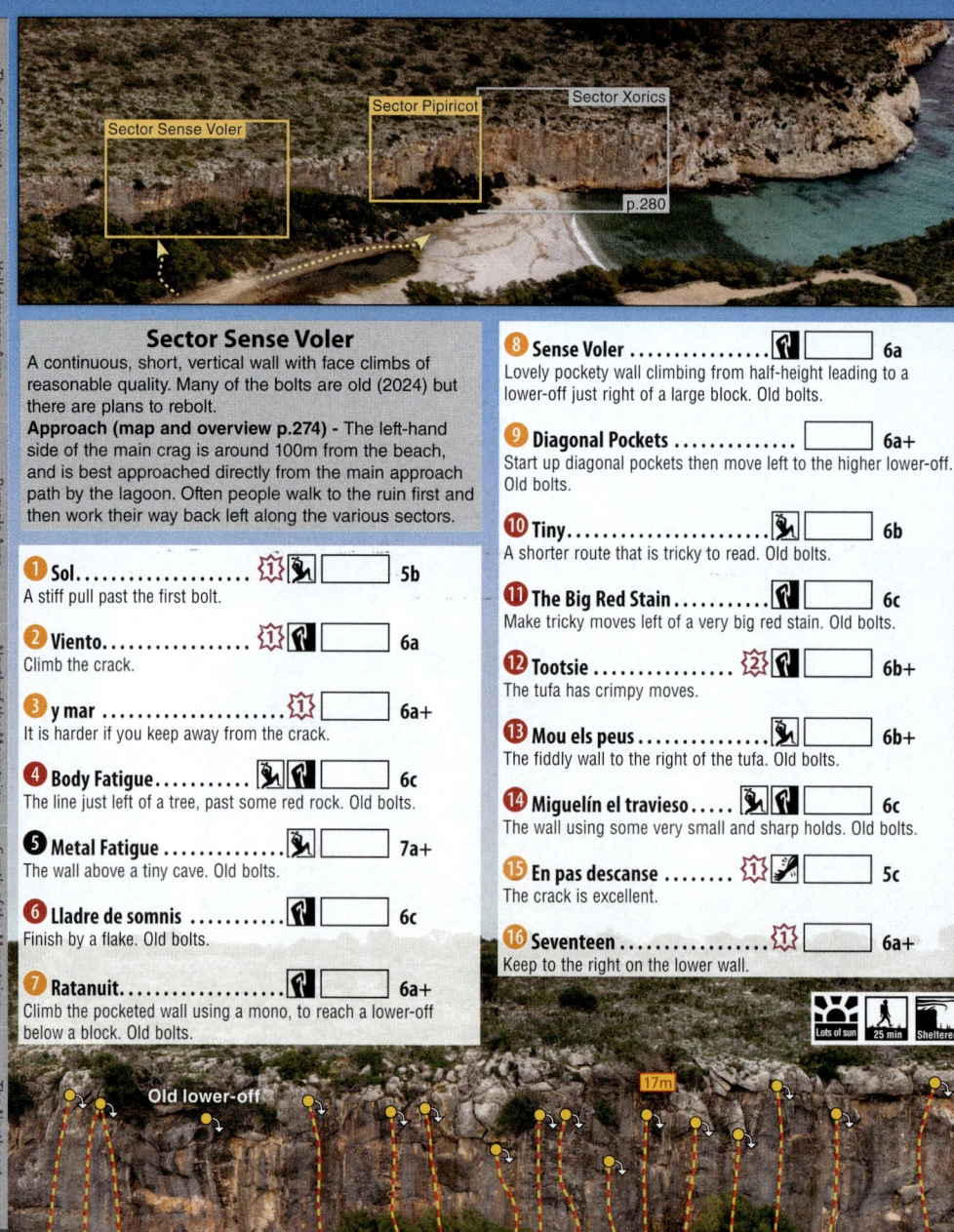

Sector Sense Voler

A continuous, short, vertical wall with face climbs of reasonable quality. Many of the bolts are old (2024) but there are plans to rebolt.

Approach (map and overview p.274) - The left-hand side of the main crag is around 100m from the beach, and is best approached directly from the main approach path by the lagoon. Often people walk to the ruin first and then work their way back left along the various sectors.

1 Sol 5b
A stiff pull past the first bolt.

2 Viento 6a
Climb the crack.

3 y mar .... 6a+
It is harder if you keep away from the crack.

4 Body Fatigue 6c
The line just left of a tree, past some red rock. Old bolts.

5 Metal Fatigue .... 7a+
The wall above a tiny cave. Old bolts.

6 Lladre de somnis 6c
Finish by a flake. Old bolts.

7 Ratanuit .... 6a+
Climb the pocketed wall using a mono, to reach a lower-off below a block. Old bolts.

8 Sense Voler 6a
Lovely pockety wall climbing from half-height leading to a lower-off just right of a large block. Old bolts.

9 Diagonal Pockets .... 6a+
Start up diagonal pockets then move left to the higher lower-off. Old bolts.

10 Tiny 6b
A shorter route that is tricky to read. Old bolts.

11 The Big Red Stain 6c
Make tricky moves left of a very big red stain. Old bolts.

12 Tootsie .... 6b+
The tufa has crimpy moves.

13 Mou els peus .... 6b+
The fiddly wall to the right of the tufa. Old bolts.

14 Miguelín el travieso 6c
The wall using some very small and sharp holds. Old bolts.

15 En pas descanse 5c
The crack is excellent.

16 Seventeen .... 6a+
Keep to the right on the lower wall.

Sector Pipiricot — Cala Magraner

Sector Pipiricot

This section has some steeper lines and a trio of good easier climbs, all on very good rock. A few routes have old bolts but most have been rebolted.

Approach (map and overview p.274) - 60m right of Sector Sense Voler, and 60m left of the ruin by the seashore, is a large, blobby cave. The first 2 routes are in this cave.

17 Cave Left .... 7a+
Direct through the cave past the tufa on the lip. Photo p.277.

18 Cave Right .... 6b+
Pull out rightwards over the lip of the cave and continue up the wall above.

19 Sa nyoscla 6a
A nice climb. Finish at a lower-off on left. Photo p.275.

20 Paramuero................. 5c
A good, technical little pitch with a tricky start.

21 Herbofilia 4a
A very nice pitch but quite polished.

22 Jardiners sense fronteres 3c
The line of staples up the scoop. A fun easy route on positive, although somewhat polished, holds.

23 Perelló 4c
Staple bolts up the groove. The start is slick.

24 Pixotades per ses galtes . 6c+
Hard moves on monos with a tricky clip.

25 Penta .... 6c+
A zig-zag line left of the cave.

26 Galiana m'engana 6c
A hard start and not much easier above.

27 Sa sesta .... 6b+
Another hard start but good higher up.

28 Pipiricot .... 6b+
Pull out right from the cave to a scoop. Old bolts.

29 Wall and Groove 5c
The pocketed wall and groove - slightly spaced bolts. There is a new alternative start on the right - that is also **5c**.

30 Florinotto 5c
The hard section is taken on the left at the grade given and is run out. Climbing direct is harder.

31 Crack.................... 5c
The crack left of the caves leads to a steep finish.

32 Reachy .... 6b+
The reachy crux can be bypassed on the left at about **6a+**.

Cala Magraner — Sector Xorics

Sector Xorics

The largest sector is at the right-hand end of the cliff right by the beach, and is where most people head to first. It is home to many excellent pitches. Most of the routes have good bolts. The beach on the right-hand side used to extend under the routes but the sea has washed it away in recent years. This may change, but until then, these routes require a traverse along to hanging belays and often result in a wet rope when you pull it.

Approach (map and overview p.274) - The crag is more open next to the beach. There is a ruined building under some large caves on its left-hand side.

① Cave Lip 7a
Hand traverse the lip of the cave then pull up into a scoop. The bolts are showing their age.

② Only you .... 6c+
Climb up through the middle of the two caves. At the top, finish either left (slopey) or right (reachy).

③ The Juggy One 5c
Steep, juggy and excellent.

④ Joc de mans 7a
Very technical climbing out of the smaller cave.

⑤ Not Dangerous ...... 6b+
Start from the right edge of the smaller cave.

⑥ Nautilus 6a
The line of staple bolts left of a bush. A good route. *Photo p.273.*

⑦ Xorics .... 6b+
At the top you can go direct or use a right-hand bypass which turns the route into an excellent 6a. The first bolt is old but the rest are okay.

⑧ Projesso Aronnax 6c
The grey scoop is very technical.

⑨ Repusai .... 6a+
Fine climbing up the vague diagonal crack.

⑩ Beachcomber .... 6a+
A great route which can be tricky if the direct line is followed.

Sector Xorics — Cala Magraner — 281

11 Ses tres Maries .... 6a+
Passing the large blob is tricky but things ease only slightly above. Staple bolts.

12 Asuquí .... 6a+
A good technical line via an overlap and crack.

13 Asulla .... 6b+
Brilliant and spectacular climbing through the upper overhangs. Only 4c to the first lower-off.

14 L'amo de Baltix m'envia 6a
Above the water's edge, climb past two scoops. Staple bolts.

The next routes are usually above the sea depending on the extent of the beach. You can take hanging belays or traverse in to them. Whatever you do, your rope is likely to get wet when you pull it after climbing.

15 Captain Nemo 5c
A fine climb with two steep sections.

16 Jetsam 5c
Follow the sustained rib and slab.

17 El vigilant de la platja 4b
A long groove gives a great lower grade route. The crux is traversing to the start of the line if the beach is low.

18 Clásica 5b
Head up the rib right of a groove. Staple bolts.

19 Ses panxetes 6a
Features a fingery start into a scoop. Staple bolts.

20 Pilla, pilla 5c
Climb the face past some small bushes.

21 The final line .... 6b+
Even further right is another old line. Climb out of the cave.

Start from hanging belays or traversing in

Cala Bota

The crag at Cala Bota is set high above the sea and composed of well-featured rock. The routes range in style from thin walls to steep cracks with much more in between. The majority of the routes are in the mid-grades and, for those operating at this level, there is plenty to go at. There are a couple of good harder lines here but this is predominantly a low to mid-grade venue. The ledge that runs under the length of the crag makes for a pleasant place to relax and belay, whilst the small beach of Cala Bota itself is not far away. The grades tend to feel tough but are consistently applied and caution is advised on your first visit to get the feel of the style and grades.

Conditions
The crag is sunny, quick drying and often sheltered. The right side offers a little shade in the late afternoon. Although there are some climbs that might stay dry in the rain, the longish approach is not an appealing prospect in wet conditions.

Charlotte Macdonald about to enter the upper groove of *Eating Hooks* (6a+) - *p.287* - at Cala Bota. The climbing at Cala Bota is extremely varied and most of the climbs pack a punch. Photo: Mark Glaister

Cala Bota

Approach
On the Ma4014 coast road, take a well-signed turning towards Cales de Mallorca and Platja. About 2km down this road is a parking area on the left. From the parking, take the gravel track to a large gate and go through the gap on its right. Follow the track to a distinct left bend and a track that heads straight on. Carry straight on (a right branch goes down to the beach). Continue for 450m to where a path on the right leads to a small stone shelter on the top of the cliff. Walk right (facing out) for 100m and scramble down a short wall to a path that leads back under the cliff to the base of the climbs.

Cala Bota 285

Cala Magraner p.272

GPS 39.477389 3.272569

Cala Bota

Stone shelter

Cala Bota - Right p.288

Big Boulder with one route on it

Cala Bota — Left Wall

Left Wall

The first section of the crag encountered on the approach has a number of spectacular lines on heavily weathered rock and some varied pitches up cracks and over low overhangs. This is a sunny spot that doesn't see much shade throughout the day.

Approach (map and overview p.285) - From the base of the approach scramble, head left (facing out) to meet good ledges and the first climbs.

❶ Bechti2go 4a
Get established on the ledge at head height then continue on huge holds to the lower-off.

❷ Schnurzelpurzel 3c
The easy-angled face is a pleasant amble that reaches a slightly tricky section to gain the lower-off.

❸ One Hand 3b
The left-hand of two slabby lines that finish at a shared lower-off just below the large roof. The rock is very smooth.

❹ Easy 3a
The right-hand line to the lower-off shared with *One Hand*.

❺ Hoog Catharijne 5c
Make some pressing moves up the initial crack and pockets to less steep (but still interesting) ground.

❻ Banita 5c
Unusual and entertaining manoeuvres up to and through the huge hole in the roof to a lower-off just above. Much steeper than first appearances might suggest.

❼ Wonder Woman .... 6a+
Spectacular moves out across the weathered beam of stone on the right-hand side of the roof.

Left Wall Cala Bota

⑧ Triunfo del Nicol ..... 6a+
A good looking line passing just to the right of the upper roof of *Wonder Woman*.

⑨ CB 1 .... 6c?
The leaning wall right of *Triunfo del Nicol*.

⑩ El vals del obrero 5c
Head up steeply left then back right on the upper wall.

⑪ Beschenka Belka .... 6a+
A mirror line to *El vals del obrero* with a slim left-slanting ramp.

⑫ Sobre el coral 6b
A tight but excellent bit of wall climbing just left of the corner of *Maria*.

⑬ Maria 5c
The corner-crack is a fine pitch and steeper that it appears. Take care with some perched boulders left of the lower-off.

⑭ Eating Hooks .... 6a+
A tough initial overhang precedes a perplexing entry into the final flared corner. *Photo p.282.*

⑮ Todo bene 7a
A tough series of powerful pulls to pass the lower overhangs gains a rest before the challenging rounded holes and headwall.

⑯ Un poco de porno 7a
Big moves up the well-chalked pockets reach the less steep upper wall.

⑰ Speer Angel Weit .... 6b+
Attain the top of the low overhang then tackle the lesser bulges and wall above.

⑱ Gusto mo palo .... 6b+
The overhung short corners and headwall just left of the arete.

Cala Bota — Right Wall

Right Wall

Rounding the arete in the centre of the crag, the character of the rock changes, adding more variety to what is on offer. Thin technical walls, corners and grooves are the main ingredients of the routes hereabouts. This section of the crag sees shade later in the day and will provide much needed relief on hot days.

Approach (map and overview p.285) - From the base of the approach scramble, head left (facing out) to meet good ledges and the first climbs on the Left Wall. Continue along the base of the crag until the arete is reached and the beginning of the Right Wall.

❶ **Elmo Love** 5c
The right side of the dominating arete is a good climb. Start at a block below a couple of low narrow grooves.

❷ **Touch the Sky** 6a
Start up the inset wide groove and then take on the holes up the wall to finish right of the capping roof. Finishing direct is **6c**.

❸ **Edelweiß** 5c
Begin up the front of a block to gain a large ledge. Climb the wide corner groove to the top.

❹ **Somos uno** 5a
The rib of a low detached pinnacle and distinctive thin flake-crack in the upper wall.

❺ **Lubeca** .... 6a+
A fine but hard-won pitch. The thin grey wall via a beefy thin layback and fingery finale.

❻ **Kalki** 6b
The line that is defined by the orange and light coloured rock has a pressing finish.

❼ **Deichwand** .... 6b+
The concave wall to a wild finish. The start is a boulder problem.

❽ **Prinzessin Sophia** .... 6a+
The dark orange streak is a striking line and gives a fine pitch.

❾ **Ça fels good** 6b
The right-hand side of the impressive arete is a good wall climb but run out.

❿ **Doktor Michi** .... 6a+
Start up *Ça fels good* and break out rightwards up the white wall.

⓫ **Marta's Stairway** 4b
Scramble up onto a large ledge then climb the slab and short corner above to the top.

12 Im vierten Monat .... 2 stars ☐ 5c
Move up easily onto a head-height ledge then take the interesting open groove to the top.

13 Hamburg Rocks .... 2 stars ☐ 5b
Begin amongst boulders and follow ledges up left to a shallow groove and crack system. Follow this to the top.

14 Hans-Peter .... 1 star ☐ 6a
A short but intense line up the undulating wall above boulders before the crag starts to drop away to the right.

15 Buzzewackele .... 2 stars ☐ 6b
An impressive pitch up the grey tufa, tough wall and final corner.

16 Big Boulder .... ☐ 6b
A huge boulder below the route *Elmo Love* has one bolted line on its landward face.

17 Dies de Sol .... 2 stars ☐ 7b+
Start at a narrowing ledge where the cliff gains height above the sea. A bouldery start precedes some face climbing and a powerful finish.

18 Big Sebastian ... 3 stars ☐ 7c+
Hard fingery climbing to a surprising finish.

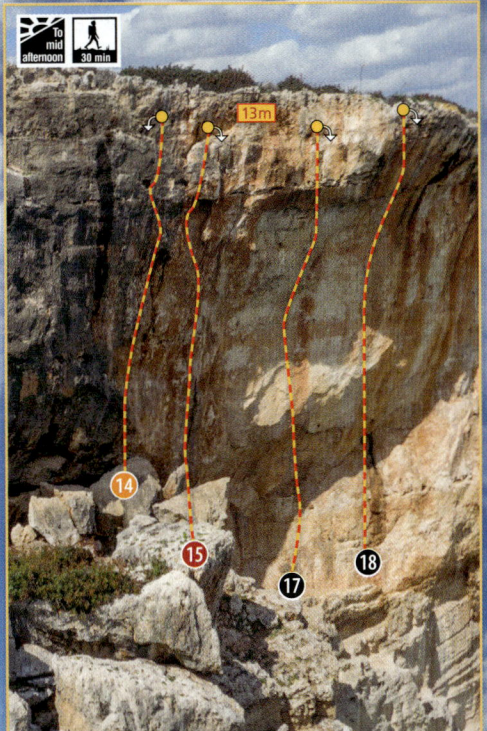

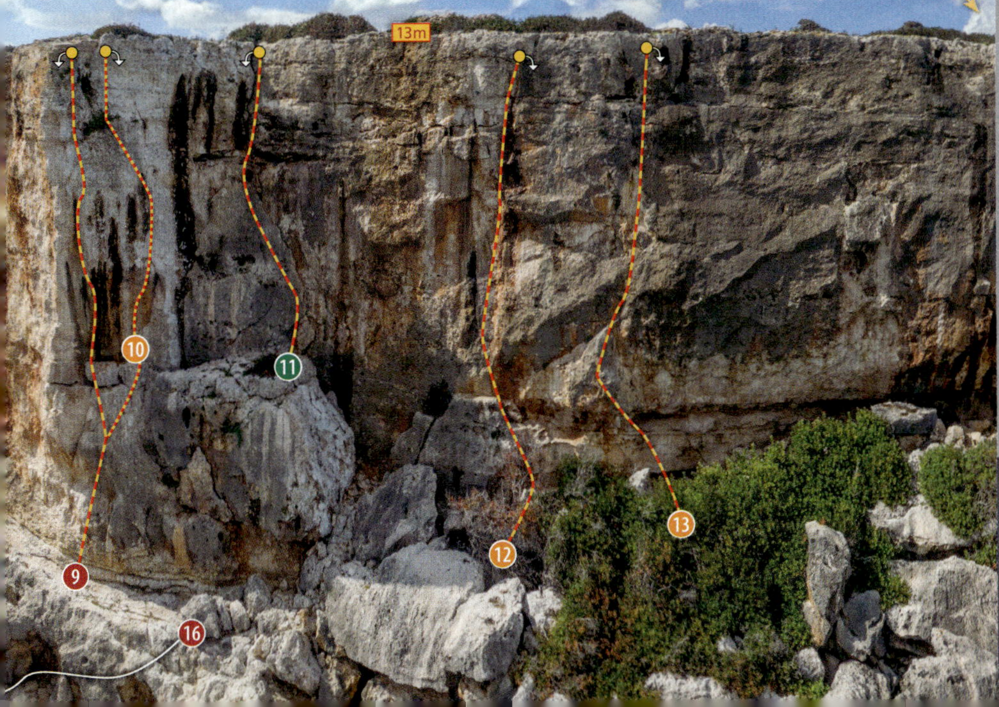

The Southwest
Valldemossa Area
Bunyola Area
North of the Mountains
South of the Mountains
The Northeast
The East Coast

Torre d'en Beu

Grade Spread | 2 | 14 | 17 | 7 | 4

Torre d'en Beu is a beautifully situated sea cliff not dissimilar to the nearby and long established Tijuana. There are fewer routes here but there is certainly potential for more. If you have run out of grade 6s at Tijuana, hop in the car and head over for a look at what is on offer. The orange-stained rock rises above a large boulder-strewn platform, and is of excellent quality on the routes covered. There is also quite a bit of bouldering on the various boulders hereabouts, but a mat is advisable.

Conditions

Torre d'en Beu mostly faces due south, and is situated on the opposite side of the island from the mountains, which means that it enjoys a much more settled climate. It is such a good suntrap that it is often too hot, even in winter. There is sometimes a sea breeze but this is usually welcome in the heat. The rock platform is well above the sea and the cliff set back from the edge so it is very unlikely that high seas will be a problem.

Jeremy Wilson on the flowstone wall of *Benas* (6b+) - *p.297* - at Torre d'en Beu. The long line of cliff faces that make up Torre d'en Beu are set above a wide platform only a minute or so from the parking above. Each sector has its own character, with those below the radar station being the most frequented having lots of climbs in the 6th grade. Photo: Mark Glaister

Torre d'en Beu

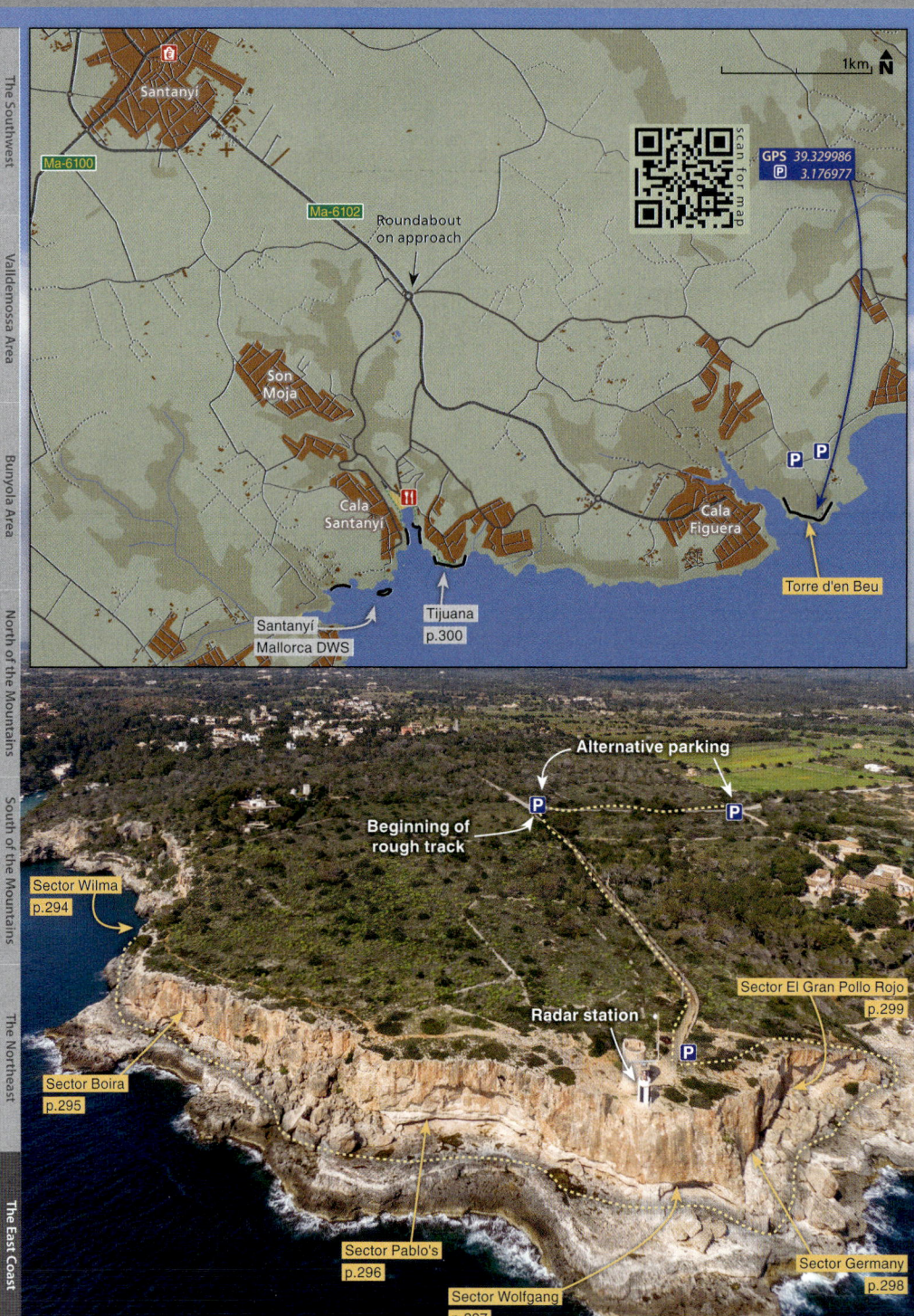

Torre d'en Beu 293

Approach
When approaching Santanyí village, follow signs for Cala Figuera and Cala Santanyí. From the outskirts of Santanyí continue for around 2km to a roundabout. Turn left here (signed 's'Amarador' - Tijuana is straight on at this roundabout). Keep right, then at the next junction turn left, then right at the one after (no real signs on this section).
At a bend, drive straight on down a rough dirt track to the parking by the tower and radar station at the end - parking is also available on the road where the rough dirt track starts. To reach the crag, head left (looking out) down a short path to the platform below the crag.

Mark Glaister on the superbly positioned rib of *Faro* (6a+) - *p.297* - at Torre d'en Beu. The structure on top of the cliff is a radar. Photo: Charlotte Macdonald

Torre d'en Beu — Sector Wilma

Sector Wilma
The wall at the very far end of the developed cliff has a couple of good easier routes.
Approach (map and overview p.292) – Continue along the crag base, past Sector Pablo's. The boulders around the corner are tricky to negotiate but eventually you reach Sector Boira. Sector Wilma is 50m further along.

Sector Wilma - 50m

1 Betty 4c
The farthest line on the left. Head up the easy-angled slab. The start is the hardest section.

2 Wilma 4a
The slab just to the right of *Betty* is easier but sustained.

3 Maquina Infernal .... 6c+
A deceptively difficult and bouldery problem.

4 Barracuda .... 6a+
The right-hand line is a brief but worthwhile pitch.

Sector Boira

This area is towards the very end of the developed section of the cliff and almost opposite the hotels of Cala Figuera. The routes are quite short but offer varied climbing with plenty of potential for new routes.

Approach (map and overview p.292) - Continue along the crag base, past Sector Pablo's. The boulders around the corner are tricky to negotiate but eventually you reach the three sections of developed climbing beyond.

5 Glenlivert .... 6c+
Tough moves through some very steep ground. The route name is not misspelled.

6 Boira .... 6a+
From the cliff-base block, follow the left-hand line of bolts past one difficult section.

7 Lucas 6b
The right-hand line is steep without any hard moves.

8 Cisne Negro 6b
Start up to the left and make a hard sequence on sharp holds to access easier ground.

9 Armin H Best Husband 6a+
A hard start to some good moves up the wall above.

10 Red Wall Left .... 6c+
Climb up onto a ramp then make a stiff pull to gain a rest before a puzzling finish.

11 Red Wall Right .... ?
The steep red wall looks to be around 7a/b?

Afternoon | 10 min | Sheltered

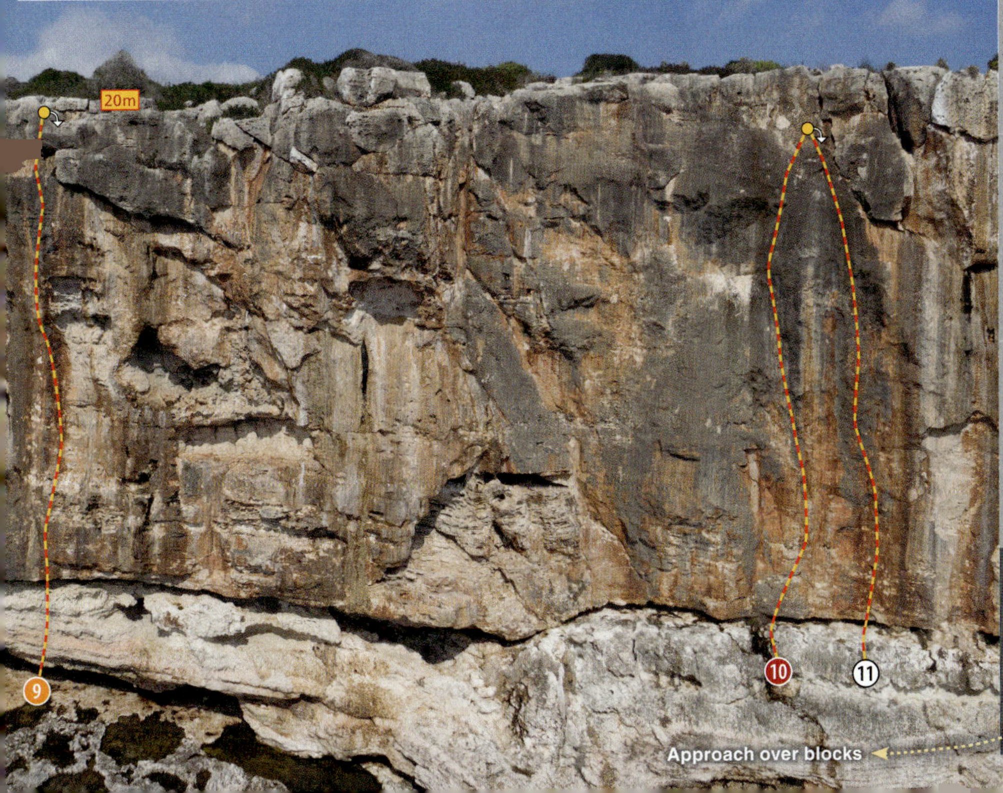

The Southwest
Valldemossa Area
Bunyola Area
North of the Mountains
South of the Mountains
The Northeast
The East Coast

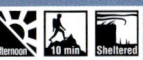

Torre d'en Beu — Sector Pablo's

Sector Pablo's

The most impressive section of Torre d'en Beu is this steep wall with a large central overhang. It has some superb routes although some of the rock is questionable, but not usually on the sections where it matters.
Approach (map and overview p.292) - Follow the platform below the crag, and around the corner under the tower/radar.

❶ Locura Temporal .... 6c+
A sandy start but great climbing above.

The next three routes all share the same start, that is a touch sandy and best started from the left.

❷ Mirame y no me Toques.. 6c
A bouldery initial sequence gains easier but sustained ground.

❸ Perpetua Demencia .. 6c
The best of the trio gives enjoyable climbing.

❹ Buscador de Cordura .... 7a+
Sustained climbing to a boulder problem finish.

❺ Heavy Metalurgia.... 7a
The central line through the main roof is impressive. Climb the corner to below the roof. Head out across the roof via burly moves and then finish up the crisp short wall.

❻ Mar de Fons .... 6b+
Easy climbing to a leftward-trending groove that has blind powerful moves on crimps. Finish in the cave.

❼ Beachball Hole 6b
A varied and challenging line with some exhilarating moves. Head up towards the beachball-sized hole. Press on up the headwall via some interesting moves.

❽ Cut Loose .... 6a+
Swing right and cut loose at a good hold. Move up to easier ground and a ledge. Finish left of the bolts. *Photo p.23*.

❾ Via del Charly 6c
Hard moves over the initial roof and up the wall gain less pressing ground left of the vegetated corner.

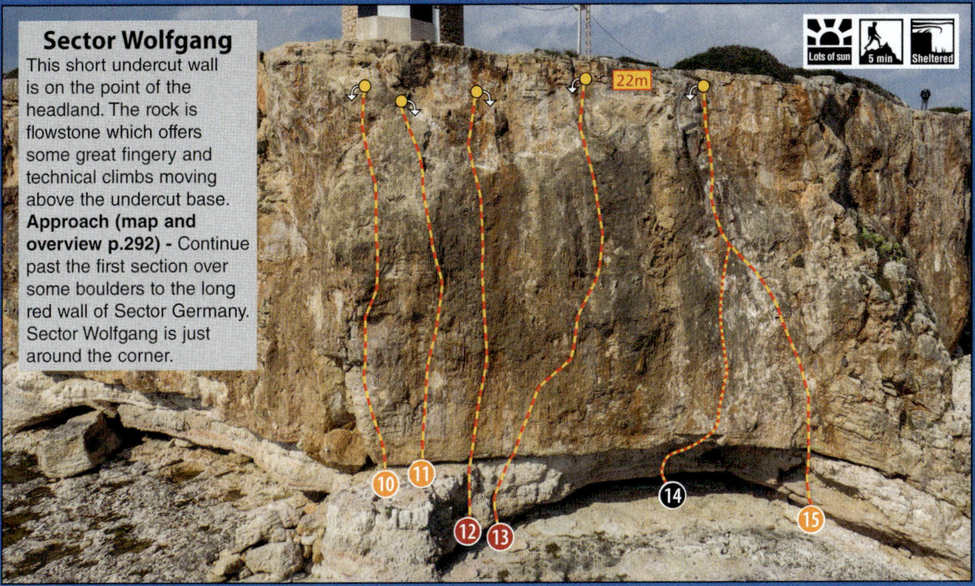

Sector Wolfgang

This short undercut wall is on the point of the headland. The rock is flowstone which offers some great fingery and technical climbs moving above the undercut base.

Approach (map and overview p.292) - Continue past the first section over some boulders to the long red wall of Sector Germany. Sector Wolfgang is just around the corner.

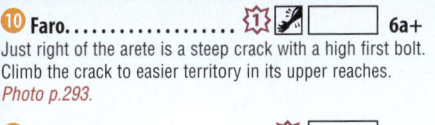

10 Faro .... 1 star .... 6a+

Just right of the arete is a steep crack with a high first bolt. Climb the crack to easier territory in its upper reaches. *Photo p.293.*

11 Thomas .... 1 star .... 6a+

The steep face, with a high initial bolt, to the right of the crack.

12 Wolfgang .... 2 stars 6b

Head directly up the wall of amazing flowstone flutings.

13 Benas .... 3 stars .... 6b+

Move up and then awkwardly right (tricky clip) on flowstone until a final thin sequence gains easier ground. *Photo p.291.*

14 Pequena Realidad .... 7b+

The low roof and wall above.

15 Diagonal .... 3 stars 5c

A delightful pitch. Climb diagonally leftwards on positive holds.

The Southwest
Valldemossa Area
Bunyola Area
North of the Mountains
South of the Mountains
The Northeast
The East Coast

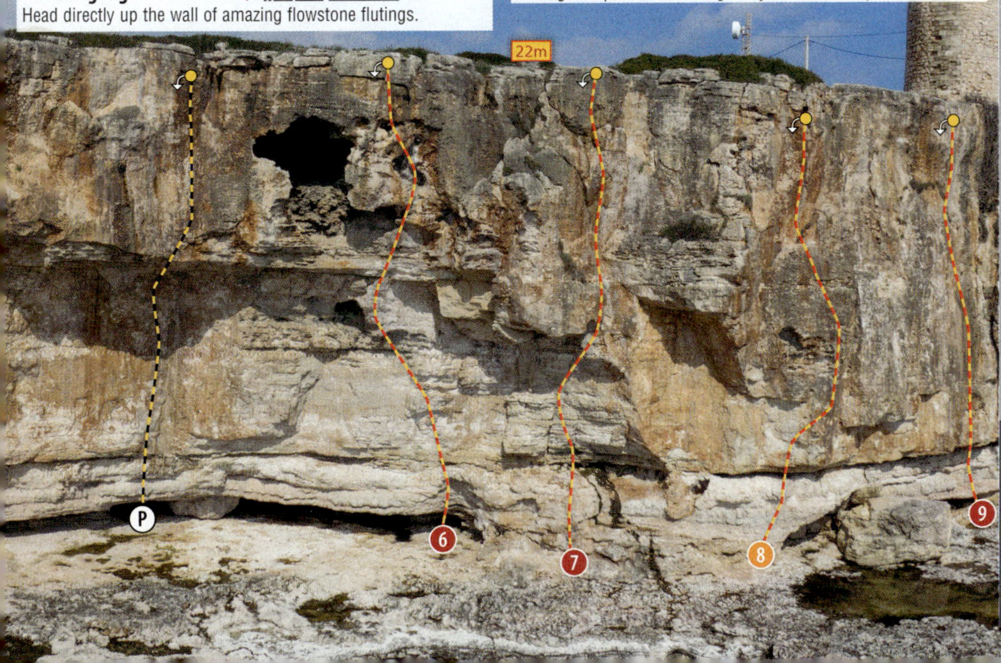

Torre d'en Beu — Sector Germany

Sector Germany
As the platform below the cliff opens out, there is a fine long wall of excellent red rock below the tower. The routes here offer great climbing and are the most popular at this crag.
Approach (map and overview p.292) - Continue past the first section over some boulders to the long red wall.

❶ **Frankllorca** 6a
Follow *Henner* to a ledge and then go left and finish direct.

❷ **Henner** 6a
The wall split by a ledge.

❸ **Hiedro** 5c
A nice climb. Ascend the slab just left of the crack, and then take the excellent steeper crack above to a lower-off.

❹ **Placa** 5c
Make a couple of moves up the crack before stepping right to the initial bolt - can be climbed direct at **6a+**. Continue up the wall direct on great holds.

❺ **Liaka** 6b
Make some fingery pulls to better holds and then move directly up the wall to a thin finish.

❻ **Germany** .... 6a+
The red streak is an excellent pitch that can sometimes seep.

❼ **Diedro** .... 6a+
The corner is quite a struggle.

❽ **Wo Ist Der Fisch?** .... 6b+
Make a slightly powerful start with a big move off crimps. Keep direct above and the holds will appear.

❾ **Derrape Left** .... 6a+
Make a powerful sequence to easier ground.

❿ **Derrape** 6b
Start up *Derrape Left* but continue direct to an interesting finish.

Sector El Gran Pollo Rojo

An attractive roof-topped wall that has unfortunately been equipped with non-stainless steel bolts. One route - the best one - has been fully rebolted.

Approach (map and overview p.292) - Continue past the first section over some boulders to the long red wall.

⓫ Ali el Quimico .... 7a+
The leftmost line. Start on the left then move back up and right.

⓬ El Secre.................... 7c
Climb up left to pass the end of the roof and finish at the lower-off of *Ali el Quimico*.

⑬ El Gran Pollo Rojo........... ?
A hard direct line through the roof.

⑭ Sese Line 8a
The central roof line.

⓯ El Caracol Loco 3 7c
Fully re-equipped. Take the corner to the roof, monkey left and up the slim groove.

⑯ El Toro Sentado............. ?
A variation on *El Caracol Loco*. Climb to the roof and then directly up the short but steep arete.

⓱ Palito de Cangrejo .... 7b+
A direct on *El Caracol Loco*. Climb to the roof and finish up the steep crack.

⓲ Sexy Line 7b
Line to the right of *El Caracol Loco*.

To mid afternoon | 5 min | Sheltered

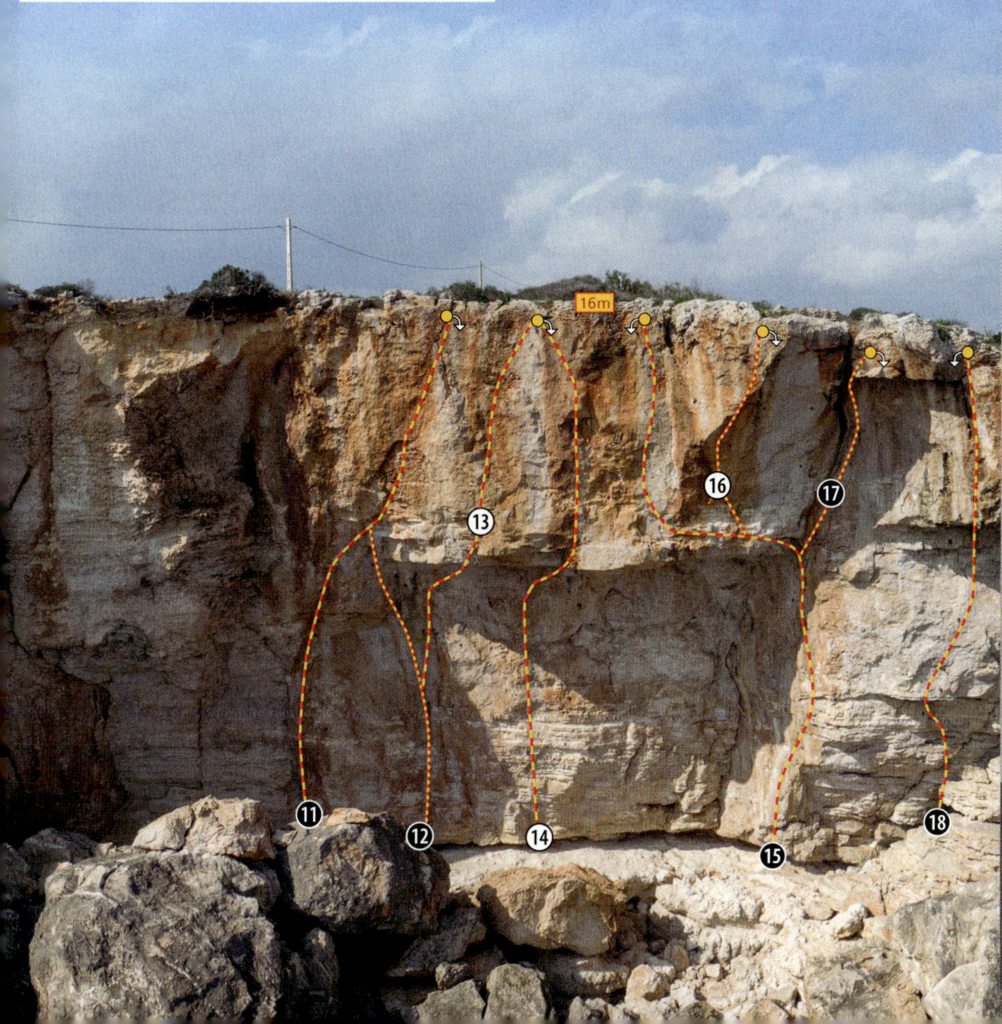

Tijuana

| Grade Spread | 1 | 10 | 28 | 22 | 10 |

This delightful location has a great holiday atmosphere. The routes are less friendly than at other venues nearby, since a good number have fierce undercut starts requiring full power the moment you step off the ground. However, once the starts are conquered the style switches to superb fingery wall climbing. Most of the routes have been re-equipped with staple bolts; treat those which haven't with extreme caution.

Conditions

Tijuana faces due south, and is situated on the opposite side of the island from the mountains, which means that it enjoys a much more settled climate. It is such a good suntrap that it is often too hot, even in winter. There is sometimes a sea breeze but this is usually welcome in the heat. The holds can be greasy, although this isn't as bad as on many sea cliffs.

Bridging up the magnificent corner of *Colesterol Party* (6a+) - *p.305* - at Tijuana. Photo: Mark Glaister

Tijuana

Approach

The cliffs of Tijuana are situated on the southeastern tip of the Island. The drive to this corner is relatively easy, although it can take a while to negotiate all the small villages and towns encountered on the way. On approaching Santanyí village, follow signs for Cala Figuera and Cala Santanyí. From the outskirts of Santanyí continue for around 2km to a roundabout. Go straight on, signed Cala Figuera. About 200m after the roundabout, bear right - this time signed to Cala Santanyí. Take the first left (unsigned) and then the first right (signed 'DRAC'). Continue along this road, to a small traffic island. Park here carefully as it is a residential area and walk past a barrier in the road to a tower on the clifftop. Follow the cliff-edge path right (looking out) until the path drops down to the base of the crag. Turn left along the platform to reach the first routes at Sector Tom and Jerry.

The Southwest
Valldemossa Area
Bunyola Area
North of the Mountains
South of the Mountains
The Northeast
The East Coast

Sector Tom and Jerry

The first feature encountered on the walk around the wave-cut platform at Tijuana is the prominent arete of *Semen de trigo*. To the left of the arete is an easy-angled wall that provides a handful of interesting easier routes. This area is in the shade until later than the other sectors and is a cool haven in the morning during hot weather.
Approach (map and overview p.301) - Walk along the wave-cut platform to the first section you arrive at.

1 Left Wing 6a
A good little route. The hard start is best approached from the left or the right. It can be a bit greasy up to the second bolt. Continue rightwards and then pull over a bulge to finish.

2 Churrito y pelete 5a
Nice climbing starting up a short groove.

3 Tom and Jerry 5c
A tricky climb with some tenuous moves up a thin slab. Harder than it used to be due to rockfall.

4 Ebam 4c
Steady and enjoyable climbing tackling the crack between the two bushes.

5 Inbetweener 5b
A direct line up the wall between *Ebam* and *Ebamsa*.

6 Ebamsa 5a
A technical, slightly polished start gains pleasant, easier climbing above.

The next routes are located to the right, around the other side of a prominent arete.

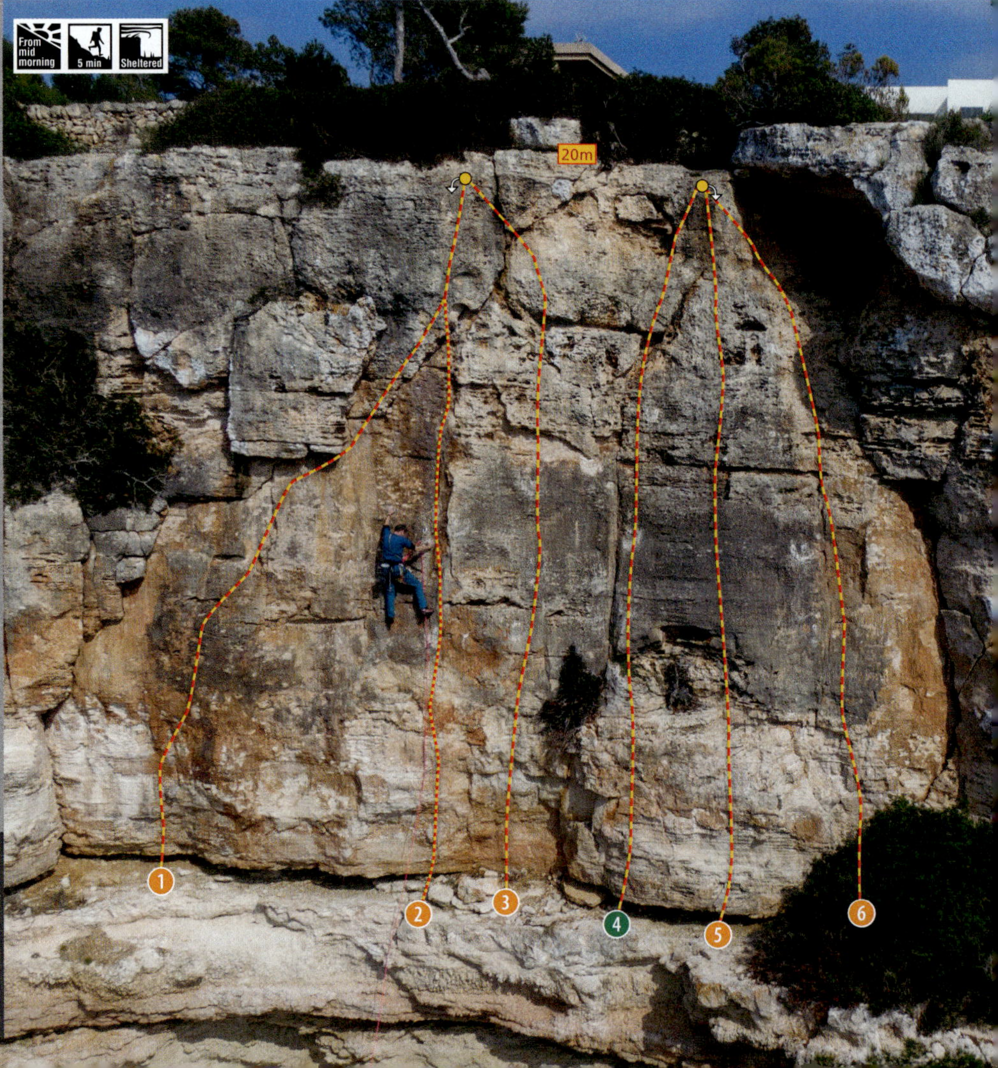

Sector Tapas **Tijuana** 303

7 Commando Foracorda ... 7a+
A steep line up the arete.

8 Semen de trigo ... 6b+
The right-hand side of the arete. Formerly called 'Arista'.

9 Finger Killer ... 6c
The direct is **6c**, the left-hand variation is only **6b+**. Either way, the climbing is very fingery.

10 Foot-hook ... 6c
A thin wall climb with a hard crux left of the corner.

11 Es diedro ... 5c
Start in the corner, then finish up the right wall.

12 Vino tinto ... 6a
The wall right of the corner. A touch polished but interesting.

13 Tapas ... 6a+
Requires a bit of a reach, or some nifty footwork.

14 Blame it on the Rain ... 6c+
Start at the right-hand end of the ledge. A very tough start.

Sector Tapas
Continuing along the wave-cut platform a little further on from Sector Tom and Jerry is the prominent arete of *Semen de trigo*. To the right of the arete is a deep corner set above the platform. Either side of the corner are steep walls with a number of technical wall climbs.
Approach (map and overview p.301) - The corner just beyond Sector Tom and Jerry.

15 Honeymoon ... 7a
Traverse right from the ledge, then up easier-angled rock.

16 Never Mind the Bollocks ... 7a
The left-hand edge of the lower roof and then the bulge and easier-angled wall above.

17 Xiscu que reiliscu ... 6b+
Thuggy! A high first clip - spotter or clipstick advised.

18 Pupé de Roqué ... 6c
The double roof to the right is spectacular.

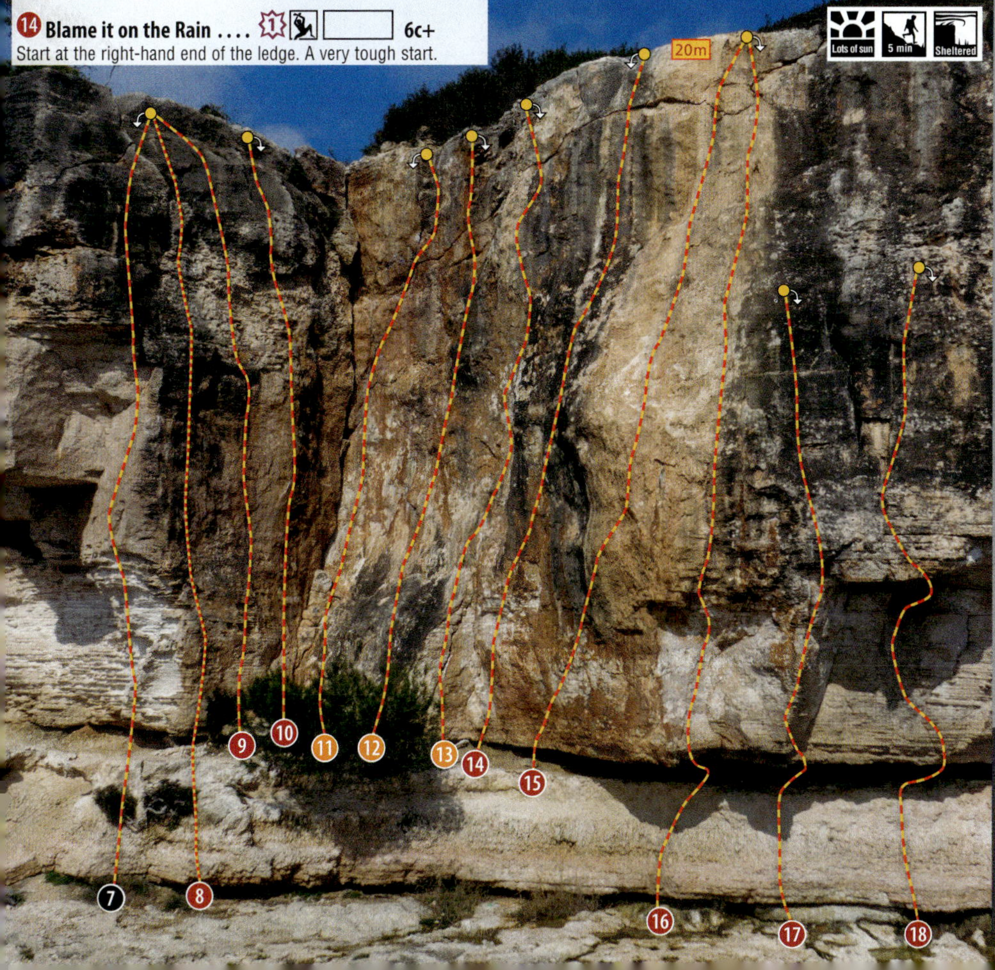

Tijuana — Sector Escuelar de Calor

Sector Escuelar de Calor

The crag here increases in height and becomes undercut at its base. The routes on this section are very impressive and a number of them require a leg-up or chipped holds to start.
Approach (map and overview p.301) - From the right-hand side of Sector Tapas there is a gap of about 50m past a section of white, crumbly overhangs.

❶ Escuelar de calor........ 6b+
Superb juggy climbing through the roofs, followed by a sustained and technical finish.

❷ Supersexi........... 7b
Start up *Escuelar de calor* and then head right. Originally the start was to the right.

**❸ Un dimange à la campange
.... 7a+**
Pull through the overhang and head left then right over a bulge onto the upper wall. Finish up the wall heading slightly right midway.

❹ Tocino for Pepino..... 7a
Start up *Un dimange à la campange* and climb direct once past the initial roof.

❺ Es Nas................ 8a
Bouldery moves out right at the first roof to a lower-off at mid-height.

❻ Siurana es panxi............... 7a+
Pull up on a rope to get established above the low overhang and then climb the corner and wall passing a small roof midway.

❼ Flesh for Dani....... 7b
The drilled roof at the start is reached from someone else's shoulders. The wall above is steep and sustained.

❽ Raixa................ 7c
Hard climbing after making the roof start of *Flesh for Dani*.

Sector Colesterol Party **Tijuana**

Sector Colesterol Party

A fine section of cliff providing an array of high quality pitches on excellent rock. Most of the routes are in the harder grades but many visit this section just to climb the classic *Colesterol Party*.

9 Come piedras .... 7b+
A desperate roof to start, followed by the black arete. Old bolts at present.

10 Cancamos 7b
The centre of the inverted 'V'. The final moves can be avoided by a slightly bold left-hand variant. The first roof is no pushover.

11 Miquel's .... 7b+
A very fine and diverse pitch - one of the best routes on the crag. Start as for *Cancamos* and continue up the sustained wall to a spectacular final groove.

12 Old Amsterdam 8a
Old bolts.

13 La calle de ritmo .... 7b+
At last a route without a hard start but it makes up for it in its higher reaches with a tough upper wall.

14 Psicomambo 6c
A subtle line that gives a memorable route. The shallow corner and grooves lead to the final thin wall.

15 La peli 7b
Glued, chipped and short - though the climbing is good.

16 Cocina ligera 7b
Brilliant climbing past the overhangs and up the arete above.

17 Na c'al les Seychelles 7b
A good route just to the left of the big corner of *Colesterol Party*.

18 Colesterol Party ..... 6a+
The most popular route on the crag. A powerful start allows access to the delightful upper open groove. *Photo p.300.*

Batchcamp - p.306

Tijuana — Sector Poseidon

Sector Poseidon

Sector Poseidon offers more great wall climbs on fantastic rock. The right-hand side of the sector has a handful of easier lines that climb a high bulging headwall, although the rock quality is not as good on these pitches and ledges break up the climbing.

Approach (map and overview p.301) - This section continues on from Colesterol Party area.

❶ Batchcamp .... 7a+
Technical climbing up the blunt arete right of the corner of *Colesterol Party*, finishing just left of the cactus.

❷ To quisqui me toca 7a
A relatively straightforward start up the groove leads to an intense technical sequence on the wall below the cactus.

③ Evola 8a
Start from a ledge level with the end of the main roof. It has a short and super-thin hard section. Formerly called 'Tenacidad'.

④ Raiworld 8b
The line of staples.

⑤ Calabruix .... 8b+
A desperate line up the next set of staples.

⑥ Poseidon 7b
An excellent pitch starting from the little ledge. A thin central section gains a strenuous finish.

Sector Poseidon — Tijuana

7 Chuteur fou .... 7b+
The steep tufa/fluting system is brilliant and slightly reachy.

8 Go Johnny 8a
Steady climbing leads to a desperate crimpy section where reach is useful.

9 Rompepiernas 7a
The wall just right is a tough cookie. Take the steep wall to the bulge. Moving up and right into the scoop is the crux.

10 Naranje 7a
The orange wall just left of the arete is hyper-technical. Old bolts.

11 Espolón .... 6b+
Climb direct. It originally started on the right at the same grade.

12 Casting .... 6b+
Slightly dodgy rock on this one.

13 Executive Producer .... 6c+
Sustained climbing just left of the two caves.

14 Cumoshot .... 6c+
This one has a thin crux move.

15 Screenplay 6c
Branch right - hard in the middle section.

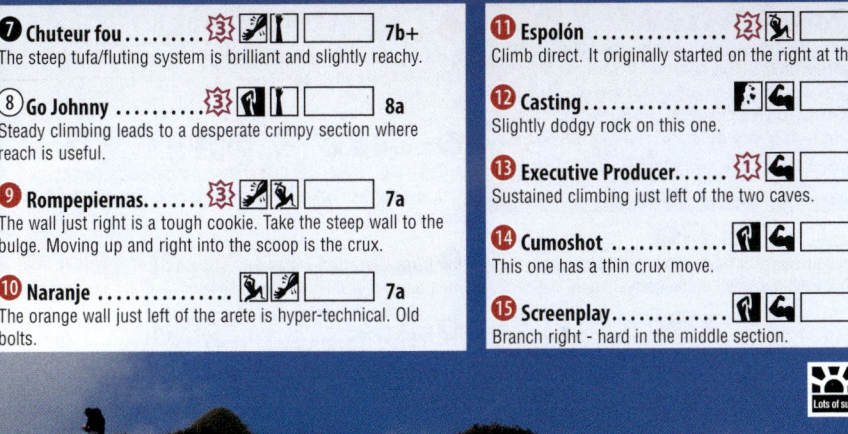

Tijuana — Sector den Jaume

Sector den Jaume
An excellent wall that has a good selection of lines and grades. All are well bolted and on very good rock. This wall also has the advantage of going into the shade late on in the afternoon - a real blessing on warm days.
Approach (map and overview p.301) - Walk along the base of the walls and around the far arete where the sector comes into view.

1 Trencaclosques .... 6a+
Start up the jamming crack, or the wall just to its right, and climb to an easing midway. Finish up the steep fingery wall.

2 S'alegria .... 6c+
A promising-looking line that unfortunately builds to a stopper finish on the very bald headwall.

3 Sa pena 7a
A good pitch up the gradually steepening wall - on some fantastic holds - to a final crux sequence just before the lower-off.

4 Postal Service .... 7a+
Another worthwhile line that starts up a gentle section of the wall and finishes with some fierce and technical sequences in its upper half.

5 Blick Uber den Telland 7b
A hard upper wall finishing on the left side of the high roof.

6 High Line .... 7a+
Start up the crack to an easing midway. The fingery crux sequence leads to a roof. Head right to the lower-off.

7 Newer Line 6c
To the left of the route *High and Wild Left* is a line with new bolts. A sandy wall leads to a final steep crux section.

8 High and Wild Left (2★) **6b+**
A spectacular pitch. Start on the left and work right into the crack-line. Move up to the overhang and climb the steep corner to some good holds at its end.

9 High and Wild Direct (2★) **6c+**
A very tough start through the roof gains the upper section of *High and Wild Left*.

10 Meteo (2★) **7c+**
Move out onto the left-hand bolt-line after the initial wall.

11 Tijuana (3★) **8a**
Move out right from *Meteo*.

12 Sa des plastics (2★) **7b+**
The direct line. *Photo p.260.*

13 Moscovita (2★) **8b**
The bolted line between *Sa des plastics* and *Welcome to Paradise*.

14 Welcome to Paradise (3★) **7b+**
A good-looking wall pitch. High in the grade.

15 Perestroika (3★) **8c**
Very technical wall climbing.

16 Moscu (2★) **8a**
A variation right-hand finish to *Perestroika*.

17 Costa sud (2★) **6c**
An excellent line that incorporates some fairly pressing moves in its mid-section.

18 Costa sud Right (1★) **6b**
A worthwhile little pitch, again with a couple of tricky moves midway.

19 Tarta Lemon (1★) **6b+**
A tough, thin crack-line.

20 Totsol com un mussol (1★) **6b+**

Lots of sun · 6 min · Sheltered

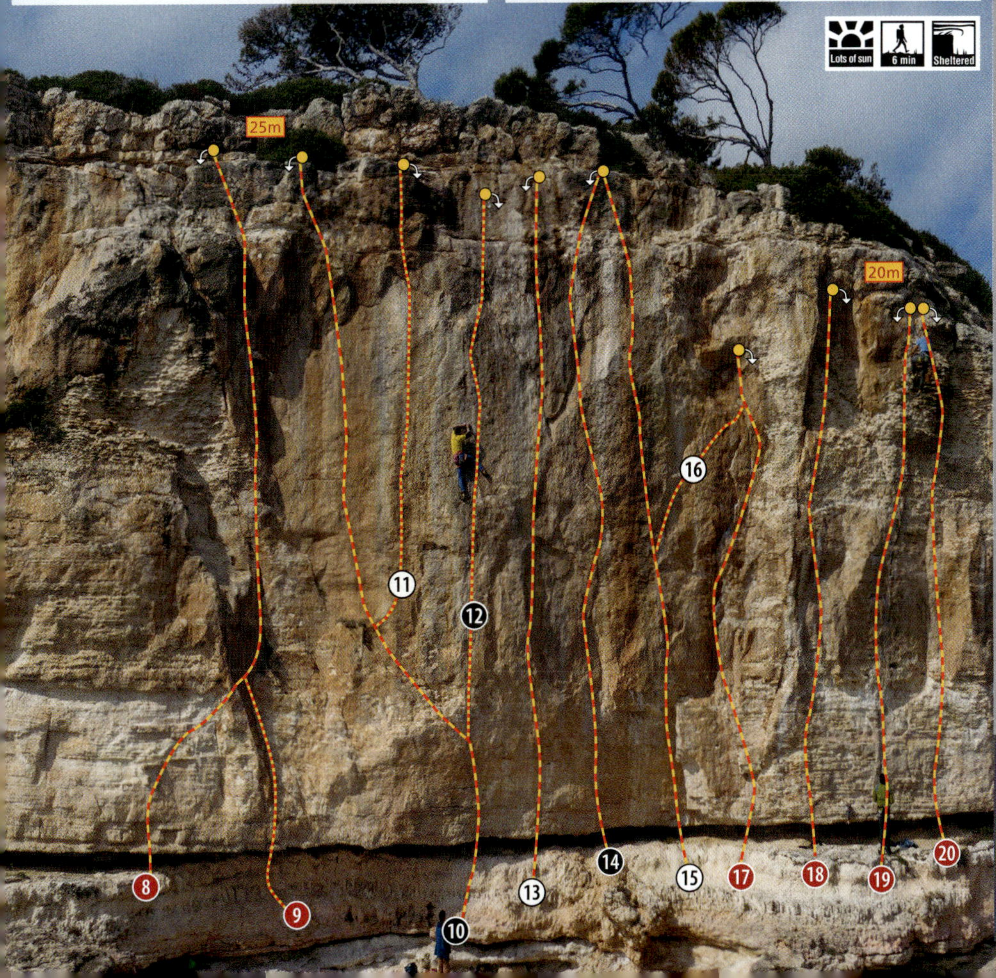

The Southwest
Valldemossa Area
Bunyola Area
North of the Mountains
South of the Mountains
The Northeast
The East Coast

Mallorca Sport Climbs — Route Index

Stars	Grade	Route	Photo	Page
**	7a+	!Mis Vecinos son Yonquis!		216
***	7c	¡Muérete ya!		202
***	7c+	¿Amigos para siempre?		202
**	4c	100 duros		250
	6b	150 Sipis		239
***	7a+	25 de agosto		184
***	6b	3D		270
*	4c	4++		271
*	6c+	666		170
*	5a	7 vidas y una más		251
	7b+	7b+ Route		226
	8a	8a Route		227
**	7b	A.		202
**	6b	Abel		46
**	6a	Abelles mortals		269
*	4c	abuela y sus pelotas, La		95
*	6c	Aferra el tul		202
**	7b	Aferrar i xapar		110
*	7c	Agárrate maldito		163
*	7c+	Agárrate Ruiz de la Prada		227
°°	8a	Agent Orange		191
*	7c	Agresió física		230
*	7b	Aguila Bonelli		102
*	6c+	Agujetas perpetuas		214
*	7c	Ai Ai		194
**	7a+	Airbus		195
*	4a	Aitornillo		91
***	7a+	Aixi es maten		230
*	6b+	Aixo es L'Habana		197
	7b+	Aixo Right		197
*	6a+	Al Capone		46
**	7a+	Al Mar		61
***	6b+	Al tanto que va de canto	75	76
*	5c	Alacran		78
***	7a+	Alan Bator		157
***	4c	Albahida (Gubia Normal)		154
	5c	Alegría		52
***	6b+	Algo salvaje	142	146
	7a+	Ali el Quimico		299
	8a	Ali-up		206
**	6c+	All Right		129
	6a	Almudaina		258
**	7c	Aloha from Hell		174
*	5a	Alternative Start (Sa Gubia)		157
*	6a	Alternative Start (Sa Mola de Felanitx)		270
*	5a	Alzheimer		250
***	7b	American	58	60
**	7c	American Airlines		71
°°°	8a	American Express		226
°°°	8b+	Amnesia		172
*	6a+	Amon Ra		130
**	7c	Amoniac amb sal		110
	7b	Anamvichi		111
	5c	Angsthase		239
*	7c+	Anti-natural		126
***	6c+	Anusqui		69
**	7a	Apendre tort		244
*	7a	Apnea		74
	5b	Approach Slab		52
*	6a	Aprendiendo a Volar		59
	4c	Aprendizaje por tercios		77
*	6b	Aquiles		103
°°°	8a	Aresta gore		126
*	6c	Arete Right		124
	7a	arete, The		197
°°	8a+	Ariestocrata		230
	7a+	Arista y diedro		137
**	6a+	Armin H Best Husband		295
**	6c	Arran		103
	7b	Arroz con leche		137
*	7a	Arrufa es cul		225
	6b+	Asteroide		53
***	6b+	Asulla		281
**	6a+	Asuquí		281
*	6a	Atila		250
°°	8a	Autoestopista, El		60
**	6b+	Average		136
*	7a	B.		202
**	5a	Baba		238
***	6b	Baixem una estrella		229
*	6b+	Balanceta		111
*	7a+	Ball de bot		226
	6b	Ball o'en banyeta verda		239
**	6a	bandido de un brazo, El		122
***	5c	Banita		286
	5a	barbut, Es		160
	6c+	Barco de rejilla		129
*	6a+	Barracuda		295
	8a+	Bart Simpson		195
*	7a+	Batchcamp		306
*	6c	Bateria baixa		90
°°°	8a	Be good		263
**	6b	Beachball Hole		296
**	6a+	Beachcomber		280
**	4a	Bechti2go		286
*	7c	Beirut		263
***	6b+	Benas	291	297
*	6c+	Bernadí Company		191
*	6a+	Beschenka Belka		287
*	4c	Betty		295
*	6a	Between the Trees	55	53
***	7a+	Bicep Blowout		120
	6b	Big Boulder		289
	8a+	Big Boy		197
°°°	8a+	Big Men	28	173
	6c	Big Red Stain, The		278
***	7c+	Big Sebastian		289
*	6c	Bilitron		77
***	7b	Billie Boy		220
*	7c	Bingo		230
*	7a	Black Block		104
	7b+	Black hole		172
**	7a+	Black Line		221
	6a+	Black Streak		239
*	6c+	Blame it on the Rain		303
*	6a	Blancanieves		248
	7b	Blick Uber den Telland		308
*	6a	Blob Indirect, The		222
	6b	Blob Right-hand, The		222
*	6c	Blob, The		222
***	6c	Blobland	180	186
**	6c	Blobland Right		186
***	7b+	Blobs 'n' Bushes		204
**	7b+	Blunt Arete		111
	6b+	Blunt Rib Left		68
	6b+	Blunt Rib Right		68
°°°	8a+	Bobo dodo		173
***	7a	Bobo dodo (L1)		173
***	7b+	Bobo dodo (L2)		173
	6c	Body Fatigue		278
*	7b+	Bofetadas de placer		165
**	6a+	Boira		295
**	7b	Boite, La		70
**	6b+	bolas del chino L1, Las		219
**	7a	bolas del chino, Las	217	219
*	6a	Bolt Whisperer		218
***	6c	Bombay Bicycle Club		129
*	7a+	Bomber torrat		127
**	6c	Bomberos Direct		157
**	4c	Bon profit		91
**	6a+	Bon vi		187
***	6b	Bona nyic		191
**	7a+	Bongo bongo		163
*	7a	Bordillo		259
*	6c	Borinot		191
*	5b	Born Slippy		128
°°°	8a	Bota Petit		227
	f6C+	Bota petit Start		227
**	6c	Botifoll		129
**	7a+	Boudica		131
	5c	Boulder Route, The		238
	7a+	Bubu		259
***	6b+	Bubu mac		188
***	7a	Buf!		207
**	6b+	Bufon		77
°°°	8a	Buitres Negros		209

Route Index — Mallorca Sport Climbs — 311

Stars	Grade	Route	Photo	Page
	7c	Bulge and Recesses		194
	?	Bulge and Wall		82
***	6a+	Bulge By-pass		203
**	7b+	Bulging Wall		136
*	6b+	Buñocracia		127
*	6c	Burandanga		130
	7a+	Buscador de Cordura		296
	7a+	Bush rit et Massacre		150
*	6c+	Busibus		120
**	6b+	Butter Fingers		130
**	6b	Buzzewackele		289
	6c	C.		202
**	6b	Ça fels good		288
*	6a+	Ca magre, puçes		239
	7c	Ca'n Bum		172
**	7b	Ca'n Furiós		221
*	7a+	Caca de colores		170
*	6c+	Cachinochalgo		219
***	7a	Cachlnochalgo Left		219
***	7a+	Cachogenesis Explosiva		61
*	6c	Cadena Perpetua		46
*	6c	Cafe del Mar.		61
**	7b	Café del Sol		78
*	6a+	Cafetut		103
*	5b	Cagadero de Gineta		130
**	5a	cagao, Las		120
*	6b+	Cain		46
***	7a+	Cain Extension		46
**	6a	Cala Bruix		76
	8b+	Calabruix		306
**	6c+	Caldero, El		46
*	6c+	Calimocho		74
ººº	8a	Calladita estás más guapa		231
**	7b+	calle de ritmo, La		305
*	6c	calvario del enano, El		225
*	7b+	Camino al infierno		77
**	5c	Camisasque	31	238
***	6b+	Campamento Balanceta		111
*	6c	Campamento para gordos		111
*	6c+	Canal Rocks		256
*	7b	Cancamos		305
***	7b+	Canibalismo vaginal		220
**	6a	Canibalismo vaginal L1		220
ºº	8a	Canibalismo variant		220
*	4c	Cannabis		160
*	4c	Cannabis in vitro		160
**	5a	Cantimplora rosa		130
*	4c	Canto de la Hormiga, El		59
**	6c	canto del loco, El		76
**	7b+	cantò, Es		113
*	7a+	Cantos picados		196
*	4b	Cap Pelat		63
*	4a	Caperucita		94
*	6b	Caperucita roja		162
**	7a+	Capiacua		232
*	7a+	Capitan gotera		225
*	5c	Captain Nemo		281
***	7c+	Capuccino		60
***	7c	Caracol Loco, El		299
	6a	Carrero de nit		129
*	7c	Casi		127
	6b+	Casting		307
**	6b	Catalina Cisna		269
**	7a+	Cave Left	277	279
*	7a	Cave Lip		280
*	6b+	Cave Right (Cala M)		279
	?	Cave Right (Santa P)		82
*	6a	Cazador, El		71
	6c?	CB 1		287
***	7b+	Cementerio de Sabo		130
*	5c	Central		222
**	6b+	Central Flake		136
**	6a	Central Pockets		69
**	6b	Central Right		136
	4a	Centro		140
**	6c+	Charismatic		165
*	7a+	Charly danone		155
**	6a	Cheers		72
**	6a+	Chelsea Smile		128
**	6a	Chicharra loca		73
ººº	8a+	Chill Out		196
	6a	Chimenea 1 (Valldemossa)		140
***	5c	Chimenea 2 (Valldemossa)		136
**	7a	Chiringuito		194
**	7a	Chisparitas		124
	6a	Chispita		248
*	6b+	Chitas marchitas		155
	7a	Choni chapa		221
***	7a+	Chorrera		78
	4c	Chris line		177
	6c+	Chu, chu, chu..		78
***	6c	Chungui chunguez		148
*	6a	Chúpamela		78
**	5a	Churrito y pelete		302
*	6a	Churro pino		177
***	7b+	Chuteur fou		307
	7a+	Circ		137
*	6b	Cisne Negro		295
*	7b	Citroën		245
***	7c	Claro de Luna		209
**	5b	Clásica		281
*	5c	Climber Gay		162
**	7b	Cloncíon		207
***	7b+	Club super tres		188
**	7b	Cocina ligera		305
*	7a+	Cocolino		221
***	6a+	Colesterol Party	300	305
***	7b	Colgao		226
**	6c	Coliflor women		229
**	6c	Colmena		74
*	6a	Colorado		245
***	7b	colores de la caliza, Los		150
***	7a+	Columna		78
*	6b	Comando rasta		177
***	7a	Combat Rock		148
***	7a	Combat Rock P1		148
	7b+	Come piedras		305
**	6a+	Comechochos		148
*	7a+	Commando Foracorda		303
ººº	8a	Commando Madrid		226
**	5a	Con el culo al aire		122
**	6a	Con el puno por debajo		218
**	6a+	Con el rabo entre las piernas	86	91
**	7b	Congo Mongo		131
**	5a	Coordina coordinator		238
º	8a	Coquito ergo sum		231
*	6c	Corbata Columbiana		128
**	6a+	Corrich		219
***	7c	Cortado		60
***	6c	Cortocircuito		163
ººº	8b	Corvus		209
**	6c	Costa sud		309
*	6b	Costa sud Right		309
**	7c+	Cotorrot		176
***	6c	Cous-cous		177
*	5b	Covas Bros		88
**	5c	Crack		279
ºº	8a	Cripta, La		70
*	5a	Cris Tocino		89
*	7a	Cristo en pel, taronges navel		222
	6c	Crozzle Pillar Left		184
*	6b	Crozzle Pillar Right		184
*	6b	Crozzly Wall		258
*	5c	crui, Es		271
	5b	Cruila fi		269
**	6a+	Cuando Los Elefantes Sueñan con la Música		68
*	6b	Cuatre pichos		74
***	6a	Cubeza de Patata	124	128
*	7c+	Cubo de Sabo		131
***	7c	Cuencamelo		174
	6a	Cuevana		196
	6c+	Cuevana Right		196
*	7a	cul mos cou, Es		111
	6a	Cul Pelut		63
**	5c	culo, El		122
	6c+	Cumoshot		307

The Southwest · Valldemossa Area · Bunyola Area · North of the Mountains · South of the Mountains · The Northeast · The East Coast

Mallorca Sport Climbs — Route Index

Stars	Grade	Route	Photo	Page
	4b	Cunilingus		78
**	5a	Curset		238
	7a	curta, La		256
*	5b	Curving Groove		222
**	6a+	Cut Loose	23	296
**	6a	D.		202
*	5c	Dali		140
*	7b+	Dame argo		72
**	6b	Danzomanía		148
**	5c	Danzomanía P1		148
	5b	Darrera sa pared		271
**	6b	Day of the Reflection		216
∞∞∞	8a	De gorrones hasta los cojones		159
**	7b+	De malas a peor		229
∞∞	8a	Debil Mente		74
***	6c+	Decadencia corporal		148
***	7a+	Decision hit		230
*	7c	Decota decotador		229
∞∞	8a	Defcon one		126
**	6b+	Deichwand		288
?		Delicatessan		276
**	7b	Delicatessan Right-hand		276
**	6c	Demencia clitorania		221
*	6a+	Demonicat		269
**	7b	Depinyolvermell		219
	4a	Derecho		140
	6b	Derecho castilla		141
***	6b	Derrape		298
**	6a+	Derrape Left		298
**	6b+	Desconocido		90
***	6a	Deshauciados, Los		53
∞∞∞	8a	Diablo		159
**	5c	Diagonal		297
***	6a	Diagonal Combination		53
	6a+	Diagonal Pockets		278
**	6b	Dias como estas		269
**	6a	Die toten hosen	267	271
***	7c	Die Toten Hosen		227
	f6C+	Die Toten Hosen Start		227
	6c	Diedre		126
**	6a+	Diedro		298
	6c	Diedro y placa		137
*	5c	diedro, Es		303
**	7b+	Dies de Sol		289
**	6c+	Dig for Gold		209
***	7a+	Dingo		276
*	6c	Dios, no puedo!		79
**	5c	Dios, si puedo!		79
*	7a+	Directe verde		127
**	7b	Directland		186
*	4b	Discópolis		68
*	7a+	Dit I fet		188
*	5c	DJ'S Club		215
*	6b	Doctor Feel Good		216
*	7a+	Doctor Jeremiah		131
*	7a+	Doctor maligno		225
*	6a	Dog Sniffer		128
**	6a+	Doktor Michi		288
*	5c	Dona Simena		76
*	6c	Doog		73
**	6c+	Dos bidedos y un destino		225
	7b	Dosis		186
**	6c+	Double Life of Marvel, The		128
**	6a	Duck		72
***	6b	Duke		244
***	7a	DVD Nasty		130
	6c	E.O.S		102
*	3a	Easy		286
*	6b+	Easy Open Groove		195
	3c	Easy Slab (Caimari)		216
	4c	Easy Slab (Sa Gubia)		160
**	6c+	Easy White		78
**	6a+	Eating Hooks	282	287
*	4c	Ebam		302
*	4c	Ebam 1		88
*	4c	Ebam 2		88
*	5a	Ebamsa		302
*	5c	Edelweiß		288
∞∞∞	8a	Efecto mariposa		231
	6a	Eliminate (S'estret)		120
	?	Eliminate (Valldemossa)		140
*	6b+	Ella ya no vive aqui		74
***	5c	Elmo Love		288
	6b+	Els corderos atacan de nuevo		238
**	6b+	Els salvatjes		187
	6c+	Els salvatjes Right		187
**	6b	Embrujada		153
***	6b+	EMI		214
	5c	EMI Right		214
?		Empalma Cantos, El		159
∞∞∞	8b	Empire State		226
**	6c	En Miquel está fumat		245
*	5c	En pas descanse		278
*	6b	Enanismo emocional		218
**	5a	End Slab 1		120
*	5b	End Slab 2		120
*	6c+	Endemicus		77
**	6c	enterrador, El		113
*	7a+	Entre dos		113
*	7a+	Entre tres		113
?		Entrepa		197
?		Equilibrium tremens		71
*	6c	Equipo Coliflor		71
*	6a	Erectus		77
***	6c+	Escaladores en la niebla		150
***	7b	Escalfament		233
***	7c	Escamas de Dragon		209
**	6c+	Esclatabutses		111
*	4c	Escoleta (Capdella)		46
	5a	Escoleta (Sa Mola de Felanitx)		270
***	6b+	Escuelar de calor		304
**	6a	Espabilaos	27	91
*	6b+	Espolón		307
	6b+	Espolon Timy		221
***	7c+	Espresso		60
**	7b+	Esteban		202
**	6c+	Esto no es Calvià		177
**	7a+	Esto no es quinto superior		146
**	7b	Estreny els dits		197
***	5c	Estricnina		148
*	7c	Eternum		146
*	6a+	Ettringen		270
**	7b+	Euribor		78
	8a	Evola		306
***	6a	Excalibur		165
*	6c+	Executive Producer		307
	7b+	Extrema Unción		70
**	6a	Facil	253	258
*	6c	Fakir		171
**	4c	Fallen Angel	115	121
*	6a	Familia Iscariote		166
	6b	Familia variante		166
**	6b	Fantasmas al amanecer		95
*	5a	Far Far Left Slab		216
*	5a	Far Left Slab		216
	7b	Far Right 7b		197
*	6a	Far right line		203
	8a+	fari aparca, El		229
**	7b	Farina de força		194
*	6a+	Faro	293	297
**	6b+	Fat Climbers		129
*	7a	Fatima		103
***	7b	ferreret, Es		113
***	7b	Fes lo que puguis		173
***	7c	Ficalito		188
***	7c	Fido Dido		263
*	6a	Fido-dido		203
**	7a	Fill de puta		194
*	6a+	Fill de ric		155
**	6b+	Fina y segura		162
	5c	Final de Ximanea		269
	6b+	final line, The		281
**	6c	Finger Killer		303
**	6c	fingidor d'orgasmes, El		230
*	7b	Firo 2014		128
	4c	First Strike		268

Route Index — Mallorca Sport Climbs

Stars	Grade	Route	Photo	Page
**	5c	Fisura (El Caló de Betlem)		255
**	6c	Fisura (Puig de Garrafa)		72
**	5c	Fisura (Valldemossa)		140
	7b	Fisura fina		137
*	6b+	Fito		139
	5c	Flake and Groove		171
*	6b	Flake and wall		113
	6a	Flake Route		82
	6b+	Flake Route Right		82
	7a	Flake to Overlap		103
***	7c+	Flashback Samurai		209
***	6c+	Flaying Machine	125	129
*	7b	Flesh for Dani		304
*	5c	Florinotto		279
***	7b	FMI		104
***	7c	Foam Party		202
*	5a	Fondo sur		95
*	6c	Foot-hook		303
ooo	8a	Football Fan		172
*	3b	Fora nirvis		88
	8b	Foracorda		159
ooo	8a+	Foracorda Junior		196
*	4c	Formigas		63
***	6c	Franceses		162
**	6a+	Franceses P1		162
	5c	Frankenjura		268
	6a	Frankllorca		298
**	7b	Freaky, The		220
*	7a	Free Tibet		245
ooo	8b	French Kiss		173
*	7a+	Frijolito		221
*	5a	Frit		203
*	7b+	Front 242		146
*	4a	fuerzas de la oposición, Las		88
**	5a	Fup		72
*	6b+	Gaditana, La		215
*	6c	Galiana m'engana		279
**	7c	Gallos Go Home!		131
***	7a+	Ganxito Perfecto		131
	7a+	Gato negro		150
**	7a	Gatos en Llamas		130
oo	8a	Gaucho		176
**	7b	Gay Power		148
**	7a	Genma		113
*	6a+	Germany		298
*	6b+	Ghandi		245
*	7a	gigante verde, La		127
**	7b	Gigoló		163
**	7c	Giramita		72
**	7b	Glasgow Kiss		128
**	7b+	Glasnost		174
***	6c+	Glenlivert		295
*	6b+	Glory Hole		271
	4c	Glückspilz		239
	7b+	Glue-ins		202
ooo	8a	Go Johnny		307
oo	8a	Gold Single Traverse		230
*	7c	golpe de gas, A		233
ooo	8a	Goo Goo Mack		171
**	7c+	Google		263
***	7c+	Gorg Blau		196
*	5a	Grade 5		226
	7c	Grado residual		196
*	6b	Gran Lubina		218
***	6b+	Gran pis		166
?		Gran Pollo Rojo, El		299
**	6c+	Gran Prepucio		129
*	5c	Gran Turismo		152
***	7b+	grau del ruc, Es		231
**	6b+	Grau, Es		104
	4c	Grey Slab Left		209
	4c	Grey Slab Right		209
*	6a	Groove		162
*	5a	Groove and Wall		91
	6b	Groove Right-hand		162
	6c	Groove, The		82
*	6c+	grupis, Las		230
*	6a	Guatón		148
***	7c+	Gueropa		194
*	4c	guerra de las galaxies, La		122
	8b	Guiris go Home		227
	8b+	Guiris Left		227
**	6b+	Gusto mo palo		287
*	6b	Hambre eterna		157
**	5b	Hamburg Rocks		289
*	6a	Hans-Peter		289
*	7c	Happy End		78
*	6b+	Hard Finish		177
	7a	Hard One, The		222
*	7b	Harissa		170
	5a	Hawaii 5-0		166
o	8a	Hay Noray!		146
***	7b+	Hay que joderse pa no caerse		71
*	6a+	Haz tu Zurollo con orgullo		130
oo	8a+	Head hunter		126
**	7a	Heavy Metalurgia		296
**	5c	Hematoma	cover	52
**	4b	Hembras		89
	6a	Henner		298
*	4a	Herbofilia		279
**	5c	Hiedro		298
*	6b	Hielo Negro		54
	6c+	Hielo Negro Left		54
**	6c+	High and Wild Direct		309
**	6b+	High and Wild Left		309
***	7a+	High Line		308
	7a	Higiene cerebral		214
	8a	Hijo de Cain		46
*	6c+	Hijo de Cain (L1)		46
**	7b	Hijo de Cain (L2)		46
**	6c+	Hippipunklperriklautico		219
*	7a	Ho passam pillo		191
***	7a	Hob nobs		206
	6a	Hola qué tal		203
**	6b+	Holland Tigger, The		129
	7a	Honeymoon		303
**	7b+	Hoodoo Gurus		227
**	5c	Hoog Catharijne		286
***	6a	Hooters		72
*	5a	Hooters Right		72
	7c	Horilous		259
*	7a	Horrible belleza		165
*	7b	Hostal Paraiso		245
*	6c+	Hot consuela		165
	8b	Hotel glamour		229
*	3b	Hoy Empieza Todo		68
***	6b+	Human Centipede		130
ooo	8a+	Humanoide		173
*	6a+	Humi		148
**	5c	Humor Amarillo		59
*	4c	Hunter's Gun, The		166
	6c	Hussein		239
	6a	Hyperion		238
	6a+	Hyperion derecho		238
*	7b+	Idem		159
***	7b+	Idiot Ballroom		204
**	6c	Ignatius		129
*	7b	Ilegales		76
**	5c	Im vierten Monat		289
**	7c	Imagine		276
*	4c	imperio contrataca, El		122
?		Impossible		191
*	5c	Imserso		215
	5c	Imserso Left		215
**	5b	Inbetweener		302
*	6a+	Inclino		63
*	6b+	Inesperda		206
***	7c	Influjos Solares		209
?		Ingravito		231
	7a	Inteligencia Artificial		70
**	7a	Interstellar Overdrive		131
	7a+	Interval training		150
**	6c	Intrépido		138
*	6a	Intricate	100	103
	7a+	invierno en Alemania es una Kaka, El		72
	6b+	Isla Bonita Original, La		162

Mallorca Sport Climbs — Route Index

Stars	Grade	Route	Photo	Page
***	6a+	Isla Bonita, La		162
*	7a	It's Tricky		268
	6a	Itchy feet		.71
	4c	Izquierdo		140
	6c	Ja me pagaràs		239
***	7a	Ja som five		188
	6c+	Jarcha		137
*	5a	jardín de la abuela, El		160
*	3c	Jardiners sense fronteres		279
**	7b	Jarribaras		220
	6a	Jarribaras L1		220
	6c	Jarribaras Left-hand		220
**	6a+	Je suis Charlie		.53
**	7a+	Jeremy		219
	6c	Jerita		238
*	5c	Jetsam		281
*	6a+	Joan 90		255
***	7c	Joan Petit		194
***	7a	Joc de mans		280
	6b+	Jódete y baila		155
*	6a	JoJo		268
	6c+	Juanchi no pudo!		.74
**	7a+	Juanma		255
*	6b	Jubilado Direct		139
*	5c	jubilado, El		138
***	7a	Judas		.46
*	5c	Juggy One, The		280
***	7a+	Jungle hop		171
	6b+	Just Married		239
***	7c	justciero, El		231
*	6c+	K.G.B		165
	6c+	Kaito		.53
	6b+	Kalandraka		214
**	6b	Kalki		288
***	7c	Karakorum		197
***	7a	Karma Cabra		131
*	6a	Karma Cabra P1		131
*	6a+	Kiko (Alaró)		209
**	6b	Kiko (Valldemossa)		138
*	7b+	Kilometre 13		229
***	7b	King Conguito		131
*	6a+	King of Quint		122
*	6a	Kirsten		137
*	5c	Kirsten II		137
*	6b	Krilin		238
°°	8a	Kudota		263
***	7a+	Kum laude		120
***	6a	L'amo de Baltix m'envia		281
*	6a	la fresca, A		225
***	7c	Labdance		.79
*	5c	Ladri di Arange		.47
*	6b+	Langostino		248
*	6a	Lanky		136
	6c+	Lastrolophithicus		239
***	7c	Le gorille a une bonne mine		172
°°°	8a	Le lapin en décomposition		150
	?	Leaning Arete		140
**	7a+	Leather Face		148
**	7a+	Leche de Milf		130
*	6b	Left Edge		138
*	6a	Left Line		204
*	6a+	Left Loop		270
*	6a	Left Pillar		170
*	6a	Left Wing		302
*	6b+	Left-slanting Crack		258
	?	Leftest Edge		138
*	7b+	Legado, El		.76
*	6b	Less Purchase		226
**	7a+	Let's deux		232
	6b+	Leuchtturm		239
*	6a	ley del deseo P1, La		155
***	6a	ley del deseo, La		157
**	6b	Liaka		298
*	6b	Lichen Muncher		131
	6c+	Link In		104
*	6b	Lion Slayer, The		.71
***	6b+	Lisa Simpson		195
	6c	Lladre de somnis		278
*	6b+	Lluvia dorado		209
***	7b	Lluvia providencial		150
*	7c+	Lo más		197
**	6c+	Locura Temporal		296
*	6c+	Lola's		197
***	7b	Lone Ranger		209
°°°	8a+	Long Beach		196
**	4c	Lord of the Rings		238
***	7c	Lorenzo Pinch, The		131
**	6a+	Lubeca		288
*	6b	Lucas (Caimari)	213	225
*	6a	Lucas (Capdella)		.46
**	6b	Lucas (Puig de Garrafa)		.74
	6a	Lucas (Sa Cantera)		.94
**	6b	Lucas (Torre d'en Beu)		295
**	6a	Lucia		.59
*	5b	Luisa en la repisa		197
**	6a	Luisa me avisa		197
**	6b+	Lulu		166
*	7a	Lumbago permanent		113
**	7c	Luna		209
°°°	8a+	lunaticos, Los		220
**	7a	Lute		204
*	6a+	lute, El		216
°°°	8b	M & M's		226
*	6a	Macaco		.77
*	6a	Macaco radiactivo		.90
°°°	8a+	Macchiato		.60
***	7c	Machado, La		186
*	7a	madura me ma pone dura, La		221
***	7a+	Magnum		205
*	5b	Makarenko		.91
*	7a	Mako 11		.53
°°°	8a	Mala llet forastera		194
**	7a	Maldito Newton		.61
*	5a	mallas de cristo, Las		203
	5a	Manada salvaje		.94
*	6a+	Manada, La		.89
*	7b	Maños moñas		130
*	6a	Mantis		225
	6c+	Maquina Infernal		295
*	6b+	Mar de Fons		296
***	6a	mar del amor, El	187	188
*	6b+	Margaritas, Las		216
*	7a	Marge Simpson		195
**	5c	Maria		287
***	5b	Mario moreno		121
***	5a	Mario moreno II		121
*	6a	Mariol.lo		102
	7b+	Marmade		177
***	6c+	Marmita, La	24	.46
*	4b	Marta's Stairway		288
*	6c	martell de Thor, El		245
*	6b+	Mas loco k el loco		130
°°°	8b+	Master Hit	223	226
*	6a	Master P1, The		155
*	6a	Master, The		157
**	7a+	Mata guiris		202
**	6a	matate chorrea, La		220
*	7c	Max Cady		191
	7c	Maximo riesgo		127
*	6a	Medizincentrum Santanyi	264	270
*	6a+	Méjico lindo		157
	6a+	Menage à trois		120
*	6a	Mes rapit suc el vent		148
*	6b	Mescalina		225
	7a+	Metal Fatigue		278
**	7c+	Meteo		309
**	6c+	Mexicans Forever		120
**	6b	Mexicans Left		120
**	6b+	Mi darmata		220
*	5b	Middle of Slab		216
***	6a	Mig día		.54
***	7c+	Miguel and the test tube babies		174
	6c	Miguelín el travieso		278
*	7b+	Miju		160
*	6c	Miko Moko		209
*	7b+	Milu		221

Route Index — Mallorca Sport Climbs 315

Stars	Grade	Route	Photo	Page
	6c	Mini yo.		225
*	7b	Mipichica.		160
***	7b+	Miquel's.		305
ooo	8b	Mirall, Es.		71
*	6c	Mirame y no me Toques.		296
*	7a+	Miseducation.		83
ooo	8b+	misión, La.		196
***	7b+	Miss Palma.		173
*	7c	Mission Possible.		78
**	6a+	Mister 40.		91
***	7a+	Misteri.		102
***	7c	Moca de pavo.		159
***	6b+	Molins de paper.		191
**	6b	Molsa blanca.		128
***	7b+	Mombasa Calling.		130
***	6b+	Mongol Express.		157
*	4c	Mongol Right.		157
*	5b	Monika.		268
**	6b	Monkey largo.		131
oo	8a	Morcilla.		130
*	5b	Moretti.		47
**	7c+	Morgue, La (Puig de Garrafa).		70
	6b+	Morgue, La (Sa Gubia).		148
***	7b	Morir Martir.		70
	8a+	Moro.		258
***	6a+	Morris.		88
*	7a+	Mort de fam.		194
**	4c	mosca, La	249	250
***	7c	Moscos fora.		231
oo	8b	Moscovita.		309
oo	8a	Moscu.		309
ooo	8a	Motorhead.		227
	f7B+	Motorhead Start Left-hand.		227
	f5c	Motorhead Start Right-hand.		227
	f7B+	Motorvisión.		227
?		Motorvisión Full.		227
	6b+	Mou els peus.		278
**	5c	Movimiento sexy.		120
oo	8a+	Mr. Magu.		197
**	6b+	Mucky.		218
**	6c+	Multi Racial.		128
*	6c	Murto.		258
?		Musaka.		263
*	7a+	Muscleman.		197
**	7a	My Princess.		271
**	7b	Na c'al les Seychelles.		305
**	7a	Na curta (Grau des Ruc).		230
	6a+	Na curta (Sa Mola de Felanitx).		271
**	7b+	Na faresta.		191
**	6a	Na guarra.		165
**	6b	Na Llarga.		270
	7c	Na Marta en el país del Indoorterror.		70
*	5c	Na palonia.		245
***	7b	Na rua.		71
	8a	Na taca.		197
*	7c+	Nakles.		73
***	6c	Namec.	35, 50	53
*	7c+	Nameless.		276
***	7a+	Nanga Parbat.	12	53
**	6c+	Nano.		89
	7a	Naranje.		307
	8a	Nas, Es.		304
oo	8a+	Natiu.		197
***	6c	Naturista, El.		60
**	6a	Nautilus.	273	280
*	7a+	negore albino, El.		130
**	6b	Negra Flor.		159
**	6c	Negracula.		124
**	5c	Neo.		94
*	7a	Never Mind the Bollocks.		303
	3c	New 3c.		250
*	7a	New 7a.		195
*	5c	New Gray Slab.		69
*	5c	New lower-off.		251
	6c	Newer Line.		308
*	7b+	Ni Araceli se agarra.		74
**	7c+	Ni quibo ni bloco.		197
*	6c	Ní-Mu.		53
*	6a	Nice One.		54
**	7c	Niño Melón.		130
ooo	7b+	No Badis.		196
**	7b	No country for plafoneros.		232
	7b	No haces más grado.		165
ooo	8b+	No Name.		174
**	7a+	No res.		203
**	7c	No vull ser com tu.		263
	8a+	Noche de los Muertos Vivientes, La.		70
*	7b+	noche me confunde, La.		197
	6a	Nordkap.		238
***	6c	Nosferatu.		224
***	6c	nostro projecte, El.		258
**	6b+	Not Dangerous.		280
*	6b+	Not Lola's.		197
	6b+	Number 1.		153
	7a+	Number 2.		153
	6c	Number 3.		153
	7a	Nuvol Kinton.		53
	5a	Nycinyatos.		191
**	6b+	O.A.T.		103
*	6b	Oasis.		157
**	7b+	Obelisco, El.		46
*	6c+	Obelix.		245
*	6b	Obi Wan.		245
*	6b	Ochobe mas.		170
***	7a	Octopussy.	3	130
***	7b	Odio a cobi.	118	127
ooo	8c+	Odissy.		226
***	7b+	Oh My God.		209
**	6c+	Ojo climico.		170
o	8a	Old Amsterdam.		305
	7b	Old Bolts (Alaró).		202
	5c	Old Bolts (El Fumat).		245
**	6b	Old Route to the Root.		268
***	7b	On es l'avi.		174
***	7b	On Line.		220
*	3b	One Hand.		286
*	6b+	Only for Women.		197
**	6c+	Only you.		280
*	5c	Òpera prima.		165
	7a	Orange Hollows.		103
	7b+	Orange Pockets.		104
?		Orange Rib, The.		83
**	6b	Orangutan nuclear.		90
**	6b	ORC.		72
*	6c+	Orion.		206
**	7b	Os habeis comido mi cerdo.		128
	8b+	otra linea, La.		171
*	6c+?	Overhang Zig Zag.		88
	7a+	Overhang, Crack and Corner.		104
*	4a	Pa los abuelos.		248
**	6a	Pa Torrat.		220
	6b+	padri, Es.		214
	7b+	Palito de Cangrejo.		299
**	7b	Palmolive.		138
***	7c+	Pantano boas.	175	174
***	5c	Papallona.	19	270
**	7a	Paparazzi.		224
*	7a+	Paparrina.		113
	7b	Papidepau.		146
**	6b+	Paprika.		124
**	6b+	Parabolt treu banya.		221
**	5c	Paramuero.		279
?		Paris Conexión.		209
*	7b	Parkinson.		194
*	6a+	Parque de diversión.		53
**	5c	Part forana.		120
*	4b	Pasión Direct.		123
***	5a	Pasión interminable.		123
*	4c	Pasión oculta.		123
*	7c+	Pasos de rellero.		229
*	6a	Pasqualín.		263
**	6c	Passenger Pigeon.		148
***	6c	Passenger Pigeon P1.		148
**	6b	Pasta Gansa.		129
*	7a	Pasta Gansa Left		129
oo	8a	Pastanaga punyetera		176

Mallorca Sport Climbs — Route Index

Stars	Grade	Route	Photo	Page
*	6a	Pastel de ochoce		170
***	7b	Pasteles de Isabel		148
***	6b+	pasto (Dog Walker), Es		256
**	6b	Patito feo	178	188
*	4c	Pedorretas		251
	7c	Peep show's barriga		177
**	6c	peladora, La		148
*	7b	peli, La		305
**	7a	Pellejo de tiburón		148
	6c	Pello frito		130
**	6a	Pena Negra		215
**	7b	Penjat		227
	8a	Pensamiento infinito		221
	f7A	Pent gurus		227
*	6c+	Penta		279
**	7c+	Penthouse		227
	f7A	Penthouse Start		227
**	6b	Pepa		139
*	6b+	Pepino		139
	7b+	Pequena Realidad		297
*	6a+	Pequeño Coatí	49	52
***	7a	Perdiuota		233
*	4c	Perelló		279
○○○	8a	Perestroika		309
*	6a+	Pérfido encanto		141
**	6c	Perpetua Demencia		296
**	6c+	Perque triunfin els canalles		146
○	8a	Perro flauta		126
**	6b	Pesadilla final		148
*	6c	Petit poi		226
*	7a+	Petit quer		112
○	8a	Petita Aixa		196
○○○	8b+	Peu deret		226
*	7a	Peur Impossible		146
	5c	Pezón		122
*	7b	Phantasmagoria		163
***	7b	Phantomas		188
○○	8a	Picados		227
**	7b+	Pijama		214
***	7b	Pilar		207
*	5c	Pilla, pilla		281
*	6b	Pin		259
*	5c	Pincha uvas		209
***	7b+	Pinchas uvas Extension		209
*	6a+	Pincho Moruno		89
*	6a	Pineapple		72
***	6a+	Pink Panther		170
***	7c+	Pinky Winki		194
*	7c	Piñón fijo		146
	6b+	Pipiricot		279
*	7a	Pitbull		74
	6c	Pitopausico		204
*	6c+	Pixotades per ses galtes		279
*	5c	Placa		298
*	6a+	Placa aspera		159
○○	8a+	Planet G		78
*	6a	Planeta Roja		53
○○	8a	Playboy	5	227
	6b	poal, Es		146
***	6a+	Poc a Poc I Bona Lletra		61
*	6a+	Pocket		222
*	6a	Pocket Right		222
	6a+	Poder fanático		88
***	7b+	Poker Face		209
**	6a	Polla boba		157
*	6c+	Pollo Amarillo		89
*	6a+	Polvoron		76
*	7b+	Pon		259
	6b+	Poor		222
**	7c+	Popeye		245
*	7b+	Popona		72
*	6c	Porcona		230
*	6b	Porrusalda, La		47
***	7b	Poseidon		306
**	7a+	Postal Service		308
*	5c	Potaje Español		160
***	7c	Precisión milimétrica		230
**	4b	Primer plato		271
***	6b	Princesa		159
*	6a+	Princesa del Pueblo, La		216
	6b+	Princesa Mara		72
	6b	Pringa mete el dedo		162
**	6a+	Prinzessin Sophia		288
	?	Project		276
	?	Project Colateral		233
	8b+	Project No More		226
*	6c	Projesso Aronnax		280
**	6a+	Proteina vegetal		166
***	7b+	Proyecto Salto Base		129
***	6c	Psicomambo		305
*	6c+	Psycho Killer		171
**	6c+	Puntas de Pollas		130
***	6a	Punto G		148
**	6c	Pupé de Roqué		303
***	7b	Pussycat		79
***	6c+	Pussycat/Soledad Combo		79
***	6a+	Puta del Pueblo, La		46
*	6a+	Puta guiri		77
*	5c	Puta Mares		269
*	6a	Puta perro	151	155
	5a	Putero perdut		94
***	5a	Quan es fa fosc		154
*	7a+	Quaranta Putes		129
*	5c	Quarried Wall		122
**	6c	Que chulo		270
○○○	8a+	Qui tub retub		231
*	7b+	Quin berenar		184
	6a	Quint		229
*	7a+	R-line		230
***	6b	Rafael Borrás	241	245
	8b	Raiworld		306
	7c	Raixa		304
**	7b	Rallito		233
*	4b	Rama Lama Dindon		91
*	4a	Rama Lama Left		91
○○○	8b	Ramadán		172
*	6a+	Ramon me ha hecho el avion		209
*	5c	Rampline		69
**	6c	Raska y Gana		128
	5c	Rata pinyada		248
	6a+	Ratanuit		278
*	5c	Ratapinyada		59
**	6b+	Reachy		279
**	7b	Realidad paralela		229
**	6c	Recluta Patoso		128
***	6b	Récords de Bunyola	237	239
	5c	Recto cresta		141
**	6b+	Red Stain		120
**	6c+	Red Wall Left		295
	?	Red Wall Right		295
*	6a+	Reggae Shark		269
***	7a	Relaja la Raja	210	220
**	6b	Relaja la Raja L1	198	220
***	6a+	Rellquies del passat	219	218
*	7b+	Remate final		231
○○	8a	Repoman		184
○	8a	Repowoman		184
*	6a+	Repusai		280
*	7a	Requena, Los		73
*	6a+	Resaca	167	166
*	6c	Reset		263
	5c	Respect the Rock		248
*	5a	retorno del Jedi, El		122
*	7a+	Retruc		110
**	7c+	Reunió de granots		196
	6a	rey de bastos, El		90
*	5c	Rib Left		215
**	6a	Rib Right		215
*	5a	Right		222
**	6b+	Right Line (Alaró)		204
*	5a	Right Line (S'estret)		127
**	7c+	Right of Corrich		219
*	5c	Right Side Slab		216
	7a+	Right-hand Roof 1		276
	7b	Right-hand Roof 2		276
*	7c+	Rigor Mortis		70

Route Index — Mallorca Sport Climbs

Stars	Grade	Route	Photo	Page	Stars	Grade	Route	Photo	Page
*	4a	roca manda, La		88	*	6b	Se mes dificil		271
***	7c+	Rock punk		174		7c	Secre, El		299
*	7a	Rocko		184	**	7a	Seis pelas		148
**	7b	Rocko Right		184	**	6a	Seis pelas P1		148
	6a+	Rompededos		141	*	6b+	Semen de trigo		303
***	7a	Rompepiernas		307	*	6b+	Sementir		177
*	5c	Rompesuelos		220		8b	Senglier		171
*	7a	Roof Route Left		140		6a	Sense Voler		278
*	7a	Roof Route Right		140	**	6b	Sensei		90
	6c	Roof, The		271		7a+	Septaplua		226
*	5c	Rosa Blanca		47	*	6a	Ses panxetes		281
*	7b+	Rosa de sanatorio		171	***	6a+	Ses tres Maries		281
	7a	Rosa dels Vents, La		152		8a	Sese Line		299
*	7b	Route 6		194	**	7b+	Setebe el plumero		176
*	6a+	Route 9		166	*	6a+	Seventeen		278
**	6b+	Roxy Foxy		89	∞∞	8a+	Sex on the Beach		79
	6c+	Rufo		184	***	6b+	Sexo débil		159
**	6b+	Rustic pogo		166	*	6b+	Sexo Rapido		63
	7c	Rusty		136		7b	Sexy Line		299
*	6a+	S-Groove		124	∞∞	8a+	Shabada		172
**	6c+	S'acabat		204	**	7a+	Sherpa		53
	6c+	S'alegria		308		7a+	Shisha Pangma		53
**	6b	S'àmfora	107	111		5b	Short Pillar Centre		69
***	6a+	S'àncora	20, 96, 108	110		5b	Short Pillar Left		69
*	7c+	S'àtic		113		4b	Short Pillar Right		69
∞∞	8b+	S'Entreforc		197	*	4c	Short Rib Route		123
*	6c	S'escorpi		194		4a	Short Slab		195
*	7c	S'Horabaixa		191	**	6a	Shorty		136
**	6b+	S'illeta		184	***	7a+	Si lo sé no vengo	147	146
	6c	S'única		113	*	7b	Si t'aplec		110
*	6b+	Sa Bruta	93	95	*	7b+	Si yo fuera presidente		126
**	6a+	Sa canal		194	*	7c	Siddhartha		46
*	6c+	Sa Cantera		94	*	4b	Siglo 21		68
	5c	Sa cova		271	**	7b	Sika-phobia		131
	5c	Sa curta		204	*	6c	Silicona		166
**	7b+	Sa des plastics	260	309	***	6b+	Sin Metros No Hay Paraido		61
***	7c	Sa festa		197	*	7b+	Sindrome		78
*	6a	Sa figuera		271	*	6c+	Siracusa mon amour		230
*	6c+	Sa figuera borda		111		6b+	Sirius		206
**	6b+	Sa figuereta		204		7a+	Siurana es panxi		304
**	6a+	Sa fisura (Sa Cantera)		95	*	7c+	Skiasical		231
*	6a	Sa fisura (Sa Mola de Felanitx)		271		6a	Skidmark		71
∞∞	8a	Sa fosca		196	**	6c	Slab 1		209
*	6c+	Sa nina va moguda		94	**	7b	Slap		112
*	6a	Sa nyoscla	275	279	**	6a+	Slow Life		159
***	7a	Sa pena		308	**	6b+	Smooth Criminal		216
*	6c+	Sa primera		197	*	5c	Snowboard		203
*	4b	Sa rampa		271	°	8a	Sobrasada power		233
**	6c	Sa roqueta		184	*	6a	Sobrassada		203
*	7a+	Sa rota magnètica		112	*	6b	Sobre el coral		287
**	6b+	Sa sesta		279	**	7c	Sobremunt		111
***	7b+	Sa taranta		194		7c	SOeScaladores en perdición		150
**	6c	Sa torre picada		184	*	5b	Sol		278
	3c	Sa via de n'Andreu		59	***	6b	Sol Solet		159
*	7a+	Saca las uñas nini		221	*	6c	Sol Solet Right Start		159
**	7a+	Sacrilegio		225	**	7a+	Soledad		79
***	6c+	Sal de arenal		146	∞∞	8b	Sóliva		197
∞∞	8a	Salpicón de menisco		171	∞∞	8a	Solo Sex		171
*	7b	salt, Es		229		6a	Som-hi		239
*	7b	Saltimbanquis		103	*	7a	Something		138
∞∞	8a+	Salto del Angel, El		73		6b	Somni bucolic		239
∞∞	8b+/c	Sam Sara		46	**	5a	Somos uno		288
	?	Sánchez		205	*	7a+	somriure de la bruixa, El		232
***	7b+	Sand Bag		276	*	6b+	sonido de la gaita, El		225
*	7c	Sangonera		111		6a	Sonrisa vertical		157
	6a+	Sant Crist, El		239		6a+	Sor-presa		153
*	5c	Sapporo		47	*	7a	Sostre		255
***	7c	Sarcofago		70		6a+	Sostre del murero		248
*	6a	Schnuddel		269	***	6c+	Sostre den burotet	1	140
**	3c	Schnurzelpurzel		286	**	7a+	Sostre Direct		140
**	7a+	Scoop Direct		215	∞∞	8a	sòtil, Es		113
**	6c+	Scoop Groove		124	*	6a	Spanky		136
*	6b+	Scoop Left (Caimari)		215	*	6b+	Speer Angel Weit		287
**	7b	Scoop Left (Valldemossa)		136	*	7a+	Spoon Man		128
*	7b	Scoop, The		83	∞∞	8a	Sportacus		196
*	6b	Scooped Runnel		138	**	7c+	Springfield		195
**	7a+	Scorpion		128	***	6b	Stalactites and Pockets	64	69
	6c	Screenplay		307		6c+	Starman		206

Mallorca Sport Climbs — Route Index

Stars	Grade	Route	Photo	Page
*	6c	Steep and slabby		127
?		Steep Arete		126
*	7a	Steep Groove		159
	7b	Still a Project?		202
**	4b	Stone Lion		251
	6b+	Strigol		130
	7a+	sudaca, El.		127
	6b+	Suegra 747		131
**	6c	Sun	183	188
**	6a+	Sun Right-hand		188
	6b+	Super calvo		129
*	6c+	Super Lopez		73
	8a	Super Natural		126
**	6c+	Super Unknown		128
***	7b	Superchorrera		205
	6a	Superchorrera access.		204
**	7a+	Superferret		229
**	6a	Supernova, Spits 'n Giggles		153
**	7b	Supersexi		304
**	6a	Suphi	134	139
*	6b	Suphi Left-hand		139
*	6b	Suquet		224
***	7b	Sweetie the Pooh		219
**	7a+	Tabasco		162
**	6c	Talaiot Corcat	105	104
**	6c	Tall en Verduc		103
?		Tall Wall Left		83
**	7a+	Tall Wall Middle		83
	7a+	Tangerine Dream		206
	5b	Tantum ergo		160
**	6c+	Tao		148
**	6b+	Tao P1		148
**	6a+	Tapas		303
**	6b+	Tarta Lemon		309
**	6a+	Tata		63
°°	8b+	Tatoo		126
**	7b+	Tatoo L1		126
	6b+	Te mastico pere no te trago		214
**	7c	Te mataràs		231
*	7b+	Tecnoverborrea		221
***	7a+	Tequila Forever		256
	6c	Terapia de grupo		239
	6b+	Teresetes		78
*	6b	terrat, El.		170
**	7c	Terre d'adventure		173
°°°	8a	Terre d'adventure plus		173
°°°	8a	Terrorvision		227
	f7C	Terrorvisión Start		227
**	7c+	Tête de pene		174
**	7c+	Tetrix		127
***	7b	Therapy		205
	7c	Thin Seam		191
*	6a+	Thomas		297
*	7c+	Tia aina		233
*	6a	Tía melis		148
	5c	Tiddler		203
**	6a+	Tierra al reves	161	159
**	6a	Tierra Doy Una/Sutra		46
*	6a+	Tight Slab		120
°°°	8a	Tijuana		309
*	6b	Tiny		278
*	5c	Tio listo		250
*	5a	Tiquis Miquis		63
**	7b+	Tira que ve peix		230
°°	8a	TNT		276
*	7a	To kiski'm'toca.		162
***	7a+	To pa ti (Alaró)	207	207
*	7a	To pa ti (Puig de Garrafa)		71
*	7a+	To quisqui me toca		306
*	7a+	To the memory of Miquel Riera		90
*	7a	Tocino for Pepino		304
*	6c	Todo bien		287
*	6a	Tofal Boxer		89
	6b+	Tofol		177
*	6c	Tom		270
*	5c	Tom and Jerry		302
**	7a+	Tongo mongui		233
**	6b+	Tootsie		278
**	7c	Tornillo Torcido		60
**	7a	Toro Sentado, El		299
	7a	Tot Disney		259
*	7b	Tot picat		258
°°°	8b+	Totes.com		196
*	6b	Totom fa el que vol		166
*	6b+	Totsol com un mussol		309
***	6a	Touch The Sky		288
	6b+	Tourist Go Home		129
	6c+	Toxica		90
*	5c	Trad Dream		270
**	7b	Tramontana		231
*	5c	Tramontana fuerza		248
*	6b	Trampera matinera		165
**	6b+	Trànsfuga		224
*	6a+	Trash Out		90
*	4c	Traverse to the left!!!		269
	6c	Travesia		137
***	6a+	Trencaclosques		308
	7c	Tres estrellas		150
**	7b+	Tres menos cuarto		146
	7b+	tres mosqueteros, Los		196
*	7c	Trio infernal		127
	6b	Triplet derecho		141
***	6c	Triquinosis		204
***	6a+	Triunfo del Nicol		287
*	7a	Truc		110
**	7a+	Trundling		221
***	7b+	Tufa Big		276
	6b+	Tufa Time		103
	6a	Tufolandia		248
*	7a	Tulipán		229
**	4b	Turbo 3		68
	6a+	Türlich Türlich		270
*	6c	Tutup		191
	6b+	Twins		91
*	7c+	Txapuz Board		227
	8a	Txino tzapa		127
*	5c	Txorrack		103
*	6a+	Ufff jajajajaja		268
	8a	último vals, El		174
*	7a+	Un dimange à la campange		304
	6a	Un final difícil		270
	6a	un metro de la Gloria, A.		79
*	7a	Un poco de porno		287
*	7a+	Un tio conflictiu		276
*	7a+	uñas de Dori, Las		215
**	6c+	Under Waikiki		140
°°	8b	Undertakers, The		70
	6a+	Uudos		245
*	7a+	Va de block		76
*	4c	Vagon roll		203
*	7a	Vall-de-mega		136
*	5c	vals del obrero, El		287
*	6b	Vampiresa		77
*	6a+	Vampiresa Direct		77
**	6b+	Vampiro		77
	6c+	Vampiro Right		77
*	5c	Variante Neo		94
*	6a+	Verger, Es		110
?		Via antigua con buriles		204
***	7a+	Via d'en Pepino		71
*	7a	Via d'Johny		214
*	7a	Via d'Juli		214
*	6b	Vía de los bomberos		157
**	6c	Via del Charly		296
*	6b+	Vía des clau		138
*	5c	Vía des vombers		216
*	6b	Via Llum de Lluna		159
*	6c	Via morito		219
*	6c	Via Terra Lliure		159
*	7a	Viagra de Abuelo		130
	7a	Viagra Direct		130
	6a+	Victorinox		214
*	7c+	Vida fácil		230
***	6c	Vidio Nasty		130
*	6a	Viento		278
*	4b	vigilant de la platja, El		281
**	6a	Vino tinto		303
°°°	8a	Virgin (Port de S)		188
**	6a	Virgin (S'estret)		120
**	6a	virgin del felpudo, La		90
***	7b+	Virgin Direct		188
°°°	8a+	vista de pájaro, A		227
**	6c	Vivan las jarras		72
*	6a	Vivan los Shandis		72
*	6b	Vive dios		225
	6b	Vívora		245
***	6b	Vol de nuit		148
**	7c	Voltor Negra (Cala Llamp)		60
***	7a+	Voltor Negra (P. d'es Grau)		102
*	7a+	Voramar		184
	8a	Voyages dans l'eau de là		150
*	7b	Vuelo del Fénix, El		68
	6a	Vuit se mes		170
*	7a	Vull fer més		110
***	6b	Waikiki		140
	6b+	Wall 'n' Crack		204
**	7c+	Wall and Bulge		276
**	7a+	Wall and Cave		82
**	5c	Wall and Groove		279
**	6c+	Wall and Overhang		138
*	7a+	Wall Eliminate		136
	6b	Wall Left (El Caló de Betlem)		255
*	6c	Wall Left (Port de S)		188
	7a+	Wall Left (Santa P)		82
*	6b+	Wall Right (El C. de Betlem)		255
**	6b	Wall Right (Port de S)		188
	?	Wall, The		83
*	6c	Wassabi		104
***	6c	Wave Scalpel		270
***	7b+	Welcome to Paradise		309
	7b	White Arete		82
	6c	White Bulging Wall		102
**	7b+	White Groove, The		83
	6c+	White pillar		69
**	6c+	White Wall		82
	6c	Why Not		137
*	6c	Why!		163
	7a+	Wild Planet		53
	7b+	Wild Spirit		53
*	4a	Wilma		295
**	6a+	Wo Ist Der Fisch?	257	255
*	6b+	Wo Ist Der Fisch?		298
	6c	Wolfgang		297
*	6a+	Wonder Woman		286
**	7a+	Xama		195
*	6a+	Xancia de Ghandi, La		129
*	7b	Xavier		209
**	7a	Ximo		195
*	6a+	Xisco jove		269
*	6a+	Xisco vell		268
**	6b+	Xiscu que reiliscu		303
**	6b+	Xorics		280
**	6a+	Xorixapes		218
**	7b+	XTR		205
*	6b	Xupamela		258
**	7b+	Xurrito		111
*	6a+	y mar		278
	7b	Yogui		259
**	6c+	Yonquis de la Broca		216
	7a	Zampabollos		195
	6b+	Zampabollos Left		195
**	6c	Zapatiazo		131
	6c	Zaragüay		163
***	7c+	Zaratrusta		230
	4c	Zarzamora		121
	3c	Zarzamora Center		121
	4c	Zarzamora Right		121
***	7c	Zatropeck		202
	6c	Ziga zaga		215
**	6a+	Ziritone	243	244
°°°	8a+	Zombieland		70
**	7a	Zona de Moda		60
**	6b+	zona mágica, La		88
	6c	Zurdo		141

Buttress and Crag Index *(Crags in **BOLD**)*

Above the Road	102
Alaró	**200**
Albahida, Sector	154
All Right, Sector	129
Bella Donna Aparcamiento	229
Blobland, Sector	186
Bobo dodo, Sector	173
Boira, Sector	295
Bomberos, Sector	157
Bomberos - Lower Left	155
Caimari	**210**
Cala Bota	**282**
Cala Llamp	**56**
Cala Magraner	**272**
C'an Formiga	**63**
C'an Nyic	**191**
Ca's Català	**88**
Cabra Zombi, Sector	124
Can Ortigues	**38**
Capdella	**40**
Cara Oeste	150
Chorreras, Sector	206
Colesterol Party, Sector	305
Colmena, Sector	74
Comuna de Caimari - Adalt	214
Comuna de Caimari - Es Raconet	218
Comuna de Caimari - Placa Rotja	221
Conguito, Sector	131
Corral, Sector	76
Cous-cous, Sector	176
Cuarentón, Sector	120
Cueva (Caimari), Sector	226
Cueva (Cala Magraner), Sector	276
del Medio, Sector	204
den Jaume, Sector	308
des Cable, Sector	196
Dragonera, Sector	52
Dragonera - Right, Sector	54
Dreta, Sector	232
Duck, Sector	72
Duke, Sector	244
East Face (El Caló de Betlem)	255
El Caló de Betlem	**252**
El Fumat	**240**
El Gran Pollo Rojo, Sector	299
Embrujada, Sector	152
Es pasto, Sector	256
Es Salt	229
Es Sotil	112
Es Torrente, Sector	197
Es Verger	**106**
Escuelar de Calor, Sector	304
Esquerra, Sector	230
Excalibur, Sector	165
Far Left Cave (Port de Sóller)	184
Football Fan, Sector	172
Fraguel	**168**
Free Tibet, Sector	245
Germany, Sector	298
Gorg Blau	**192**
Goo Goo Mack, Sector	171
Hairpin Wall	222
Iniciación, Sector	59
Isla Bonita, Sector	162
La Creveta	**236**
Left Wall (Cala Bota)	286
Main Crag (Valldemossa)	138
Main Wall (La Creveta)	238
Main Wall (Penyal d'es Grau)	102
Mario, Sector	121
Mejicano, Sector	126
Mont Port	**48**
Muro de Caimari	224
North Buttress (Puig St. Marti)	248
Nuevo, Sector	184
Oasis, Sector	60
Pablo's, Sector	296
Paret de sa Porta	202
Paret dels Coloms	146
Pasión, Sector	122
Penyal d'es Grau	**98**
Pink Panther, Sector	170
Pipe, Sector	122
Pipiricot, Sector	279
Plaques, Sector	194
Port de Sóller	**180**
Poseidon, Sector	306
Potaje Español, Sector	160
Princesa, Sector	159
Puig de Garrafa	**64**
Puig St. Marti	**246**
Radio 3	68
Raska y Gana, Sector	128
Right Wall (Cala Bota)	288
Rigor Mortis, Sector	70
Roadside Buttress	141
Rock Punk, Sector	174
Sa Cantera	**94**
Sa Cova (Es Verger)	110
Sa Cova, Sector (Port de Sóller)	188
Sa Gubia	**144**
Sa Mola de Felanitx	**268**
Salto, Sector	73
Santa Ponça	**82**
Sense Voler, Sector	278
S'estret	**114**
Silicona, Sector	166
Sombra, Sector	78
Son Servera	**263**
Subte, Sector	259
Tapas, Sector	303
The Cathedral	45
Tijuana	**300**
To pa ti, Sector	71
Tom and Jerry, Sector	302
Torre d'en Beu	**290**
Upper Crag (Valldemossa)	136
Valldemossa	**132**
Waikiki, Sector	140
West Face (El Caló de Betlem)	258
West Face (Puig St. Marti)	250
Wilma, Sector	295
Wolfgang, Sector	297
Xorics, Sector	280
Xurasco, Sector	130

Mallorca Sport Climbs — Map and General Index

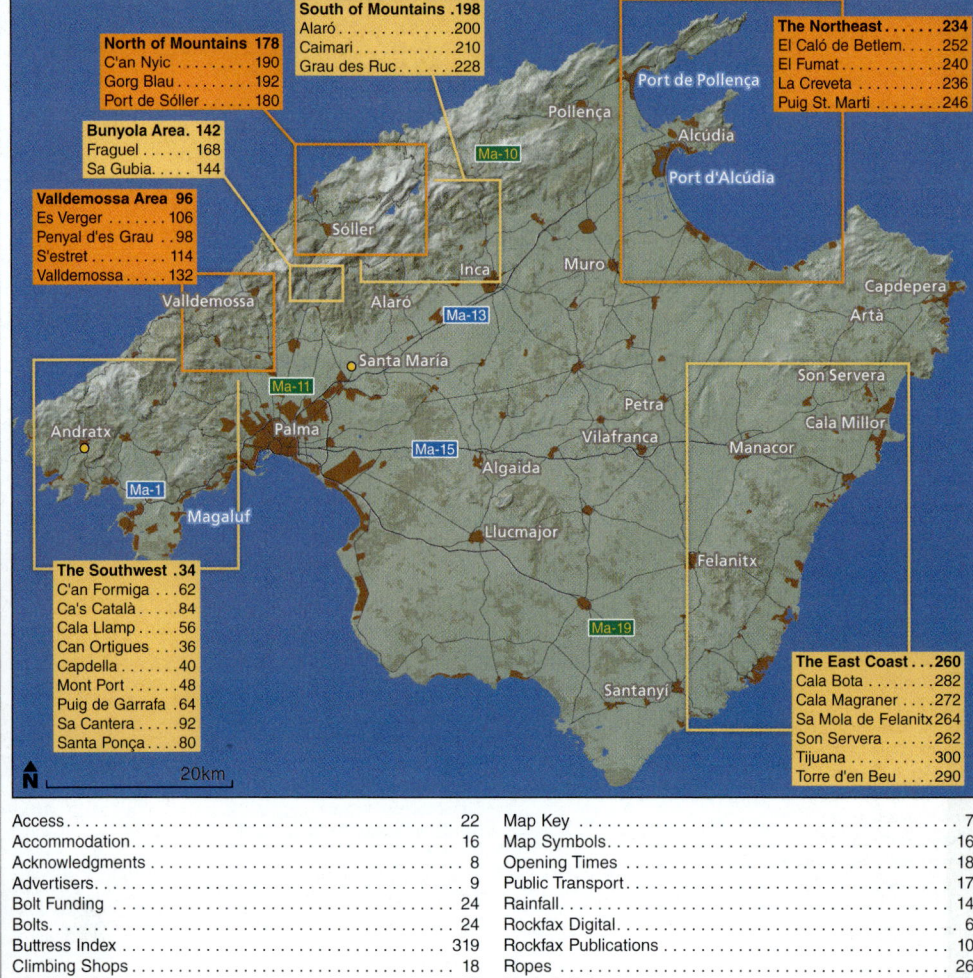

South of Mountains .198
Alaró 200
Caimari 210
Grau des Ruc 228

North of Mountains 178
C'an Nyic 190
Gorg Blau 192
Port de Sóller 180

The Northeast 234
El Caló de Betlem . . . 252
El Fumat 240
La Creveta 236
Puig St. Marti 246

Bunyola Area. 142
Fraguel 168
Sa Gubia. 144

Valldemossa Area 96
Es Verger 106
Penyal d'es Grau . . 98
S'estret 114
Valldemossa 132

The Southwest .34
C'an Formiga . . . 62
Ca's Català 84
Cala Llamp 56
Can Ortigues . . . 36
Capdella 40
Mont Port 48
Puig de Garrafa . 64
Sa Cantera 92
Santa Ponça 80

The East Coast . . . 260
Cala Bota 282
Cala Magraner . . . 272
Sa Mola de Felanitx 264
Son Servera 262
Tijuana 300
Torre d'en Beu . . . 290

20km

Access. 22		Map Key 7	
Accommodation. 16		Map Symbols. 16	
Acknowledgments 8		Opening Times 18	
Advertisers. 9		Public Transport. 17	
Bolt Funding 24		Rainfall. 14	
Bolts. 24		Rockfax Digital. 6	
Buttress Index 319		Rockfax Publications 10	
Climbing Shops. 18		Ropes 26	
Climbing Walls. 18		Route Index 310	
Destination Planner. 32		Route Lengths 27	
Flights 14		Route Names. 22	
Gear. 26		Secret Crags 22	
Getting Around. 17		Shops 18	
Getting There. 14		Symbol Key 7	
Getting there by Air 14		Temperature. 14	
Getting there Without Flying 14		The Book. 4	
Grade Colour Codes 26		Topo Key 7	
Grade Table 26		Tourist Information Offices. 18	
Graded List 29		Travel Insurance 14	
Grades. 26		UKBoltFund.org. 24	
Guidebooks 22		UKClimbing Logbook. 6	
Guiding Services 18		Weather. 14	
Introduction 4		Websites. 22	
Lowering Off 27		When to Go 14	
Map 16, 320		Where to Stay 16	

Mountain Rescue

Dial 112 - Ensure you have details of your location and what the incident involves.
This number works on any mobile on a Spanish network.